The Bonds of Love, Revisited

Jessica Benjamin is one of the most important and influential psychoanalysts of the last four decades. She is one of the founders of relational psychoanalysis, a movement that has by now expanded over the globe, and one of the first to introduce feminism and gender studies into psychoanalytic thought. Jessica Benjamin's is of the most known and quoted representative of these two movements within world psychoanalysis and beyond, in philosophy, gender/women's studies, and cultural studies departments everywhere.

The publication of her book, "The Bonds of Love" (1989) was nothing short of a revolution. Psychoanalysis was until then a field immune to a changing world, to the unrest of the 60s, to the feminist and queer liberation movements, to the new philosophies of the Frankfurt School in Germany and post-structuralism in France. The book was a game changer. It called psychoanalysis to doubt its most basic premises on the human condition. It read Freud through a feminist framework, and through Hegel, forever tipping our perspective on infancy, gender, and the interplay of power and dependence that drives human relationships from the start.

This volume marks the 25th anniversary of Benjamin's work. Pulling together 14 international scholars, it looks back on the book's first impact, as well as on its continued relevance to psychoanalysis and gender studies today. The chapters offer theoretical deliberations and elaborations of the book's original themes as well as reflecting on it from more intimate angles, as a source of personal and professional inspiration for feminists and clinicians around the world.

This book was originally published as a special issue of *Studies in Gender and Sexuality.*

Eyal Rozmarin, Ph.D. is co-editor of the journal *Studies in Gender and Sexuality* and Associate Editor of the Routledge book series Relational Perspectives. He has published book chapters, and articles in psychoanalytic Journals, including *Psychoanalytic Dialogues, Contemporary Psychoanalysis,* and *Studies in Gender and Sexuality*. His research takes place in the intersection of psychoanalysis and social theory, and explores the relations between subjectivity, society, and history.

The Bonds of Love, Revisited

Edited by
Eyal Rozmarin

LONDON AND NEW YORK

First published 2015
by Routledge
2 Park Square, Milton Park, Abingdon, Oxon, OX14 4RN, UK

and by Routledge
711 Third Avenue, New York, NY 10017, USA

Routledge is an imprint of the Taylor & Francis Group, an informa business

© 2015 Taylor & Francis

All rights reserved. No part of this book may be reprinted or reproduced or utilised in any form or by any electronic, mechanical, or other means, now known or hereafter invented, including photocopying and recording, or in any information storage or retrieval system, without permission in writing from the publishers.

Trademark notice: Product or corporate names may be trademarks or registered trademarks, and are used only for identification and explanation without intent to infringe.

British Library Cataloguing in Publication Data
A catalogue record for this book is available from the British Library

ISBN 13: 978-1-138-83062-2

Typeset in Times New Roman
by RefineCatch Limited, Bungay, Suffolk

Publisher's Note
The publisher accepts responsibility for any inconsistencies that may have arisen during the conversion of this book from journal articles to book chapters, namely the possible inclusion of journal terminology. In this case, the chapters have been rearranged so that the order is different to that appearing in the introductory chapter.

Disclaimer
Every effort has been made to contact copyright holders for their permission to reprint material in this book. The publishers would be grateful to hear from any copyright holder who is not here acknowledged and will undertake to rectify any errors or omissions in future editions of this book.

Contents

Citation Information vii
Notes on Contributors xi

1. Introduction: *The Bonds of Love* at 25 1
   Eyal Rozmarin

2. The Racialization of the Mind in Intimate Spaces: The "Nanny" and the Failure of Recognition 4
   Gillian Straker

3. Loosening the Bonds: Psychoanalysis, Feminism, and the Problem of the Group 17
   Francisco J. González

4. Bondless Love 32
   Stephen Hartman

5. What's Love Got to Do with It? Sexuality, Shame, and the Use of the Other 48
   Galit Atlas

6. Revisiting *The Bonds of Love* 56
   Fran Bartkowski

7. *The Bonds of Love*: Looking Backward 59
   Jessica Benjamin

8. The Benjamin Chreode 74
   Uri Hadar

9. The Cat Ate Our Tongue—But We Got It Back: Benjamin's Journey From Domination to Surrender 93
   Boaz Shalgi

10. Intersubjectivity and French Psychoanalysis: A Misunderstanding? 111
    Régine Waintrater

11. Beyond Intersubjectivity: Science, the Real World, and the Third in Psychoanalysis 119
    Martin Altmeyer

CONTENTS

12. "Here I Am!"—Irreducible Invocation of the Other 138
    Noreen O'Connor

13. Reading Jessica 147
    Andrea Celenza

14. A Day at the Zoo Through the Lens of Jessica Benjamin's *Bonds of Love* 153
    Donna Bassin

    Index 165

Citation Information

The chapters in this book were originally published as a special issue of *Studies in Gender and Sexuality*, volume 13, number 4, (October–December 2012) and volume 14, number 1, (January–March 2013). When citing this material, please use the original page numbering for each article, as follows:

Chapter 1
Introduction: The Bonds of Love *at 25*
Eyal Rozmarin
Studies in Gender and Sexuality, volume 13, number 4, (October–December 2012) pp. 237–239

Chapter 2
The Racialization of the Mind in Intimate Spaces: The "Nanny" and the Failure of Recognition
Gillian Straker
Studies in Gender and Sexuality, volume 13, number 4, (October–December 2012) pp. 240–252

Chapter 3
Loosening the Bonds: Psychoanalysis, Feminism, and the Problem of the Group
Francisco J. González
Studies in Gender and Sexuality, volume 13, number 4, (October–December 2012) pp. 253–267

Chapter 4
Bondless Love
Stephen Hartman
Studies in Gender and Sexuality, volume 14, number 1, (January–March 2013) pp. 35–50

Chapter 5
What's Love Got to Do with It? Sexuality, Shame, and the Use of the Other
Galit Atlas
Studies in Gender and Sexuality, volume 14, number 1, (January–March 2013) pp. 51–58

CITATION INFORMATION

Chapter 6
Revisiting The Bonds of Love
Fran Bartkowski
Studies in Gender and Sexuality, volume 13, number 4, (October–December 2012) pp. 274–276

Chapter 7
The Bonds of Love*: Looking Backward*
Jessica Benjamin
Studies in Gender and Sexuality, volume 14, number 1, (January–March 2013) pp. 1–15

Chapter 8
The Benjamin Chreode
Uri Hadar
Studies in Gender and Sexuality, volume 14, number 1, (January–March 2013) pp. 16–34

Chapter 9
The Cat Ate Our Tongue—But We Got It Back: Benjamin's Journey From Domination to Surrender
Boaz Shalgi
Studies in Gender and Sexuality, volume 13, number 4, (October–December 2012) pp. 277–294

Chapter 10
Intersubjectivity and French Psychoanalysis: A Misunderstanding?
Régine Waintrater
Studies in Gender and Sexuality, volume 13, number 4, (October–December 2012) pp. 295–302

Chapter 11
Beyond Intersubjectivity: Science, the Real World, and the Third in Psychoanalysis
Martin Altmeyer
Studies in Gender and Sexuality, volume 14, number 1, (January–March 2013) pp. 59–77

Chapter 12
"Here I Am!"—Irreducible Invocation of the Other
Noreen O'Connor
Studies in Gender and Sexuality, volume 14, number 1, (January–March 2013) pp. 78–86

Chapter 13
Reading Jessica
Andrea Celenza
Studies in Gender and Sexuality, volume 13, number 4, (October–December 2012) pp. 268–273

CITATION INFORMATION

Chapter 14
A Day at the Zoo Through the Lens of Jessica Benjamin's Bonds of Love
Donna Bassin
Studies in Gender and Sexuality, volume 14, number 1, (January–March 2013) pp. 87–97

Please direct any queries you may have about the citations to
clsuk.permissions@cengage.com

Notes on Contributors

Martin Altmeyer, Psy.D. is a psychotherapist in Frankfurt/Main and Private Lecturer of Psychoanalytic Psychology, University of Kassel, and Supervisor of Bund Deutscher Psychologinnen und Psychologen (BDP). He co-edited *Die vernetzte Seele: Die intersubjektive Wende in der Psychoanalyse* (Klett-Cotta, 2006) with Helmut Thomae.

Galit Atlas, Ph.D. is a psychoanalyst, creative arts therapist, and clinical supervisor in private practice in Manhattan. She is on the faculty at New York University Postdoctoral Program in Psychotherapy and Psychoanalysis and the Four Year Adult and National Training Programs at National Institute for the Psychotherapies. She is an author of articles and book chapters that focus primarily on gender and sexuality.

Fran Bartkowski, Ph.D. is Professor of English at Rutgers University–Newark and author of *Kissing Cousins: A New Kinship Bestiary* (2008).

Donna Bassin, Ph.D. is Visiting Associate Professor at Pratt Institute's Department of Creative Arts Therapy, Brooklyn, NY, and in private practice psychoanalysis and psychotherapy, Manhattan, NY.

Jessica Benjamin, Ph.D. is a practicing psychoanalyst in New York City, where she is a supervising faculty member at the New York University Postdoctoral Psychology program in Psychotherapy and Psychoanalysis and a faculty and founding board member of the Stephen Mitchell Center for Relational Studies. She is known as a contributor to the development of relational psychoanalysis and its interrelation with feminism as well as the theory of intersubjectivity. She is the author of three books: *The Bonds of Love* (1988), *Like Subjects, Love Objects* (Yale University Press, 1995), and *Shadow of the Other* (1998). Her most frequently cited article is "Beyond Doer and Done to: An Intersubjective View of Thirdness" (*Psychoanalytic Quarterly*, 2004).

Andrea Celenza, Ph.D. is an Assistant Clinical Professor at Harvard Medical School, Faculty at the Boston Psychoanalytic Society and Institute, Faculty at Massachusetts Institute for Psychoanalysis, and author of *Sexual Boundary Violations: Therapeutic, Supervisory and Academic Contexts* (2007). Dr Celenza has authored numerous papers on the evaluation and treatment of therapists who have engaged in sexual misconduct, focusing on training and supervisory issues. She has been the recipient of several awards, including the Karl A. Menninger Memorial Award, the Felix & Helena Deutsch Prize, and the Symonds Prize. She is currently working on a new book: *Erotic Transference, Erotic Countertransference, and Erotic Perversion in the Analytic Setting*. She is in private practice in Lexington, Massachusetts.

Francisco J. González, M.D. is a graduate analyst and faculty of the Psychoanalytic Institute of Northern California.

Uri Hadar, Ph.D. is Professor of Psychology at Tel Aviv University (TAU). He received a B.A. in mathematics and psychology and an M.A. in clinical psychology from TAU as well as a Ph.D. in experimental psychology from the University of London. His research interests include Relational and Lacanian psychoanalysis, functional neuroimaging of language, and coverbal gesture. He is the author of two Hebrew books on psychoanalytic psychotherapy. His third book, *Psychoanalysis and Social Involvement*, is forthcoming.

Stephen Hartman, Ph.D. is a co-editor of *Studies in Gender and Sexuality* and an associate editor for *Psychoanalytic Dialogues*. He co-chairs the faculty of the Psychoanalytic Institute of Northern California.

Noreen O'Connor, Ph.D. (Contemporary European Philosophy), Dip. Psychoanalytic Psychotherapy, is a psychoanalytic psychotherapist in private practice in North London. Her experience includes working as a training analyst, supervisor, and teacher on psychoanalytic trainings and in universities in Britain and Ireland. She is co-author with Joanna Ryan of *Wild Desires and Mistaken Identities: Lesbianism and Psychoanalysis* (1993; 1994; 2003) and, with Mary Lynne Ellis, *Questioning Identities: Philosophy in Psychoanalytic Practice* (2010). She is a member of The Relational School, London and the International Association of Relational Psychoanalysis and Psychotherapy (IARPP).

Eyal Rozmarin, Ph.D. is co-editor of the journal *Studies in Gender and Sexuality* and Associate Editor of the Routledge book series Relational Perspectives. He has published book chapters, and articles in psychoanalytic Journals, including *Psychoanalytic Dialogues*, *Contemporary Psychoanalysis*, and *Studies in Gender and Sexuality*. His research takes place in the intersection of psychoanalysis and social theory, and explores the relations between subjectivity, society, and history.

Boaz Shalgi, Ph.D. is a clinical psychologist. He is a faculty member at the Department of Psychology, Bar-Ilan University, and a teacher and supervisor at the Psychoanalytic Psychotherapy Program of Tel-Aviv University and at the Winnicott Center in Israel. He maintains a private practice in Hod-Hasharon, Israel.

Gillian Straker, Ph.D. is a Mellon Foundation Distinguished Scholar and visiting Research Professor at the University of Witwatersrand and Clinical Professor in Psychiatry at the University of Sydney. She has published papers in the areas of psychoanalysis and race, and psychoanalysis and trauma and is the director of the Centre for Advanced Studies in Psychotherapy and Counselling.

Régine Waintrater, Ph.D. is Associate Professor in Clinical Psychology and Psychopathology at the Department of Psychoanalytical Studies of the University Paris 7-Diderot. She recently wrote the introduction to the French edition of Jessica Benjamin's *Like Subjects, Love Objects* and is the author of *Sortir du génocide: Témoignage et survivance* [Exit from Genocide: Testimony and Survival] (2003).

Introduction: *The Bonds of Love* at 25

Eyal Rozmarin, Ph.D.

New York University Postdoctoral Program in Psychotherapy and Psychoanalysis

In this brief introduction to the collection of essays that follows, I point to what in my mind are some of the most pertinent and powerful aspects of Jessica Benjamin's *The Bonds of Love* (1988), the author and book to whom this collection is dedicated. I tell of my first encounter with Jessica Benjamin and the impact the encounter had on me. I comment briefly on the book's place in contemporary psychoanalysis. Using Jessica Benjamin's own words, I highlight what in my mind is one of the book's greatest achievements: the reframing of the relations between knowledge and ethics in the light of a feminist critique of gender.

The Bonds of Love, which burst into our discourse in 1988 and changed it forever, is in its very name a fantastic reminder of the full ambition of psychoanalysis: making sense of and taking a stance toward love and domination, that is, human relations, their conflicting drives, their confounding expressions, their spiraling power structures and paradoxical consequences. *The Bonds of Love* was, and remains, a path-blazing effort to survey the field of human relations and to reexamine the psychoanalytic expedition still making its way through its enigmatic landscape. It is at the same time a scathing critique and a love letter, to both human relations and psychoanalysis, as they are and as they should be. It is a project steeped in the ambition that gives Jessica Benjamin's entire oeuvre its unique power, the ambition to not only account for things as they are but also to propose ways to make things better. It is, as it should be by its own dialectical measure, a work of negation and recognition, a living, desiring paradox for which the characterization "theoretical" is an understatement. "My conclusion," writes Benjamin in the last paragraph of the book, tracing its entire trajectory,

> is both modest and utopian. The renewal of mutual recognition in the wake of its breakdown is not a final, redemptive "end of history"; rather, it is a necessary part of the continuing process of individual and social change. . . . To attempt to recover recognition in personal life does not mean to politicize personal life relentlessly or to evade politics and give up the hope of transformation—although all of these failures happen in real life. It means to see that the personal and social are interconnected, and to understand that if we suffocate our personal longings for recognition, we will suffocate our hope for social transformation as well [Benjamin, 1988, p. 224].

The Bonds of Love created one of those rare psychoanalytic moments, hardly seen since the days of Red Vienna and the Kinderseminar at the Berlin institute, where psychoanalysis attempted to address both the intimacies of individual and familial life and their ideological underpinning, to reveal their interdependence in the service of both knowledge and progress. This unique lacing together of psychology, social critique, and ethics is one reason *The Bonds of Love* is such an important contribution to the psychoanalytic project.

My own first encounter with Jessica Benjamin was as a graduate student at the New School. I participated in a seminar she led as part of the New School's short-lived psychoanalytic studies program on psychoanalysis and feminism. Attending that seminar changed the course of my thinking, and perhaps my very life, dramatically. We read many important texts, each leaving its own mark. But the one that stood out for me then, and still does, was *The Straight Mind* by Monique Wittig (1992). For someone who came to clinical psychology from pre-postmodern philosophy, with my own cobbled-up readings in mostly classical and object relations psychoanalysis, that seminar offered nothing short of a revolution. I still remember the last sentence in Wittig's essay: "Lesbians are not women" (1992, p. 32). Lesbians are, of course, not women in the sense that "woman" has in what we have come to call heterosexist discourse. But this "of course," that is, the necessity of observing concepts in their socio-historical contexts, was far from evident to me then, and it was foreign to mainstream psychoanalytic discourse. It was Jessica who put such texts on our reading list at the New School, and she was one of the first to put them, with *The Bonds of Love* and the books that followed, on psychoanalytic reading lists everywhere. The encounters with feminism and with critical theory that permeate *The Bonds of Love* gave me and others in my generation the kind of license we needed to begin thinking both psychologically and critically, both against and through a subject, to make a socio-historical analysis of premises a premise in the study of human psychology. Jessica's work has been part of a movement: a feminist, gender, and queer conscious critical confrontation of traditional psychoanalysis that, with contributions by the likes of Nancy Chodorow, Adrienne Harris, Muriel Dimen, Virginia Goldner, Ken Corbett, and others, brought about a true expansion of psychoanalytic theory and technique. Without that movement, gender and sexuality would have retained their traditional ahistorical character, there would have been no relational psychoanalysis with its achievements and controversies, and all of us would remain closeted in our strangeness masking as countertransference and our authority masking as neutrality. Twenty years later, almost to the day, now a co-editor of a journal that was born of this movement, I, and all of us at *Studies in Gender and Sexuality*, cannot be more pleased to be able to recognize Jessica's monumental contribution to our undeniable collective progress.

The collection of articles presented here traces, by necessity, only some of the themes addressed by and following *The Bonds of Love*. Some of the contributors to the collection are Jessica's contemporaries reflecting on their encounter with the book and its resonance with their own work and circumstances. Some represent a second generation of thinkers who look back and forward as they contemplate and elaborate on the book's contribution to our discourse. The essays come to us from the West and East coasts of the United States, from the United Kingdom, Germany, France, Israel, and Australia. Some of the contributions are more personal, some more theoretical. There are quite a few poetic moments to be found, and there are even photographs to look at. Finally, there is an essay by Jessica. There is a lot. And so we have decided to publish these essays, 14 in all, including this introduction, in two consecutive issues of the journal.

This first issue includes essays by Gillian Straker, Francisco J. González, Andrea Celenza, Fran Bartkowski, Boaz Shalgi, and Régine Waintrater. The second issue will include essays

THE BONDS OF LOVE, REVISITED

by Jessica Benjamin, Uri Hadar, Galit Atlas-Koch, Noreen O'Connor, Martin Altmeyer, Stephen Hartman, and Donna Bassin.

All of us at *Studies in Gender and Sexuality* wish to extend our deepest gratitude to the contributors to this collection. *The Bonds of Love* is an immensely inspired and far-reaching text and for that very reason not an easy one to comment on. The contributors took upon themselves a formidable task when they agreed to take part in this project. The result is a resounding testimony to the reach of the book, now 25 years after its publication, but no less so to the depth and potency of contemporary psychoanalytic thinking.

As will become evident when you read through the essays that follow, each of the contributors found in *The Bonds of Love* his or her own idiom to respond to. For me, it is the way the book pivots around and succeeds in reframing our most basic conception of the relations between knowledge and ethics vis-à-vis a feminist critique of gender. In Jessica's words,

> Let me be clear about the stakes of this critique: it is not a matter merely of exposing bias, or of the exclusion of women from a world they wish to enter. If the rational, autonomous individual's claim to neutrality is compromised, then so is his claim to universality. If his way of being in the world is not simply human, but specifically masculine, then it is not universal. And this means that his way is not the only or inevitable way of doing things. Furthermore, if this subject establishes his identity by splitting off certain human capabilities, called feminine, and by refusing to recognize the subjectivity of this feminine other, than his claim to stand for equality, liberty, free thought, and recognition of the other is also invalidated. And this means that his way cannot be the best way of doing things [Benjamin, 1988, pp. 188–189].

REFERENCES

Benjamin, J. (1988). *The Bonds of Love: Psychoanalysis, Feminism, and the Problem of Domination*. New York, NY: Pantheon Books.
Wittig, M. (1992). *The Straight Mind*. Boston, MA: Beacon Press.

The Racialization of the Mind in Intimate Spaces: The "Nanny" and the Failure of Recognition

Gillian Straker, Ph.D.
University of Witwatersrand and University of Sydney

Jessica Benjamin's (1988) notion that relations of dominance and submission reflect an original difficulty between child and caretaker is reviewed. The need for caretakers to be affected by the child's robust attempts to control them while at the same time neither retaliating nor capitulating is affirmed as is the idea that gender relations can compromise this endeavor. This article then takes further Benjamin's focus on gender relations in the family to include an exploration of the role of siblings. The article then moves to expand Benjamin's focus on gender relations in society to include race relations. The intersection of race and gender relations in apartheid South Africa is explored with special reference to the "nanny." Within this context I question Benjamin's placing of an ethical obligation on the oppressed to establish themselves as subjects and explore the complexity of this issue. However, I validate Benjamin's fine analysis of the factors that may inhibit some oppressors' attempts to be subjects in the face of the oppressed; these factors include a bypassing of shame and attempts to short-circuit the anger of the oppressed.

When Eyal Rozmarin asked me to write a piece in honor of Jessica Benjamin's (1988) book, I found myself pulled back to a Sunday afternoon at the home of a friend, Rise, in South Africa; we shared much in common and read many books together, mostly novels with a feminist slant. It was with Rise that I first began to read *Bonds of Love*. It is a testament to the groundbreaking nature of this book that I remember not only its contents but also the context in which I first encountered it so many years ago. This is especially so as there is much I have forgotten about my own personal life during that tumultuous political time.

My knowledge of feminism at that time came mainly from novels, for two reasons: first, South Africa was in the midst of an academic boycott; second, the academic reading and writing I was engaged in was dominated by the urgency of engaging with issues of racism and apartheid. It was a double pleasure therefore to receive Jessica's book, sent to me as a gift by Melanie Suchet, a South African living in the United States and now known by many readers of *Studies in Gender and Sexuality*. In it was a note that read, "Hey Gilly read this book. It's great." It certainly is.

Jessica's book presents an analysis of human relations of great relevance to issues of apartheid and racism, even though this is not its explicit agenda. My only regret is that I did not have access to it earlier when I was writing a paper on the institution of the "nanny" and its role in the development of racism. My paper was published in 1990, two years after Jessica's book was published in New York. However, I received the book only after I had written my paper. Her insights would have substantially furthered my understanding, and I intend now, in this article, to revisit questions raised in my original paper, with the additional insights Jessica offers into the roots of domination and submission, a mode of relating that characterizes racism of all kinds. In doing so, I hope that you, the reader, will factor into the equation that gender relations is not my area of expertise; I hope nevertheless to honor Jessica's work and to acknowledge its contribution to our understanding of all relationships of dominance and submission. What follows are thoughts and ideas stimulated by Jessica's work, which I present for discussion and development, as they are works in process.

The first idea pertains to the possibility of extending Jessica's ideas concerning gender relations to race relations. The second idea pertains to extending family influences that shape gender relations to encompassing the role of siblings. A further thought pertains to the possibility, or, more accurately, the impossibility of resisting such shaping. In this regard, I applaud Jessica's notion that each of us might have an ethical responsibility to resist submission and assert ourselves as subjects when we are members of an oppressed group. However, I question the viability of this in circumstances of extreme oppression. My final thoughts pertain to Jessica's extension of the idea of dominance and submission to notions of sadism and how this might explain some of the more extreme forms of racism that continue to plague postapartheid South Africa.

I begin with recapping my understanding of Jessica's thoughts concerning how it is that patterns of domination and submission come to be sedimented into our being in the first place. I choose as my specific focus Jessica's notions concerning the influence of the mother-child relationship on the development of this mode of relating. I leave out of the equation Jessica's focus on the father, not because he is unimportant, and indeed, it is a strength of Jessica's work that she highlights his function. I do so because my focus is on the role of the nanny in the development of relationships of dominance and submission based on race. As such, my focus is on women and the role of the mother. I am well aware of the distinction between mothers and fathers as women and men, and maternal and paternal functions, which can operate independently of the gender of the person. However, it remains true that in most societies there is a strong tendency to assign these functions according to gender. Thus, my focus on women in this article is also a focus on the maternal function and the effects of its failure.

BENJAMIN ON RECOGNITION

Benjamin (1988) essentially argues that a preoccupation with domination and submission is the result of a breakdown of equal, mutual relationships. She sees the capacity for mutual relationships as having its roots in childhood. Mutuality is based on the development of the capacity for recognition of the other. The development of recognition has several moments. The first of these is the pleasure that infant and caretaker may share in the experience of similar affects. This pleasure is experienced when both parties share a positive affect generated in mutual play, and each recognizes the smile on the face of the other, so to speak. The second of these, usually at about 10 months, is the moment when the infant and caretaker can both look at an object in the world and enjoy it together. Alternatively, as is often the case, the caretaker enjoys the infant's enjoyment, that is, the caretaker enjoys contacting the infant's state of mind. These first and the second moments of the infant's experience may be summarized, respectively, as follows: We are feeling this. I know that you who are another mind are feeling this same feeling as me. In this second moment the infant realizes that there are separate minds out there, but, as yet, these minds do not seem to be independent from the infant (Benjamin, 1990).

However, at about 2 years old the child becomes aware that he or she and the caretaker may feel differently, and this precipitates a crisis. It is the successful negotiation of this crisis that sets the scene for mutuality and the failure of negotiation that sets the scene for relationships of domination and submission (Benjamin, 1988). In her assertions that the failure of negotiation of the crisis of difference and separateness is at the basis of a preoccupation with dominance and submission, Benjamin (1988) draws on the developmental work of Winnicott (1971) and the philosophical work of Hegel (1807).

Winnicott (1971) asserts that, at the moment the child realizes that he or she and the *mother* feel differently, he becomes threatened by her independence and the fact that satisfaction of his needs, wishes, and desires are dependent upon her. This compromises his omnipotence and his absoluteness. The child attempts to deal with this by employing multiple strategies to assert control over the mother and to reestablish his sense of omnipotence. However, the child is in a conundrum. If he fails to assert his omnipotence, he has to acknowledge his dependence on her. However, if he succeeds, he finds himself in an unsafe world. He might then be king, but there is nobody stronger and bigger than him to take care of him. He is also left at the mercy of his own aggression. This aggression, which arises as a tension within, requires regulation. If the mother collapses in the face of this aggression and cannot stand her own ground, his aggression comes to be felt as a destructive force. It is no longer an unconscious phantasy, but has a destructive effect in the external world. This is a terrifying experience for the child and does not allow him to establish a sense of difference between internal objects and people in the external world. Thus, he is prone to symbolic equivalence and all the terrors that can attach thereto. Therefore, Winnicott believes that the greatest gift a mother can give her child is the capacity to destroy her in phantasy while she survives in reality by standing her ground against the aggression expressed toward her. It is her survival of his aggression, real and imagined, that helps the child to distinguish between his internal world of objects and introjects and the external world of people and events.

For the mother to give her child this gift, she has to be able to withstand his or her aggression without fragmenting and becoming submissive or retaliating and becoming dominating. If she is unable to stay her ground and endlessly capitulates to the demands of the child, or if she fragments in the face of his aggression, he is unlikely to moderate his own narcissism. He is likely to become tyrannical in interpersonal relationships and to dominate others. If she becomes retaliatory and dominating herself, the child is likely to become submissive and struggle to have a sense of self outside of a compliant adaptation to the other.

Benjamin (1988) adds to Winnicott (1971) in arguing that these two different modes of relating to the child by the mother are likely to be influenced by the gender of the child. Mothers relate differently to male and female children. They are more likely to be submissive in relation to male children and to dominate the female children. This is because, in the home, it is likely that the mother herself is required to be more submissive to her male partner than he is required to be in relation to her, presuming of course the family is a heterosexual one. These differences based on gender are carried over in the way in which the mother relates to her children. It is these differences that Benjamin highlights in her discussion of the evolution of relationships of dominance and submission.

There is no doubt in my mind that Benjamin (1988) is correct that gender relations between parents shape patterns of dominance and submission in their children, but it is my belief that, in addition to parents, siblings play a crucial role in the maintenance of relationships of dominance and submission. It is not only how the caretakers (both mothers and fathers) relate to their children that solidify these gender relations but also how all the children in the family are shaped into relating to one another.

SIBLINGS AND GENDER RELATIONS IN THE HOME

This role of siblings in shaping gender relations in the home is poignantly expressed in the following autobiographical snippet given to me by a highly intelligent, creative, and intuitive colleague who spoke of her lifelong struggle to free herself from compliance forged in the domestic bonds of love that Benjamin (1988) has described:

> In our family there were Dad and Mum, my two sisters, Jenny and Elaine, and me. I am the eldest. We did not have any pets but we did have some chooks in our backyard.
>
> But our family was not finished yet because we didn't have a boy.
>
> We had three bedrooms in our house. The third one was a tiny room at the end of the kitchen. Because I was the oldest of the three girls, I was allowed to have this room by myself when I was seven.
>
> One night when I should have been safely asleep in my cosy flannelette pyjamas, I overheard my parents talking in the kitchen. "What will we do if it's not a boy this time, David?" asked my mum. "We'll try again, Marj. We'll try again" he replied. But we didn't have to.
>
> Our boy arrived a few weeks later. And I knew just how special he was. We all knew how special he was. We took good care of him and we loved watching mum change his nappy on the kitchen table and see his little penis send a jet of wee high into the air. He was different. He was very special.
>
> With three sisters and a mother to look after him, he would want for nothing. As he grew we learnt to read his little signs and alert mum to them in case she hadn't noticed. Watching him twist his little fingers around each other we would call to her, "Mum, he wants a drink." And keep at her until he got it.
>
> Of course, he was slow learning to talk; he had no need. But how clever we were in learning his language, so that we could serve him, our special boy. The only one who could carry on the family name.
>
> We loved him so much. We loved his beautiful, long, fair curls. We wished that we had long, fair curls too. His hair grew so long and beautiful that mum would not cut it. When I took him for a walk around the streets in his little blue stroller, ladies would stop me and say, "What lovely curls she's got!" "No, no, he's a boy!" I would say.
>
> As soon as we got home I begged her, "Mum, please, please cut his hair. People think he's a girl."
>
> When he was two and we had made the move to our new house at Miranda, he would not go to sleep some nights. So I'd lie beside him on the bed and stroke his soft, soft hair and the side of his dear little cheek. I did not mind lying there, stroking him and felt so proud, creeping out to announce, "He's asleep!"
>
> I could be sure of a word of praise or thanks. It was worth it!
>
> And where was Dad? Not home. Or sitting in his chair, reading, but still not really there. Not with us. And we were minding his boy, his special one. Then we could be special too!

What is illuminating about this story is how it depicts the home as a total institution, to borrow a term from Goffman (1961). It is geared to support the narcissism of boys and the compliance of girls. Doubtless, at the time that my 60+ colleague grew up, all state institutions reflected these values. Thus, there was unlikely to be any counterpoint to my colleague's experiences in her family offered at school or elsewhere.

It is of note in this story that the dad is perceived to be absent, even while his influence is ever present and ubiquitous. This again would be characteristic of family structures of the time and place of my colleague's childhood (Mitchell, 1974; Dinnerstein, 1976; Chodorow, 1978; Dimen, 1991). What is also of note is the degree to which the mother is perceived to be present and active in solidifying the gender relations the father approves of, not only by enacting them in relation to him but also in shaping these gender relations between the siblings. The role of the mother in regulating sibling relations not only in regard to gender, but more generally, has been termed by Mitchell (2003) "the law of the mother," a law that in my view has been undertheorized in psychoanalytic work. It is a counterpoint to the much-written-about law of the father. It is the law of the father, or the name of the father, in Lacanian terms (Fink, 1997), which determines how we relate to authority on a more vertical plane. How we negotiate this law is conventionally considered to determine how we manage Oedipus and our entry to the Lacanian Symbolic order and the social contract that this implies (Fink, 1997).

However, it seems to me, in accordance with Mitchell (2003), that the first inklings we may have of fairness and justice come from the law of the mother. It is this law that regulates the negotiations that take place between the more potentially equal relations between siblings rather than the more vertical relations between parents and children, albeit that there are also hierarchies between siblings as seen in the aforementioned vignette. Nevertheless, in this vignette, it is the ever present law of the mother that gives voice to the law of the father and that sets the scene for a variety of social contracts between siblings. It is her voice that actively determines whether siblings will come to recognize one another in Benjamin's (1988) meaning of the term *recognition*. It is she who gives expression to the father's views and establishes a hierarchy of dominance and submission between siblings. She shapes our entry into broader social contracts. She, herself, may be regulated by the law of the father, but it is her law that first regulates the sibling relationships. As such, I believe the law of the mother to be crucial in the negotiation of the kind of reciprocity and mutuality that Benjamin (1990) speaks about. In her story, my colleague does not comment directly on her relationship with her mother. However, the degree to which this colleague experienced herself to be subject to the demand of the mother to care for her brother ahead of herself does not bode well. I have read other stories that my colleague has written, and it is clear in these further stories, as well as in discussions with this colleague, that she has had a very difficult relationship with her mother. She also had extreme difficulty freeing herself from the prison of her own mind, which demanded that she comply with the demand of the other, a demand forged in these familial bonds of love. Nevertheless, my colleague has taken on board the task of freeing herself, both through her writing and through a lifelong journey of personal exploration. Thus, she has shouldered the ethical responsibility that Benjamin (1998) believes we all have to establish ourselves as subjects.

OBLIGATIONS AND OPPRESSION

Thinking through Benjamin's (1998) notion that we all have a responsibility to establish ourselves as subjects, I find myself ambivalent. In theory I agree with Benjamin about the importance of resistance and thus take Benjamin's point that the oppressed have an obligation, an ethical responsibility, to establish themselves as subjects when confronted with those who oppress them (Benjamin, 1998). However, in practice, I believe Benjamin (1998) underestimates the difficulties of shouldering such an obligation, and I elaborate on this in my discussion of the extreme oppression that pertained to domestic workers in South Africa. I further believe that Benjamin underestimates the shame and guilt that oppressed people may feel if they feel obligated, and, at the same time, feel unable to fulfill this obligation. There is also the question of who we are, and how we are positioned in society, when we speak of the obligations of the oppressed.

Indeed, the issue of obliging the oppressed to mutuality was challenged in a different key in the context of the Truth and Reconciliation Commission (TRC) in South Africa. In this situation, the obligation was less to assert oneself as a subject from the position of the oppressed but rather to forgive the erstwhile oppressor and thereby return to the possibility of a mutual recognition of each other as subjects. This obligation was a subtle undercurrent in the TRC and was criticized as the requirement to forgive was experienced by many as another form of oppression (Straker, 1999; Moosa, Straker, and Eagle, 2004).

It is in the light of these concerns that I return to Benjamin (1998) and to her sense that the oppressed have an ethical responsibility to assert their subjecthood in the face of their oppressors. Although Benjamin states her position in regard to this obligation most directly in *The Shadow of the Other* (1998), it is implicit in all her work.

In *The Shadow of the Other* (1998), Benjamin speaks of Mandela taking an ethical responsibility for being a subject before symmetrical power relations had been achieved in South Africa, and she goes on to extend this ethical responsibility to all. Thus, she states, "any subject's primary responsibility to the other subject is to be her intervening or surviving other" (Benjamin, 1998, p. 99). However, Mandela is an exceptional human being, and, as Benjamin (1998) points out, he had the solidarity and backing of the African National Congress. Mandela is exceptional precisely because he was able, against the odds, to assert himself as a subject. I believe that Benjamin underestimates the enormity of these odds when more extreme forms of oppression pertain than in the political context in which Benjamin herself lives.

Oppression, including gender oppression, is more virulent in many countries than in the United States, both when *Bonds of Love* was written and at the current time. Certainly, during apartheid, the conditions of most black women employed as domestic workers and caretakers of white children were extraordinarily oppressive. These women who were expected to care for white children up to 7 hr a day and more (Wulfsohn, 1988) had almost no opportunity to establish themselves as subjects without risking the most onerous consequences.

THE "NANNY" IN THE CONTEXT OF APARTHIED

Cock (1980), in her groundbreaking book *Maids and Madams,* describes the exploitation and conditions of extreme dependence suffered by black women during the apartheid years. She points out that domestic workers were not only dependent on their employers for their livelihood but also they frequently resided on the property where they worked. Loss of employment for domestic workers, therefore, often meant not only a loss of income but a loss of abode as well. Furthermore, under the pass laws, loss of employment often meant loss of the right to remain in a particular residential area at all.

Thus, loss of employment could be catastrophic for black women. This was especially so as domestic workers were often illiterate and poorly educated. This was a result both of the poor quality of education offered to blacks and because domestic work was available to less skilled individuals (Kuzwayo, 1985). Lacking in education and skills, and operating in a society where there were high levels of unemployment, the black nanny under apartheid was open to extreme exploitation. Because she frequently lived at the site of her employment, her private life as well as her work life came under the scrutiny and control of her employer. The times at which she was allowed visitors, and whether they could spend the night, whether her own children could stay with her, and many other personal and intimate aspects of her life were controlled by her employers (Cock, 1980).

Thus, the black nanny operated in a system that underlined her powerlessness. This powerlessness was a fact in the external world, and, although individuals took up different positions in relation to this, and some may have succumbed to a surplus submission whereas others resisted it, there is no doubt that submission was demanded, not on pain of death, but certainly with life-threatening consequences for self and family. Is it any wonder therefore that many black women were unable to consistently assert themselves as subjects, even though there may have been moments of resistance? Whether or not black women resisted their objectification, and the degree to which black women were not seen as subjects by whites, is captured in comments recorded in one of the very few studies conducted during the apartheid years.

THE OBJECTIFICATION OF THE BLACK NANNY

The degree to which white women objectified the black nanny who looked after their children is exemplified in the following comments in a study conducted by Wulfsohn (1988) on the mother's relationship with the nanny and her perception of the child's relationship with the nanny:

> My daughter knows the nanny can't sit with us at the table and sit on the same furniture—my children have been brought up that way [p. 170].

> When we're eating at the table and her sister asks the girl to come and sit with us, she tells her sister that the nanny may not come and sit with us at the table [p. 170].

> We don't take the girl on holiday. I need a break from her, too, because she does sometimes intrude on our family life. Also it's such a hassle to organise her special food, you know like boys-meat and mealie-meal [p. 173].

> I don't talk to Blacks much, I don't think it's a good idea [p. 172].

It is little wonder that, with such parental endorsement of children's lack of recognition of the nanny and with iniquitous social structures in place, black women struggled to assert themselves against their white charges. Concomitantly, is it any wonder that many white children developed an extreme sense of entitlement in relation to black people and perpetuated the racism in which they were immersed from birth? Certainly, narcissism and entitlement characterized adult relations of whites to blacks during the apartheid years. Furthermore, as I now live in Australia, I am aware that some Australians believe that many South African immigrants demonstrate this entitlement in other spheres. Having said this, it behooves us to remember that, in general, the culture of the West has been labeled the "Culture of Narcissism" (Lasch, 1979).

White South Africans are not alone in being thought of as narcissistic, but then the United States also has a slave heritage and a history of black women caring for white children. Perhaps this should give us some pause for thought, and even as we pause for thought, it is important to factor into the equation that mothers, as well as nannies, were involved in caretaking. Given this, it is likely that mothers who were more empowered than their black employees were better able to assert themselves in relation to their children. This would offset a more generalized narcissism while not offsetting the entitlement and demand of their white children in relation to their black nannies and by extension to black people in general. It is also important to note that, although the comments made by mothers in Wulfsohn's (1988) study were not uncommon, they also were not universal, and in many homes there was a focus on children having some respect for the generational divide that operated between children and their nannies. However, even in these homes, it was often the case that the nanny's inequality remained deeply embedded in everyday practices. Racism and inequality were expressed in the use of everyday objects as in most white homes the nanny was not allowed to drink from the same cups or eat from the same plates. Everyday objects were an ever present reminder of inequalities and relations of submission and domination.

In commenting thus on the role of the home in supporting racism, I am aware that what happened in the home was only possible because of the legal, economic, and social structures that underpinned the racism of apartheid. I do not underestimate the crucial importance of these structures. Nevertheless, the home played its part in establishing apartheid of the mind. Given the degree to which childcare was outsourced to black women under apartheid, it is hard to believe that white children, to their detriment, would not feel the effects of the radical disempowerment of their black caretakers in the very intimate space of the home. I believe this to be so, even though the nanny was seen by many children as a shadowy figure who lacked the substance of the mother (Wulfsohn, 1988). Indeed, this subjective experience of the nanny as a shadowy figure could be seen, in and of itself, to be an indicator of the child's difficulty in recognizing the nanny as a person and subject in her own right.

The degree to which white children lacked empathy for their black caretakers, and the degree to which they did not see them as subjects, is reflected in further comments from Wulfsohn's (1988) study. Before presenting these comments, however, I wish to reiterate once again my belief that black women were not in a position to push back against these children without running the risk of severe consequences to their livelihoods and existence. Given their living and working conditions, these women were well aware that to be a good employee meant being a grateful and endlessly patient worker. Thus, for white children the feedback required not only for the development of a sense of the other as subject but also for a sense of empathy was absent. The degree to which this empathy was absent is reflected in the following comments from Wulfsohn's study, as mothers reflected on their children's attitude toward the nanny:

> When I ask my child to clean up his mess he tells me that he's not a nanny.

> When my child has to tidy up, she responds, "Anna will do it; she's just the maid."

The devastating interpersonal consequences of this lack of empathy and objectification of the other is further illustrated Wulfsohn's (1988) observations of the children in her study:

> When the child came into the house, she took off her wet shoes and handed them over to the nanny without looking at or greeting the nanny [p. 172].

> Not once did this child glance in the direction of its nanny, who was vacuuming in the same room in the course of the testing [p. 173].

> The child snatched her leotard from her nanny without any sign of appreciation or recognition for the time the nanny had spent hunting for it at the whining demand of the child [p. 173].

Although the aforementioned quotes reflect all too clearly distorted interpersonal relationships focused on relations of submission and domination, in my opinion they stop short of sadism, and I find myself wishing to end my own exploration of the issue of racism here. Indeed, at this point my previous paper ended. However, as Benjamin (1988, 1995) has taken us further into the murkiness of sadism in gender relations, I find myself challenged to continue this exploration in relation to race relations.

SADISM, RELATIONSHIPS OF DOMINATION/SUBMISSION, AND RACE

It is a strength of Benjamin's (1988, 1995) work that she takes us beyond narcissism and entitlement to an exploration of sadism. Unlike Klein (1984), who is more inclined to see sadism as constitutional, Benjamin sees it as a flow on effect of the fusion of sex and aggression fostered in relationships based on dominance and submission. When the child's aggression is extreme, and the caretaker is unable to modulate this aggression interpersonally, the child remains in the sway of an unconscious fantasy or *phantasy* to use the Kleinian (1984) term. As Benjamin (1995, 1998) indicates the child depends on the mother to push back adequately without fragmenting or being retaliatory in order to establish himself or herself as a real person. This idea that the mother needs to push back and contain the child's aggression by processing it without capitulating to it reflects both the views of Winnicott (1971) and Klein (1984) despite Klein's greater emphasis on constitutional factors. Both these theorists see the child as engaged in unconscious phantasies of destruction of the all-powerful mother, who is also fearsome as she is imagined as retaliatory and as requiring an omnipotence to manage this retaliation, an omnipotence the child imagines that he has. When the mother does not contain the child's aggression but fragments or retaliates, the child is left at the mercy of his phantasies, which involve not only a self that is omnipotent but also a mother who is terrifying and monstrous as both her retaliation and her fragmentation in the face of his aggression are feared. If the mother does not set limits on the child's aggression in the world outside his phantasies, it is hard for the child to escape from his inner world and the images it contains. This lays the groundwork for an attack upon the terrifying mother, both internally and externally, an attack that may become sexually tinged as the child's awareness of his own sexuality and the mother's/caretaker's enters the frame.

It is this dynamic of fusion of sex and aggression that might explain some of the continuing racial violence in South Africa, where the institution of the nanny persists. A recent incident that was widely reported in the press involved a group of white university students who humiliated black women cleaners caring for them in their student residence. These students videotaped themselves forcing these women to eat food that it appeared the students had urinated in while they watched with sadistic enjoyment. In her analysis of this incident, Shaffer (2012) points to the sexual connotations that were seen to inhabit this event, both by interviewees and by discussants. Thus, Shaffer lends support to the notion that the fusion of sex and aggression underpins sadism. This fusion can be seen very early on in a quote from a white South African child in

Wulfsohn's (1988) study. What is also clear in this quote is the extremity of the powerlessness of the nanny:

> When Catherine bathes my brother and me, I can see her titties. I try and pull her clothes away, I splash her with water. She gets cross with me so I smack her on her titties. It doesn't matter, she is just the maid [p. 158].

Reflected in this quote is this young boy's acute awareness of the powerless position of the nanny even as she tries to push back. Indeed, it is clear that when Catherine does try to push back, and her charge recognizes this, he ups the ante and overrides her attempt. He clearly believes himself to be safe in the protection of his white parents, a protection that ironically leaves him very unsafe indeed. He is left unsafe because Catherine, his caretaker and substitute mother, cannot contain his aggression and thus leaves him at its mercy and in a compromised mind state that may indeed become enacted in sadism.

As I end this article, hoping to have achieved my intention of extending Benjamin's ideas concerning dominance and submission in gender relations to a consideration of race relations, I wish to add a caveat.

CAVEAT

In indicating the extensive objectification of black women by white children and the difficulty that black women had in establishing themselves as subjects, I am mindful of the fact that not all white South African children related to their childcare workers in this way. There were also white employers who may have related in ways designed to empower the childcare worker as far as possible in this situation of general second-class citizenship.

I am also mindful that in particular moments many black women were able to resist their subjugation. As individuals, we all have many self-states. However, I believe the penalties for too vigorous and sustained overt resistance by black women in domestic employment would often have led to dismissal, and they would no longer be employed as childcare workers. Sustained overt, personal resistance was therefore unlikely although there may well have been moments of assertion of the self as subject. As Shireen Ally (personal communication, 2012) points out, this difficulty in establishing oneself as subject in the face of the other did not preclude domestic workers from engaging in covert resistance. She cites a book on apartheid by Ginsberg (2011) in which there is a chapter called "House Rules," which indicates how domestic workers break house rules in numerous ways as acts of resistance and subversion. However, Ally questions the relationship between these acts of resistance and the establishment of oneself as subject and indicates that they may not be equivalent. It is my view that they are not as the establishment of oneself as subject can only occur in a relational context whereas resistance can occur outside of this.

It is of note that the Apartheid Archive Project, initiated to collect experiences of apartheid in everyday life, does not yet offer stories of resistance by childcare workers. If there were more stories in the Apartheid Archive Project from these workers, a different picture might well emerge as indicated by Ally (2012). There are, however, many stories that pertain to the cost of being a nanny both to the person involved and to her own children. There are also stories from whites concerning their perception of resistance by their own nannies, but this resistance was still a resistance sanctioned by their white parents and not an assertion against white employers, as exemplified in the following story:

> Both my parents worked for their entire working lives. During my formative years, I was brought up by a Zulu maid, C Z, who we called "Zaza." She came to work for us when I was five years old, in about 1967. My expectation that she would approach our relationship from a position of complete subservience was sorely misplaced. When Zaza told me to pick up my clothes from the floor, I did not feel the need to take her seriously. I uttered a few choice words to her, with racial connotations, and received in turn a few hard slaps to the bottom. My first corporal reprimand from Zaza was met with unbridled indignation. When my parents came home from work, I told them of this "gratuitous" assault on me, and expected her to receive the appropriate sanction. My hopes were dashed when my mother asked her what had happened, and preferred her version to mine (Zaza did not lie). In my presence Zaza was given full permission to use whatever force it took to discipline me. I have to commend my mother for her endorsement of Zaza's authority. Zaza had full control of our household. She would decide what we ate for supper. She would decide how to feed and attend to my two baby brothers. She would decide what groceries needed to be bought, and she would look after us when my parents came home late from work. Zaza became my authority figure and I had to answer to her... Zaza was one tough cookie. (SN37, white, female, 40 s) [Apartheid Archive Project, 2009].

However, as Shaffer (2012) points out, this show of power was only possible through the authorization of the white parents. She points out further that the white mother is commended for "allowing" Zaza such authority. The limitations of this aside, especially from Zaza's point of view, it is nevertheless clear that this narrator does not lack empathy in the same way as the children in Wulfsohn's (1988) study do, and it would not seem far-fetched to believe that this was, at least partly, due to the fact that Zaza, when given the opportunity, stood her ground.

This story is not the only story in the Apartheid Archive Project that indicates the deep attachment of white children to black nannies. Some of these stories are discussed in more depth in my paper "Shaping Subjectivities," in which I also refer to Suchet's (2007) moving account of her relationship with Dora, whose second name is not mentioned, perhaps because it was not known (Straker, 2011).

Thus, even positive attachments between white children and their black caretakers were complicated by the contexts in which they occurred. Frequently, intense attachments occurred in situations where the white children were unhappy in the home, and their black nanny was their only source of solace. The following quote from the Apartheid Archive Project reflects an attachment of this nature:

> Mrs. M was my substitute mother during the many long hours that my own mother was at work. It is difficult to explain the relationship between a black female domestic worker and a white child in apartheid South Africa. We were both separated out of necessity from our biological family and so a bond developed between our two fractured hearts. (N60, white woman, 40s) [Apartheid Archive Project, 2009].

What Mrs. M's own feelings were we do not know. However, what we do know from our knowledge of some of the Apartheid Archive Project contributors is that white children in these circumstances often became activists in later life. Nevertheless, in taking up these positions we could still ask whether there was an unconscious phantasy of being a rescuer, a phantasy that might embody the power relations they had learned in the home. The rescuer occupies a position of power in relation to the one to be rescued. How these power relations are then negotiated requires much thought and reflection. It is easy in this position to be paternalistic without even realizing it, as indicated in many of the apartheid narratives (Straker, 2011).

Furthermore, having said this, I am not oblivious to the irony that my focus is on white children and the damage I believe they sustained as an effect of exposure to the unequal power relations that are intrinsic to the institution of the "nanny." It was black women and their children who suffered most tangibly as a result not only of this institution but also the whole system that sustained it, and indeed, there are narratives in the Apartheid Archive Project that attest to this:

> So I grew up knowing my place: As far away from the white person as possible. The white person had power to invade my mother's privacy, and to decide when she could see her kids. I had to be as quiet as possible around a white person. Any marker of my existence disturbed her/him. (N31, male, black, 50s) [Apartheid Archive Project, 2009].

> I watched my mother bringing up white kids, serving white people to ensure that we were fed. With each year that passed, I watch her energy slipping away, ounce by ounce, punctuated by unceremonious dismissals if my mom dared express an opinion. (N31 male, black, 50s) [Apartheid Archive Project, 2009].

However, I choose to focus on white experience, not simply to document it but also to try to understand the roots of racism to attempt to ameliorate it. In this, I hope to go beyond description and to try to take into account criticisms such as that leveled against the recent film *The Help*, which looked at domestic service across race lines. The film, set in the Deep South before the success of the civil rights movement, was criticized by the Association of Black Women Historians (2011). Despite the film's clear disapproval of the exploitation of black women by white women, the film was seen to erase the voice of the black worker herself. I am aware that I am not exempt from this criticism; however, I hope this article goes beyond the depiction of the experience of whites benefitting from blacks to use these experiences along with Benjamin's (1988) insights to come to a deeper understanding of the perpetuation of racism.

CONCLUSION

In concluding, I reiterate my appreciation of Benjamin's enormously important work. I wish, in ending, to align myself with her thinking about ethical responsibilities of the oppressor. Although I believe that in circumstances of extreme oppression it is problematic for any person outside of the particular circumstances of oppression to designate it to be an ethical responsibility of the oppressed to establish subjecthood, I also believe that we as oppressors do well to think of the responsibilities Benjamin points toward. There are many like myself who may feel guilt and shame for having been both a witting and unwitting oppressor. Benjamin (1998) speaks to us. She reminds us of the dangers of fleeing our guilt, either by attacking the victim or by losing our own subjectivity, and fragmenting in the face of the other's expressed distress and anger. If we fragment, or attack, we in effect refuse to negotiate a true recognition of ourselves as subjects or to recognize the other as subject in relation to the self. We thus leave the victim to cope with his or her own anger without the opportunity of interpersonal modulation as we sink into the narcissistic morass of our own shame and guilt.

I thank you, Jessica, for reminding me of this. It is indeed true, and I take it on board as much as I can. However, just as I believe that the oppressed need legal and social structures that facilitate the establishment of self as subject (as indeed Jessica believes), so too I believe oppressors need legal and social structures that provide for reparation and restitution of wrongs, not in order to allow us to bypass personal responsibility but to help us to better own our own responsibility with the support of a well-functioning symbolic order.

REFERENCES

Apartheid Archive Project. (2009). http://www.apartheidarchive.org/site/index.php
Association of Black Women Historians. (2011). *An Open Statement to the Fans of The Help*. Retrieved from http://www.abwh.org/index.php?option=com_content&view=article&id=2:open-statement-the-help&catid = 1:latest-news
Benjamin, J. (1988). *The Bonds of Love*. New York, NY: Pantheon.
———. (1990). An outline of intersubjectivity. *Psychoanalytic Psychology*, 7S, 33–46.
———. (1995). *Like Subjects, Love Objects*. New Haven, CT: Yale University Press.
———. (1998). *The Shadow of the Other*. New York, NY: Routledge.
Chodorow, N. (1978). *The Reproduction of Mothering*. Berkeley: University of California Press.
Cock, J. (1980). *Maids and Madams*. Johannesburg, South Africa: Ravan Press.
Dimen, M. (1991). Deconstructing difference: Gender splitting & transitional space. *Psychoanalytic Dialogues*, 1, 335–352.
Dinnerstein, D. (1976). *The Mermaid and the Minotaur*. New York, NY: Harper & Row.
Fink, B. (1997). *A Clinical Introduction to Lacanian Psychoanalysis*. Cambridge, MA: Harvard University Press.
Ginsberg, R. (2011). *At Home with Apartheid*. Charlottesville, Virginia: University of Virginia Press.
Goffman, E. (1961). *Asylums: Essays on the social situation of mental patients and other inmates*. New York, NY: Anchor Books.
Hegel, G. W. F. (1807). *Phenomenologie des Geistes* [Phenomenology of Sprit]. Hamburg, Germany: Felix Meiner Verlag, 1952.
Klein, M. (1984). *Envy and Gratitude and Other Works 1946–1963*. London, UK: Hogarth Press.
Kuzwayo, E. (1985). *Call me Woman*. Johannesburg, South Africa: Ravan Press.
Lasch, C. (1979). *The Culture of Narcissism: American Life in an Age of Diminishing Expectations*. New York, NY: Norton.
Mitchell, J. (1974). *Psychoanalysis and Feminism*. New York, NY: Pantheon.
———. (2003). *Siblings*. Oxford, UK: Polity Press.
Moosa, F., Straker, G., & Eagle, G. (2004). Forgiveness in the context of political trauma. In: *Forgiveness in a Changing Age*, eds. S. Ransley, & T. Spy, New York, NY: Brunner Routledge, pp. 128–150.
Shaffer, T. (2012). Fraught tenderness: Narratives on domestic workers in memories of apartheid. *Journal of Peace Psychology*, 18(3), 307–317.
Straker, G. (1999). Psychoanalytic reflections on the South African Truth and Reconciliation Commission. *Psychoanalytic Dialogues*, 9(2), 245–274.
———. (2011). Shaping subjectivities: Private memories, public archives. *Psychoanalytic Dialogues*, 21, 1–15.
Suchet, M. (2007). Unraveling whiteness. *Psychoanalytic Dialogues*, 17, 867–886.
Winnicott, D. W. (1971). *Playing and Reality*. London, UK: Tavistock.
Wulfsohn, (1988). *The impact of the South African nanny on the young child* (Doctoral thesis, University of South Africa, Johannesburg, South Africa).

Loosening the Bonds: Psychoanalysis, Feminism, and the Problem of the Group

Francisco J. González, M.D.
Psychoanalytic Institute of Northern California

This article reflects on Jessica Benjamin's important first book, *The Bonds of Love* (1988), considering one of its greatest contributions to be the cultural shift it helped inaugurate in the psychoanalytic understanding of gender and its ethos of reworking and historicizing core psychoanalytic concepts. In this spirit, and following Benjamin's reference to Freud's *Group Psychology and the Analysis of the Ego* (1921), it offers a reconceptualization of the Oedipus, adding to it the psychoanalytic idea of the group. Using groups to theorize gender allows greater flexibility and a more nuanced description of the intersection of the social with subjectivity than do more traditional readings that rely on individual accounts of identification.

. . . and so from the very first individual psychology . . . is at the same time social psychology as well.
—Freud (1921)

Published squarely in what we might now refer to as the age of Reagan, a period seized by the panics of a crumbling modernity, Jessica Benjamin's *The Bonds of Love* (1988) stands in a line of generative works (one hesitates to use the word *seminal*) that mark an important historical turn in psychoanalytic theorizing. Books like Juliet Mitchell's *Psychoanalysis and Feminism* (1974) had marked the crossroads of these two often contentious disciplines, but in *The Bonds of Love*, Benjamin's closest interlocutors and companions are Dorothy Dinnerstein's *The Mermaid and the Minotaur* (1976), Nancy Chodorow's *The Reproduction of Mothering* (1978), and Carol Gilligan's *In a Different Voice* (1982). These writers, and of course many others who would shortly burst upon the scene (notably Dimen, 1991, 1995; Goldner, 1991; Harris, 1991, 1997; Corbett, 1993, 1996; Elise, 1997, 1998; see also Dimen and Goldner, 2002) reinvigorated and fundamentally reshaped the landscape of psychoanalytic thinking about gender. The beauty of their projects is partly to be found in the powerful ways they unfolded and reworked psychoanalytic theory, not merely through a critical dismantling of established analytic shibboleths but also through nuanced reinscriptions and novel readings of existing ideas. That is, not through repudiation but through elaboration. Repudiation, of course, is taken to task in *The Bonds of Love* as a highly problematic mechanism. (Masculinity can hardly be said to have a bedrock, but whatever its foundation, Benjamin insists, its geology must surely be more complex than a simple rejection of "the feminine"). A different strategy prevails, one that calls for ties with past objects to be reworked, reclaimed, and continually resituated in wider contexts and from the vantage points of new developments. Benjamin and her cohort found a complex critical engagement with psychoanalysis, despite its redolent patriarchy, at a time when many repudiating feminists were all too ready to throw the Freudian project overboard.

The kind of relation to theory this work represents—a historicizing one—is in keeping with the psychoanalytic ethos of remembering and reworking and working through. In a way, such reworking is at the heart of most theoretical advancements in psychoanalysis. Even an old patriarch like Melanie Klein, setting her investigations on a much earlier developmental stage than Freud, was able to move the theme of envy from penis to breast and thereby develop a more fundamental, more perdurable theory of psychic motivation. Like clinical work with individual histories in the consulting room, theoretical reworking preserves a lively link to the past while casting it in new lights—thereby changing the past by its relationship to the present. What early theoretical revisions largely did not do, however, was locate the old theory in history, demonstrate its cultural saturation, unpack the ideologies inherent within it. Although we might say Melanie Klein made moves with feminist implications (like radically shifting the analytic limelight from the father to the mother), she did not have the benefit of feminism, at least not as a robust construction for making theory.

There is no doubt that Jessica Benjamin does. Coming two years before the publication of Judith Butler's *Gender Trouble* (1990), *The Bonds of Love* (1988) is an apogee of the very late second wave, kissed by Foucault, acknowledging homosexuality (mostly in the form of homoeroticism between fathers and sons), and quite willing to take on the likes of Andrea Dworkin and Catherine MacKinnon. These last two bastions of essentializing feminism are criticized for failing to recognize the true roots of male domination in *societal* rationality rather than in the direct expression of *personal* violence (p. 216). This move to the social from the personal—or more accurately, this move to an analysis of the close imbrication and resonance between the social and the personal, of their subtle and profound call and response—is the brilliance and the heart of Benjamin's book. In this way, it is a book that does important political work, though it would be facile to call it principally political. As Benjamin (1988) writes in the closing sentences,

> To attempt to recover recognition in personal life does not mean to politicize life relentlessly or to evade politics and give up hope of transformation—though all these failures do happen in real life. It means to see that the personal and the social are interconnected, and to understand that if we suffocate our personal longings for recognition, we will suffocate our hope for social transformation as well [p. 224].

Here, personal longing for recognition becomes the animating engine for social change. Surely this speaks of Benjamin's own longings as a theoretician, a woman who wants theory to "see" and reflect her experience of coming to subjectivity. Rather than follow the erstwhile and reductive feminist call to arms that the *personal is political*—unpacking the practices of the psychopathology of everyday life as the battlegrounds of political emancipation—Benjamin asserts more fundamentally that who we are as persons is already saturated with an unconscious politics, that the process of becoming a subject is itself subject to the inscriptions of the political orders of domination, and further still, that the inequities in the operations of power *as it is gendered* permeate the very theory we have for understanding the psychoanalytic formations of those processes.

It is valuable to return to this book a quarter of a century after it was written to see the deeper warp and woof of relational psychoanalysis itself. The *Bonds of Love* was published the same year as Stephen Mitchell's *Relational Concepts in Psychoanalysis* (1988), and it certainly weaves together intersubjectivity theory and object relations, stitching it through with the attachment theory and infant research that established relational qualities of subjectivity from the earliest developmental stages. But it also illuminates the fascinating backdrop of the narcissism wars (Kohut and Kernberg, yes, but also the "popular narcissism" of Lasch) and particularly just how indispensable were feminism and critical theory. Indeed it is very difficult, impossible really, to imagine a relational psychoanalysis without these theoretical frames.

We often think of relational theory as an emerging from the troubles postmodernism brought to a one-person psychology, but feminism and the critical theory of the Frankfurt School provide indispensable scaffolding. Adorno, Horkheimer, Habermas, Fromm, Marcuse, and their predecessors Marx, Hegel, Weber, and Lukacs all make important appearances in *The Bonds of Love* (1988). Following their theoretical program, Benjamin positions psychoanalytic theory in a wider historical flux, articulating the ideologies that shape the very means of psychoanalytic understanding. It is this interdisciplinary weaving that gives the book its power, as when Benjamin famously braids the Hegelian idea of recognition with intersubjectivity theory in her intricate reading of the *Story of O* and thereby develops a deeply psychoanalytic notion of recognition that continues to retain its currency today.

In a powerful and ingenious turn of turning the method in on itself, she demonstrates the unconscious gendering at work in the very tenets of the Frankfurt School. Thus, the conclusion that the detached, instrumental organization of modern society, one that denigrates dependency and extols self-sufficient autonomy and a rationalist objectivity, are primarily the hallmarks of a masculinist ethos. Instrumental rationality in this analysis is itself primarily an effect of the gendered splitting of parental functioning, and "the state, that purveyor of instrumental rationality, really is symbolically equated with the detached father" (Benjamin, 1988, p. 204).

What *The Bonds of Love* (1988) so usefully does, then, is what all good analysis does: it loosens the too-tight grip we have on interpretation and shakes our convictions in the unassailable "truth" of history, awakening our curiosity, revealing what we thought to be transparent and self-evident as opaque and dense with unformulated meaning. It does this at the level of our theory. In this way it is an analysis of analysis, working in an interdisciplinary fashion to pry open our dearest ideas, so that we can think them anew.

Benjamin's reading of the Oedipus, unquestionably one of the crucibles of gender, is a wonderful example of this kind of opening, and it is here that I wish to concentrate my explorations. As she herself writes in a later contribution (Benjamin, 1992), any psychoanalytic approach to gender inflected by postmodernism will necessarily be overinclusive, paradoxical, and rife with multiplicity: such an approach "is best realized not by excluding old concepts and metaphors so much as by learning to play with them, reinvent and reorder them, to see all the layers of meaning that are part of their cultural and psychic sediment" (p. 423).

I am very sympathetic to this way of thinking. Rather than throw the oedipal baby out with the stagnant psychoanalytic bathwater, she would have us reconstruct the scene. Stephen Mitchell (2000) in his engagement with Benjamin's work, worries about this kind of historical re-reading, finding it at times "formulaic" or "abstract," and concerned that the stress on the preservation of ideas protects outdated concepts that need to be "jettisoned" (p. 265). There is a scientific imperative in his critique, one that rightly stresses the importance of clarity and applicability and hews to a certain narrative of theoretical progress but which neglects, I think, the aesthetic rigor of our particularly psychoanalytic methodology: one that operates in time, through *nachträglichkeit*. The present collection of essays is just such a study. Returning to older ideas and recontextualizing them is itself a praxis of investigation. To continue to work with Oedipus, Freud's or Benjamin's, in a way that strives toward relevancy, is neither clinging to dead ideas nor a facile matter of refurbishing them. It is not simply an attempt to strip off the encumbering "cultural patina" in order to reveal a rationalist algebra of Oedipus underneath (though it can be very useful to desaturate ideas, to make variables of constants while preserving the relations between the elements). It is also to mark and excavate a site of theoretical density in our history that posits more than it can explicate, that carries what we cannot yet quite think or put into words, a kind of "unthought known" (Bollas, 1987) for our theorizing. To do this is to reshape our collective thinking as a discipline. Then, Oedipus becomes more than a positivist formula; it becomes one of the things we put in play with one another, the creative toy of our very serious game, our rubric's cube.

I take up Benjamin's Oedipus in the spirit of such play.

First, let me review her argument about "The Oedipal Riddle" (as one of her chapters is called). Oedipalization here is the principal route to individual subjectivity and the foundry of agency. In the conventional—one must here explicitly read heterosexual—configuration, the roadway to individuality runs through the father and specifically through identificatory love for him. Other authors have noted the kind of "male imaginary" that is preserved in Benjamin's use of paternal identification (Harris, 2005), which continues to privilege the heterosexual father as the guarantor of subjectivity, but the question of identificatory love remains quite fascinating and useful if we expand it, introducing other imaginaries. (Developing the language for these other imaginaries is daunting. Despite our acknowledgment of an array of multiple kinds of family structures and subjective formations, we are still deeply tied in our theoretical language to constellations of Oedipus that devolve on the idea of the holy family of mother, father, and baby.)

For now, Benjamin (1988) would have us understand that the fundamental problem in this scene is that the road to freedom implicates a perverse split between "a father of liberation and a mother of dependency": "it means that being a subject of desire requires repudiation of the maternal role, of feminine identity itself" (pp. 133–134). There is a troubling way in which feminine identity is here once again conflated with the maternal (and perhaps therefore, more insidiously, with reproduction), but Benjamin's project is to demonstrate the unfair burden women (or perhaps even femininity) carry through such a division of psychic labor. This split between "a mother of attachment and a father of separation" (p. 134) is literally embodied in the figure of a male father and a female mother (the redundancy in this expression already demonstrating how conflated are gender and paternity) and serves to gender a whole host of qualities. Thus, separateness, independence, agency, desire, rationality, and subjectivity are the purview of the father and masculinity, whereas dependence, attachment, nurturance, subjection, irrationality, and fusion are the domain of the mother and the feminine. (That this division of labor is also indicative of a larger economy, namely, the most traditional forms of coupledom in heterosexuality, is another matter.) The father rides in on his white horse, triumphant over the forces of maternal tyranny. Not so fast, Benjamin says. The idealization of the good father of sanity, individuality, and freedom is purchased at the expense of the subjugation of women. The father is riding a Trojan horse, if any horse at all, which disguises a covert identification with the pleasures of domination and power, his idealization based on the erotics of ideal love.

It is here that Benjamin embarks on a deeper elaboration of her concept of identificatory love, one of the singular contributions in her work. We can understand this now as part of a larger project of reconstructing theories of heterosexuality because Benjamin's use of the concept of identificatory love challenges the logic of either/or common in reductionistic versions of Oedipus, a logic that mutually excludes erotic object love and identification. In such a system, being a woman means loving a man. In 1988, Benjamin imagines a world in which children of both sexes can use both mother and father as figures of attachment and separation in a culturally validated way (how far, and how little, we have progressed since then). Following Fast's (1984) idea of "overinclusiveness," Benjamin (1988) sees toddlers as having "identification not yet limited by identity" (p. 113) in which "the core sense of belonging to one sex or the other is not compromised by cross-sex identifications or behaviors" (p. 113). The child is free to identify with either sex parent without falling into much gender trouble (Butler, 1990). As *The Bonds of Love* is largely uninfluenced by queer theory, the understanding of identification here can often feel undergirded by a dichotomy of gender ultimately grounded in an essentialized difference between the sexes, though Benjamin is explicitly laying ground for the deconstruction of these categories. (Later, of course, with the efflorescence of queer and trans theory, things will get much more complicated.)

Benjamin takes up her elaboration of identificatory love via Freud's *Group Psychology and the Analysis of the Ego* (1921) and opens an interesting door for us with this text, for there is indeed something very important happening at the level of groups when we think about gender. The "group" is not a term we have made much use of in our gender theory, though it has enormous relevance as a particularly psychoanalytic category (Freud, 1921; Bion, 1961; Foulkes, 1964; Bleger, 1970; Dalal, 1998, 2002; Hopper, 2003; Kaës, 2007). Or rather, we do make regular use of one specific group—the family—though we tend not to treat it as such. This article aims to loosen the bonds we have on thinking about the family as if it were the only constitutive group for gender and sexuality.

As a text, *Group Psychology* (1921) is pregnant and fascinating, a nodal point in Freud in which he is beginning to elaborate a series of intertwined ideas: identificatory love, the ego ideal, and a theory of groups. These ideas will find more refinement later, but in this originary exposition they exist in a strange mix-up, in the myth of the primal horde. Now, the primal horde myth is surely one of the stranger passages in all of Freud, the kind of place where we tend to avert our gaze, but it becomes more palatable as a narrative of gendered group formation, particularly in the way group formation is braided with identification and supra-egoic structures (the ego ideal and superego). I take up a reading of the primal horde later but first need to return to Benjamin's idea of identificatory love.

It is not surprising that Benjamin turns to identificatory love because identification theory is the analytic workhorse for our models of social inscription in the individual subject. Following Freud, the installation of the superego is the internalization of the law and social order (classically aligned with the register of the father, as Benjamin shows). Gender theory in particular is built up on the mechanism of identification (Stoller, 1968; Fast, 1984; Harris, 2005). In being like his father, a boy becomes masculine; in being like his mother, he becomes feminine. Adrienne Harris (2005) has called for a "significant deconstruction" (p. 126) of the process of identification regarding gender theory, suggesting that we need to describe the variegated and diverse forms, textures, and qualities of this mechanism. Benjamin's contribution to this project in *The Bonds of Love* was to take it up at its source, so to speak, to draw from the spring in Freud (and therefore in psychoanalytic history) where identification had not yet split off from erotic attachment.

For Freud (1921) such identification could take both an ordinary form leading to normal development and a more pernicious one leading to psychic bondage or enslavement. In the ordinary form it comprises an early emotional tie and is a precursor to object love. In a passage Benjamin quotes, Freud writes,

> A little boy will exhibit a special interest in his father; he would like to grow like him and be like him, and take his place everywhere. We may simply say he takes his father as his ideal. This behavior has nothing to do with a passive or feminine attitude toward his father (and toward males in general); it is on the contrary typically masculine. It fits in very well with the Oedipus complex, for which it helps to prepare the way [Freud, 1921, p. 105, as cited in Benjamin, 1988, p. 133].

Lacking the theoretical idiom we might use today, Freud seems to distinguish gender ("typically masculine") from sexuality ("nothing to do with a passive or feminine attitude") and subtly aligns gender with the mechanism of identification, thus setting the stage for the conventional Oedipus. Even here, there is a subtle nod to a gendered group ("males in general"). We do well to recognize that in both the concepts of gender and of sexuality, we implicate broad categories of others. Even when we invoke simplified and conventional notions of identification and sexuality (I, a man like my father, take women as my sexual objects), there is a subtle but profound movement from taking the individual mother as an erotic object to the displacement of that object love onto an entire category of women—a movement from singular to plural. Erotic longing and identification are necessarily shuttled through something collective, a sense of membership in a group that shares a common characteristic (whether sex, certain modes of socialized sexuality, or gender).

But Benjamin will use Freud's ideas to consider a more individual development, though one with a tie to socialized norms. The ordinary "special interest" of identificatory love can become perverted, she explains, in adult life when we fail to live up to our ideals and make of the identificatory object a master, putting it in the place of a harsh and demanding ego ideal. Benjamin follows Adorno but adds a gender twist to analyze the hypnotic surrender to fascistic leaders: the early *male* object of identificatory love fails to return recognition, leaving the child hungry for an idealized paternal object and subservient to its draconian internalized representation in the psyche, now become a pernicious *Vaterland*. This perverted constellation of the ego ideal later becomes in Freud the "pure culture of the death drive" (Freud, 1923, p. 53) in the form of the sadistic and deadening superego. In a sympathetic reading of Adorno, Rozmarin (2011) describes an ego left under the "spell" (p. 325) of this superego, a psychic installation of social control, though one that also carries with it a hope of reconciliation through a being-with-others founded on an identification with the collective.

Several threads are braided here: questions of sameness and difference, enthrallment and sexuality, and links to the social.

The enthralled, spellbound quality of the ego's relationship to the superego or the ego ideal has something to do with the proximity of love with identification. Freud himself struggles to differentiate these types of emotional bonds in *Group Psychology* (1921). Identification there is viewed as an early, incorporative kind of love, roughly corresponding to the oral phase and the desire to devour the object, to make one out of two. It is because of their close relationship, he writes, that object love can so easily slip back into identification (pp. 105–107). Here identificatory love has the same flavor as Fast's (1984) notion of gender overinclusivity: an indeterminate or undifferentiated psychic platform open to potentiality. The blurred overlap of love and identification, an undifferentiated state of simultaneously wanting, having, and being the object, creates a kind of enchantment that transfixes the child in idealization of the father and the ego of the ego ideal. Freud (1921) describes this state in terms of being in love or being hypnotized: entrancements. Here sameness and difference magically meet.

In Benjamin's (1988) exposition, "for girls as well as for boys, the homoerotic identification with the father informs the image of autonomy" (p. 122). This homoerotic identification is not with a sameness to be found in the body of the father (though Benjamin will see in the penis-as-phallus a representation of the power with which the child seeks to identify) but with a sense of agency and desire, that is, not identification at the level of anatomy but of autonomy. The "homoerotic" Benjamin points to is a correspondence of sameness as subjects: the recognition each other as *like* one another has something of the erotic about it. This is not surprising. Identification is that powerful and mysterious operation, our psychic gizmo, that discovers sameness in difference. As a mechanism of in-between, it paradoxically establishes and names a gap by eliminating it, or rather it names a similarity and leaves unnamed, but implicit, a difference. And so, even at this very early level, identification itself contains the substrate of pleasures that will later be seen as sexual: of merger emerging from separation and the dissolution of boundaries premised on their constitution.

The link between erotic love and identification had also been elaborated in *Mourning and Melancholia* (Freud, 1917). Here too, identification and erotic love are closely tied, with identification as the consequence of erotic love lost. Butler (1995) uses this link to ground her theory of gender as melancholic identification. Gender in this reading *is* melancholia: a love that is not mourned because not recognized, foreclosed as something that "never was and never was lost" (p. 165). Here, conventional masculinity and femininity are the unmarked graves of homoerotic object love. In *Group Psychology* (1921) we also see the shimmering of homo-eros in the shadows in Freud's reference to Leonardo—if also the confusion that will haunt psychoanalysis on this score for the better part of the next century as homosexuality becomes one of the slippery slides of psychoanalytic theory, a conflation point for so many critical terms (blurred distinctions between self and other in narcissism and object love, a confusion of tongues in distinguishing between oedipal and preoedipal levels of development, to name just two important sets). Such is the insidious working of ideology, a point that has been elaborated by a number of analytic writers (Lewes, 1988; Butler, 1990; Corbett, 2009).

But the Freudian text Benjamin points us to is primarily concerned not with individual identifications but with understanding group psychology. By invoking the group, we return to one of our most captivating contemporary questions: How do we understand the social link in psychoanalysis? This question has at least two sides, which are inextricable. One has to do with how psychoanalysis is positioned in the social (how does ideology work within our theorizing to reinforce and perpetuate hierarchies of power, say). The other has to do with how we understand social inscription in the individual.

We now have a raft of established writers, particularly in relational psychoanalysis (Benjamin, 1988, 1995, 1998; Butler, 1990, 1997; Goldner, 1991; Aron, 1996; Elise, 1997, 1998; Dimen, 2001; Dimen and Goldner, 2002; Layton, 2002, 2004, 2006; Harris, 2005; Corbett, 2009), who like Benjamin have refreshed our thinking by articulating the stultifying effects of hegemonic forces in our gender theory. Work of this nature happens almost inevitably in the beneficent shadow of Foucault with an emphasis—sometimes overt, sometimes quite subtle—on discourse and its regulatory, normalizing effects. We postmodern analysts readily recognize that there is no way out of our social embeddedness, and we are ready to accept cultural contingency as a limit on our understanding, but we struggle, I think, to find ways to put all of this in truly psychoanalytic terms (Stern, 2011). Discourse, after all, takes place in a nonhuman realm.

Gender has been one the most productive sites of this investigation, thanks in part to the pioneering work of books like Benjamin's. Rozmarin (2011) puts the matter succinctly when he writes, "The relations between how one is gendered and how one is subject-in-collective cannot but be mutually constitutive. In other words, gender trouble... is also trouble in the relations between the subject and the collective and there is no preset hierarchy in the equation; neither is primary" (p. 335). Neither the constitution of subjectivity in the collective nor formations of gender can be presumed primary; neither is a starting point for the other. And further, gendered being *necessarily* concerns this tension of being a subject in, against, with, and of the collective. The relatively underused concept of the group may help us navigate these complexities in a theoretically useful way. The notion of the group provides a stepping-stone across a great theoretical divide between realms of discourse and ideology on the one hand and the lived experiences of individual subjectivity on the other. It is with this in mind that I turn to a reading of the primal horde myth through the lens of group theory.

The primal horde is Freud's (1921) ur-myth of group psychology, a "Just-So Story," as he calls it, that although little more than conjecture, may be able "to bring coherence and understanding into more and more new regions" (p. 122). To review: the horde is a primitive world of men—tellingly, this a strongly gendered story—a father and his sons as a band of brothers. The filial tie is mythological: less strictly familial, more clannish or tribal. The tension depicted is between individual psychology in the form of the all-powerful and independent father and the group psychology of the subjugated horde. The primal father dominates his sons by prohibiting sexual satisfaction; it is specifically this prohibition that constellates them as a group: "he forced them, so to speak, into group psychology" (p. 124). Thus sexuality, gender, and group formation are linked.

Contemporary groups of all kinds, Freud (1921) postulates, evoke the primal horde. Like the sons, members of any constituted group are bound together in identificatory love with a thirst for authority; the leader of such a group sits in the place of the primal father: "A primary group of this kind is a number of individuals who have put one and the same object in the place of their ego ideal and have consequently identified themselves with one another in their ego" (p. 116). An external object (the leader) thus collectivizes individuals, promoting identifications in two directions: vertically with the position of ur-father, horizontally with each other as mythological brothers.

Thus, in the structure of the ego ideal we have a pivot between individual psychology and group membership, an "intermediate formation" (Kaës, 2007, p. 158) that acts as a link between two orders of reality, namely, that of the single subject as separate entity and the collective subject of the social order.

It is important to note, then, group membership begins to describe an aspect of subjectivity, a seat of agency, or ego formation, that is specifically collective in its constitution. Although even dyadic structures might be seen as "a group formation with two members" (Freud, 1921, p. 115), we tend to conceptualize dyadic and triadic relationships and structures at the level of individual objects rather than groups or collectivities. Group membership, on the other hand, describes a psychological relationship in which the object is not individualized and which constructs a corresponding psychic structure that is likewise not individual but groupal, a "we-ego" (Dalal, 1998, pp. 194–195). The subject is thus most properly an "intersubject" (Kaës, 2007, p. 238): "divided between the demands imposed on him by the necessity of serving his own purposes and those that derive from his status and function as a member of an intersubjective chain [in a group], of which he is at one and the same time the servant, the link of transmission, the heir, and the actor" (p. 241).

We might then say that the identificatory father as ego ideal stands in the place of a leader of a group that constitutes gender, calling into being a type of collective subjectivity. Vertical and horizontal elements of this identification are interlaced: identification with the father, "vertically," mediates and establishes identification within the band of brothers, "horizontally." Juliet Mitchell (2003) has similarly linked gender, sibling kinship, and horizontal identification (though she stresses individual sibling relationships grounded in reproductive and blood ties). I emphasize that the horizontal identification I am indicating designates a different kind of object relationship from what we usually consider: it is not a tie to an individual object in the classic psychoanalytic sense, and neither is it a tie to abstractions at the level of, say, the "big Other" of Lacanian theory, discursively aligned with History, Language, and the Symbolic. It is rather a relation that begins with a group-object as a roughly unified collection of multiple individual objects that are quotidian, local, and intimate and builds in complexity over time. The level is of *we-them* rather than *I-you*; the grammar of its subjectivity is plural (Moss, 2003).

I flesh out these ideas by following a simplified example of conventionally constituted heterosexual masculinity before turning to a more general theory. In designating a collectivity constituted by gender, the primal father establishes and names a group of men and boys with extension beyond the family (he also names other groups, women and girls, most readily in this context). This primal father can be seen as an agent of interpellation (Althusser, 1971), who calls the child into social existence in the gender order. He fulfills what Kaës (2007, p. 161) has called a *phoric* function (from the Greek, *phorein*, meaning to transport or displace). Kaës is describing the functioning of group members who act as intermediates, providing a bridge between intrapsychic spaces and shared or common spaces; these members hold or say something for the group. They transport or carry speech, dreams, symptoms, or ideals, for example, on the behalf of others: "they bear or carry them as much as they are borne or carried by them; they bear the trace of that which created them and of that on which they were founded" (p. 161). The primal father fulfills such a phoric function; he speaks on behalf of the child in naming his membership in the group constituted by gender.

This reading is a mythological construct, of course, because both parents are carrying something on behalf of gender to the child. The early primal father is not acting single-handedly. Rather, "primal father" is the name we can give to a process that represents a wider, more complex naming and reiteration of group constellations and one that includes the active participation of the mother. For the mother is likewise a phoric bearer that carries prohibitions and norms through her speech and manner (Castoriadis-Aulagnier, 1975, as cited in Kaës, 2007). The very division of emotional labor that Benjamin describes between mother and father in the conventional oedipal scenario bears testament to a couple functioning as a group of two, each working to carry or bear something of gender to the newest member, the child.

For this primal father of conventional heterosexual masculinity we might read the Freudian injunction against sexual satisfaction through the prism of identificatory love and discover here the prohibition of homosexuality. As we have seen, identificatory love is stitched through with the "homo-eros" of sameness as the tie that binds (named, demarcated, and organized by sex in the heterosexual normative); this is a slippery tie that slides easily into object love. The erotic dimension of love implicit in identification is what must be renounced as one of the conditions of entry into this particular group of "men." This renunciation is melancholic in its structure, unrecognized and unmourned (Butler, 1995). The repudiation of the erotic tie, the foreclosure of homosexual eros, becomes part of the foundation of gender in the conventional heterosexual masculine. Membership in this club is franked by the renunciation of femininity in all of its forms and everything that might be associated with it, including homoerotism.

Seen from this vantage then, Benjamin's (1988) analysis in *The Bonds of Love* is a thick description of what constitutes membership in a group we can call conventional—or precarious or brittle—male heterosexuality (González, 2011). In this grouping, certain qualities (tenderness, care, dependence) are gendered as feminine and unconsciously split off because they do not conform to particular masculine norms of modern Western culture (Layton, 2002, 2006). Such a division of labor already points to the larger economy it sustains, namely, a particular variant of heterosexual groupality and the reproductive and traditional couple that is its primary instantiation.

The melancholic identification that anchors this kind of masculinity should not be read merely as the internalization of an individual object relationship but also as a specifically social link that operates by constituting and binding a psychic group through a particular formation of gender. Not identification exclusively with the father as much as identification in and with a group. The father transmits and enacts an "unconscious alliance" at the level of a group that organizes and binds its members (Kaës, 2007), but there is also an ongoing alliance of men and boys as a collective, bound to each other.

Gender in this view is a collective symptom, compromise formation, or organizing agreement enacted through the transmission of an unconscious alliance between the members of a group. It can be analogized to the mutually enacted elements of the analytic dyad (whether in pathological forms or in the salutary establishment of a productive frame). Such alliances are structuring as "measures for reduplicating the repression and denial, since they concern not only unconscious contents but the alliance itself: the latter remains unaware of the unconscious it produces and maintains" (Kaës, 2007, p. 241). Or to put it a different way, "recognized" boys fall under the thrall of the idealized father of a particular kind of masculinity as much as "unrecognized" girls do, though the enchantments and enslavements take different forms in each case and accord differing privileges and possibilities. Recognition is always gendered and must imply concurrent misrecognition because there can be no recognition of subjectivity in an absolute or pure way outside the constraints of social categories. Mutual recognition at the level of gender occurs not only between father and son but also between boys and men of all sorts, and this gendered formation is not separable from a constitution of agency or desire. These elements of subjectivity will always carry a gender valence. The spell cast in this particular unconscious alliance is the "naturalized" gender of unreconstructed heterosexual masculinity, largely based on the repudiation of the feminine in many forms of American modern culture. Repudiation is a bond of (unacknowledged) love between these kinds of men. Groups, we understand, are defined in large measure by whom they exclude (Dalal, 2002; Moss, 2003).

The domain of this gendered group extends beyond the immediate family and identification with parents and siblings. Blood kinship itself is pierced, intercalated, mingled, or imbricated with nonkin ties to form the "band of brothers." A network of brothers, uncles, grandparents, and cousins is interpenetrated by a network of playmates and friends of the family and later by teachers, doctors, firemen, cowboys, and astronauts: the whole clan that will appear in reality and fantasy to answer the question repeatedly put to the aspiring boy: What do you want to be when you grow up? (That is, what sort of man?) Groupings of men and boys are reiterated and reassembled in a variety of constellations and configurations: at home and in the emerging social world of infancy and childhood, interpersonally and in fantasy representations. For the boy, this iteration begins to describe a sense of *belonging-to* a class or category of maleness. Members of the group, in and outside of the family, begin to fall under the umbrella of what it means to be male, a collectivity that designates "us" in the first-person plural of social subjectivity (Moss, 2003). We can imagine this conventional boy's internal narrative: *I am one of them, or rather, one of us . . . as surely and deeply as I am named to and belong to this family, I am named to and belong to the group of men that extends beyond this family.*

In this view, the child of the oedipal scenario is not only identifying with the person of father and his romance with the outside world but also complexly linking to groups of extradomestic others. To the extent that the oedipal father represents the world to the child, I suggest he also represents groups to that child, a beginning sense that there are other boys, other families. The entry into the Oedipus thus represents more than the opening drama in the travails of establishing thirdness; it also represents the beginnings of a move from the domestic sphere of the nuclear family and individual identifications into the public realm of the social and of collective identifications. The process of triangularization is therefore not only a question of how "I" relate to these two others, the parents (in the most reductionistic and common domestic form of Oedipus) but is also a question of who "we" are: "we" boys, "we" children, "we" dark-skinned ones, "we" who speak another language, and so forth. Even the classical articulation of the differences found in the oedipal situation—the difference between the sexes, the difference between generations—speaks subtly to this question of groups, designating as they do a class of people of the same sex or the same generation. The categories of gender only gain real currency as they break out of the confines of the individualized Oedipus with their extension beyond the domestic and into the world of other boys and girls, other fathers and mothers. Gender, in short, is a psychic group constituted in the social domain.

To be more accurate, we must complicate this picture. The kind of membership in gendered groups I am talking about is not static; it is not a simple, concretized, and actual gathering of the same few men and boys who meet consistently and repeatedly. Rather, such membership is abstracted and built up over time: an initially named set of gendered others acquires robustness as a category as "new members" are brought within its parameters. Such a group undergoes dynamic evolution governed by stochastic processes and organized as a nonlinear emergent phenomena (Seligman, 2005). Harris (2005) has taught us that gender is this kind of soft assembly: a collection of self-states, relational templates, bodily experience, and a whole host of other schemas softly assembled with only relative coherence, held together by the strange attractors of psychic gravity. To this multiplicity of self-states we might add the qualities of membership in iterating gender groups as part of the schema of a social self that is composed of group objects and collective identifications.

Gender as a group is thus not one actually assembled entity. Gender grouping is iterative, an emergent phenomenon that gains only contingent coherence over time. I am named a "boy" and this membership grouping is variously actualized in diverse social settings and within particular cultural conventions. To return to the conventions of the traditional heterosexual masculine: I may enter a gendered group of father and brothers whose masculinity is based on the kind of psychic splitting Benjamin describes; this group may grow with other "boys" at school whose masculinity is similarly constituted. But eventually I may start finding different boys and men who do not fit so easily within this socially instantiated grouping. Subgroupings, with their subcultures, appear and provide further elaborated points of group identification—good boys, goths, skateboarders, cholos, geeks, gamers, jocks, girlyboys, queers. ... The process of soft assembly is not continuous and progressive: groups are constantly and naturally split by tensions that threaten their coherence. The group of "men" is continuously divided, contested, shot through with fissures and new constellating currents; it is inflected by ethnicity, race, and class. These new groupings provide support and stability for new configurations of gender or sexuality.

Isn't this why *group* recognition and mirroring is so important for marginalized populations? Not only because recognition for nonconforming parts of the self may not have been available by individual formative objects but also because it is imperative to constitute a specifically *social* form of subjectivity that may not have previously existed because it had not been socially recognized. Thus, the power of coming out for gay subjects and of queer countermovements that complicate and trouble gay subjectivity. In its most conventional (and perhaps rigid) configuration we know the kind of stabilization that acquires over time through membership in multiple groups as identity. The psychopathology, and psychotherapy, of everyday life in identity politics can be found here because public "mutual" recognition in a group (recognition by the group of the individual who in turn avows acknowledged membership in it) begins to provide a pathway to cultural intelligibility (Butler, 1990; Dimen, 2011) for marginalized group subjectivity.

Adding a psychoanalytic conception of groups to our thinking about gender has several advantages. First, it provides us another way to conceptualize the inscription of the social within the individual and to do so using psychoanalytic theory because theories of groups can provide a missing link between the levels of individual subjectivity and the discursive. We are developing an increasingly sophisticated psychoanalytic language for nuanced theoretical descriptions of this intersection.[1] A theory of groups regarding gender is one more tool in that kit. Thinking groups allows us to get more specific, to pursue the post-Foucauldian analysis of the social without losing the focus on subjectivity.

Second, it helps us to continue building wider theories of gender formation that extend beyond the saturations of the oedipal family. We cannot always turn to recursive oedipal explanations as the deus ex machina, as when we invoke the traditional family setup to explain the transmission of gender to the boy raised by the single mother or in the increasing complexity of queer families. In psychoanalysis we have restricted ourselves—mostly because of the reproductive imperatives of a naturalized heterosexuality, which has until relatively recently enjoyed almost universal cultural dominion—to sanctifying the "first" group of three, installing it in an idealized configuration. We have no doubt gained a rich and highly nuanced theoretical language by keeping ourselves to this simplified three-body problem operating under the sign of the "straight mind" (Wittig, 1992), but we have paid a substantial cost in narrowing our

---

[1] To name a just a few concepts: the intergenerational transmission of trauma, the political psyche (Samuels, 1993, 2007); the cut-out unconscious (Davoine and Gaudilliere, 2004); the collective (Rozmarin, 2009, 2011); normative unconscious process (Layton, 2006); the third-person plural (Moss, 2003); interpolation (Althusser, 1971); and cultural intelligibility (Butler, 1990). For psychoanalytic elaborations of the last two, see among others, *Studies in Gender and Sexuality,* Vol. 12, 2011.

capability for rigorously theorizing nonnormative structures of gender and sexuality. The conventional stereotypical heterosexual family of a kind of Leave-It-to-Beaver oedipality is obviously only one specific instance of a broader construction of primal gender groupings.

Ideas about groups might help us desaturate our thinking about new ways of making families; they would let us put families into play. We might start by trying to desaturate the concept of "father" and "mother." Father, of course, cannot simply be equated with "head of household, male," nor can we assume that the white knight of liberation, autonomy, and subjective desire will necessarily be draped in masculinity. We must assume that there are feminine fathers and female ones, lesbian and male-to-female trans fathers—and that this array of variously gendered fathers will strike all manner of unconscious alliances with their sons and daughters and with children who could not be accurately classed as either son or daughter as they enter the social world of gendered groups. Rather than fathers we might consider *farther* objects, those primordial objects just a little beyond the horizon of the "first" object traditionally known as mother, and why not, as long as this (m)Other can be a "he" as well.

Finally, a theory of groups helps elaborate a mechanism for cultural change—for the evolution of different types of culturally stabilized gender formations. As a dynamic entity, the group is an extraordinarily rich locus of subjective transformation with potential to both shape and be shaped by individual subjectivity. Certainly, it is true that groups commandeer individuals: "the group receives them, captures them, uses them, manages them, and transforms them according to its logic and its own processes" (Kaës, 2007, p. 116). Gender conformity is this kind of commandeering. But it is also true that individual psyches shape and reconfigure the culture of the group and that, in turn, groups have the power to resist, fortify, influence, modify, produce, overthrow, and transform dominant sociocultural structures and the modes of figurability that make subjects culturally intelligible. There is no individual agent of social change without a supporting or constituting group. This is not to imply a return to unreflective identity politics, which perhaps failed to understand the relentless dynamism of groups and their often unconscious mechanisms of engagement with power. Identity is politically, as well as psychologically, necessary, but it can become a stultifying bastion in either domain that resists evolution and transformative growth.

Though we have traveled some way, through the rabbit hole of Freud's (1921) *Group Psychology,* we are not that far afield from *The Bonds of Love*. What Benjamin (1988) does there is open a window on cultural change: she does this by *making* culture. The book calls us to recognition, and not only at the level of coming to understand something insidious and perhaps inherent in the constructions of gender work and the traditional family. It helps to create and develop the cultural conditions whereby a girl might be more readily acknowledged as a desiring subject. This is group work. Benjamin speaks something on behalf of the large group of our discipline, something now entering the realms of discourse, larger than any of us. You and I as individuals, and we as a collective in our various and interlocking bonds, are called to engage with that discourse, to complicate it, question it, and reinvent it.

REFERENCES

Althusser, L. (1971). *Lenin and Philosophy.* New York, NY: Monthly Review Press.
Aron, L. (1996). *A Meeting of the Minds: Mutuality in Psychoanalysis.* Hillsdale, NJ: Analytic Press.

Benjamin, J. (1988). *The Bonds of Love: Psychoanalysis, Feminism, and the Problem of Domination*. New York, NY: Pantheon Books.
———. (1992). Reply to Schwartz. *Psychoanalytic Dialogues*, 2, 417–424.
———. (1995). *Like Subjects, Love Objects*. New Haven, CT: Yale University Press.
———. (1998). *The Shadow of the Other*. New York, NY: Routledge.
Bion, W. R. (1961). *Experiences in Groups and Other Papers*. London, UK: Tavistock.
Bleger, J. (1970). *Temas de Psicología: Entrevistas y Grupos* [Themes in Psychology: Interviews and Groups]. Buenos Aires, Argentina: Nueva Vision.
Bollas, C. (1987). *The Shadow of the Object: Psychoanalysis of the Unthought Known*. London, UK: Free Association Books.
Butler, J. (1990). *Gender Trouble: Feminism and the Subversion of Identity*. New York, NY: Routledge.
———. (1995). Melancholy gender: Refused identification. *Psychoanalytic Dialogues*, 5, 165–180.
———. (1997). *The Psychic Life of Power: Theories in Subjection*. Stanford, CA: Stanford University Press.
Castoriadis-Aulagnier, P. (1975). *La violence de l'interpretation: Du pictogramme a l'énoncé*. Paris, France: Presses Universitaires de France [The violence of interpretation, trans. A. Sheridan. London, UK: Brunner-Routledge, 2001].
Chodorow, N. (1978). *The Reproduction of Mothering*. Berkeley: University of California Press.
Corbett, K. (1993). The mystery of homosexuality. *Psychoanalytic Psychology*, 10, 345–357.
———. (1996). Homosexual boyhood: Notes on girlyboys. *Gender and Psychoanalysis*, 1, 429–461.
———. (2009). *Boyhoods: Rethinking Masculinities*. New Haven, CT: Yale University Press.
Dalal, F. (1998). *Taking the Group Seriously: Towards a Post-Foulkesian Group Analytic Theory*. London, UK, and Philadelphia, PA: Jessica Kingsley.
———. (2002). *Race, Colour and the Process of Racialization: New Perspectives From Group Analysis, Psychoanalysis and Sociology*. London, UK: Routledge.
Davoine, F. & Gaudilliere, J.-M. (2004). *History Beyond Trauma*. New York, NY: Other Press.
Dimen, M. (1991). Deconstructing difference: Gender, splitting, and transitional space. *Psychoanalytic Dialogues*, 1, 335–352.
———. (1995). The third step: Freud, the feminists, and postmodernism. *American Journal of Psychoanalysis*, 55, 303–319.
———. (2001). Perversion is us? Eight notes. *Psychoanalytic Dialogues*, 11, 825–860.
———. (2011). With culture in mind: The social third. Introduction: Writing the clinical and social. *Studies in Gender and Sexuality*, 12, 1–3.
Dimen, M. & Goldner, V., eds. (2002). *Gender in Psychoanalytic Space: Between Clinic and Culture*. New York, NY: Other Press.
Dinnerstein, D. (1976). *The Mermaid and the Minotaur*. New York, NY: Harper & Row.
Elise, D. (1997). Primary femininity, bisexuality and the female ego ideal: A re-examination of female developmental theory. *Psychoanalytic Quarterly*, 66, 489–517.
———. (1998). Gender repertoire: Body, mind, and bisexuality. *Psychoanalytic Dialogues*, 8, 353–371.
Fast, I. (1984). *Gender Identity: A Differentiation Model*. Hillsdale, NJ: Analytic Press.
Foulkes, S. H. (1964). *Introduction to Group-Analytic Psychotherapy*. London, UK: Heinemann.
———. (1917). Mourning and melancholia. *Standard Edition*, 14. London, UK: Hogarth Press, pp. 237–258.
Freud, S. (1921). Group psychology and the analysis of the ego. *Standard Edition*, 18. London, UK: Hogarth Press, pp. 65–144.
———. (1923). The ego and the id. *Standard Edition*, 19. London, UK: Hogarth Press, pp. 1–66.
Gilligan, C. (1982). *In a Different Voice: Psychological Theory and Women's Development*. Cambridge, MA: Harvard University Press.
Goldner, V. (1991). Toward a critical relational theory of gender. *Psychoanalytic Dialogues*, 1, 249–272.
González, F. J. (2011). Brittle triumph: Precarious male heterosexuality in *Revanche. fort da*, 17, 102–106.
Harris, A. (1991). Gender as contradiction. *Psychoanalytic Dialogues*, 1, 197–224.
———. (1997). Beyond/outside gender dichotomies: Introduction. New forms of constituting subjectivity and difference. *Psychoanalytic Dialogues*, 7, 363–366.
———. (2005). *Gender as Soft Assembly*. New York, NY: Routledge.
Hopper, E. (2003). *The Social Unconscious: Selected Papers*. International Library of Group Analysis 22. London, UK: Jessica Kingsley.
Kaës, R. (2007). *Linking, Alliances, and Shared Space: Groups and the Psychoanalyst*. London, UK: International Psychoanalytic Association.

Lasch, C. (1977). *The Culture of Narcissism*. New York, NY: Norton.
Layton, L. (2002). Cultural hierarchies, splitting, and the heterosexist unconscious. In: *Bringing the Plague: Toward a Postmodern Psychoanalysis*, eds. S. Fairfield, L. Layton, & C. Stack. New York, NY: Other Press.
———. (2004). *Who's That Girl? Who's That Boy? Clinical Practice Meets Postmodern Gender Theory*. Hillsdale, NJ: Analytic Press, pp. 195–223.
———. (2006). Racial identities, racial enactments, and normative unconscious processes. *Psychoanalytic Quarterly*, 75, 237–269.
Lewes, K. (1988). *The Psychoanalytic Theory of Male Homosexuality*. New York, NY: Simon & Schuster.
Mitchell, J. (1974). *Psychoanalysis and Feminism: A Radical Reassessment of Freudian Psychoanalysis*. New York, NY: Pantheon.
———. (2003). *Siblings*. Cambridge, UK: Polity.
Mitchell, S. A. (1988). *Relational Concepts in Psychoanalysis: An Integration*. Cambridge, MA: Harvard University Press.
———. (2000). Juggling paradoxes: Commentary on the work of Jessica Benjamin. *Studies in Gender and Sexuality*, 1, 251–269.
Moss, D., ed. (2003). *Hating the First Person Plural: Psychoanalytic Essays on Racism, Homophobia, Misogyny, and Terror*. New York, NY: Other Press.
Rozmarin, E. (2009). I am yourself: Subjectivity and the collective. *Psychoanalytic Dialogues*, 19, 604–616.
———. (2011). To be is to betray: On the place of collective history and freedom in psychoanalysis. *Psychoanalytic Dialogues*, 21, 320–345.
Samuels, A. (1993). *The Political Psyche*. London, UK: Routledge.
———. (2007). *Politics on the Couch: Citizenship and Internal Life*. London, UK: Karnac.
Seligman, S. (2005). Dynamic systems theories as a metaframework for psychoanalysis. *Psychoanalytic Dialogues*, 15, 285–319.
Stern, D. (2011). Ethics and liberation: Commentary on paper by Eyal Rozmarin. *Psychoanalytic Dialogues*, 21, 346–353.
Stoller, R. (1968). *Sex and Gender*, Vol. 1. New York, NY: Pantheon Books.
Wittig, M. (1992). *The Straight Mind and Other Essays*. Boston, MA: Beacon Press.

Bondless Love

Stephen Hartman, Ph.D.
Psychoanalytic Institute of Northern California

Given this opportunity to reflect on *The Bonds of Love* (Benjamin, 1988) 25 years later, I read Benjamin's text as a bridge between political theory and psychoanalytic practice. In so doing, I hope to recognize Benjamin's profound influence on my thinking about recognition and destruction in collective erotic experience. I suggest that Benjamin opens the door to the investigation of *eros* in a collective unconscious. Yet, perhaps because *The Bonds of Love* predates the rise of the Internet, aspects of recognition that connote libidinization by an erotic collective are sequestered from intrapsychic phenomena and housed in a protointersubjective realm, *the ideal*, sustaining a long held psychoanalytic priority on loss and narcissistic injury in subject formation. I champion opening the intrapsychic realm to the fantasmatic collective by discussing Grindr, an iPhone app that provides public space for homoerotic desire.

From a social standpoint, dependence denotes a power rather than a weakness; it involves interdependence. There is always a danger that increased personal independence will decrease the social capacity of an individual. In making him more self-reliant, it may make him more self-sufficient; it may lead to aloofness and indifference. It often makes an individual so insensitive in his relations to others as to develop an illusion of being really able to stand and act alone—an unnamed form of insanity which is responsible for a large part of the remediable suffering of the world.
—John Dewey, *Democracy and Education*, 1916

BONDS AND BEYOND

I discover Jessica Benjamin's influence in my work every day and in my personal life too—moored to a sense of myself in episodes of recognition and destruction, tending to like subjects and love objects, leaning into the rhythmic third, witnessing: all these matters of going on being.

I remember first encountering *The Bonds of Love* (Benjamin, 1988) at Barnes & Noble back when bookstores were still a place where strangers might meet by planned coincidence. (Choosing the right book, lingering by the shelf, subtle glances right and left, ambling slowly down to the checkout level: all part of some restless search for a like subject). I was so glued to the page that when the high-speed escalator met the landing, *Bonds* and I went flying smack into a display of books about Bush 41. Soon after the crash I decided to give up a career in political theory and pursue psychoanalysis. Thanks in large part to Jessica's mentoring, my trajectory appears obvious but, that day at Barnes & Noble, it felt like a demolition derby. I am grateful to *Studies in Gender and Sexuality* and Eyal Rozmarin for offering me this opportunity to celebrate Benjamin's achievement and to acknowledge how ever present Jessica's voice is as I train my own.[1]

I've decided to approach *The Bonds of Love* (Benjamin, 1988) from where I now write considering what preoccupied me when I began to read Jessica 25 years ago. I jump back and forth in time partly to tell a story but also to place Benjamin's contribution to relational theory in political time. I'll cull from two projects that I am working on (Hartman, 2009, 2011a, 2012, in press) to demonstrate Benjamin's enduring influence on my thinking while noting a historical anachronism in the theory of intersubjectivity that prompts this question: Do recognition and destruction of the subjective object necessarily happen at the level of the individual?

Once it became evident that psychoanalysis must grasp the subject as "steeped in sociopolitical forces, that psychic life is made equally of inner and outer worlds, and that they have found ways to talk about it that sacrifices neither dimension" (Dimen, 2011, p. 3), might we take Jessica's keen description of recognition and destruction in *The Bonds of Love* (Benjamin, 1988) a step further? I suggest that Benjamin opens the door to the investigation of *eros* in a collective unconscious. Yet, given the individualistic default of "collectivist" politics during the late 20th century under the sway of rights discourse, and perhaps because *The Bonds of Love* predates the rise of collective bonding on the Internet, aspects of recognition that connote libidinization by an erotic collective are sequestered from intrapsychic phenomena. Benjamin houses collective recognition in the protointersubjective realm of *the ideal*, sustaining a long held psychoanalytic priority on loss and narcissistic injury in subject formation. I champion opening the intrapsychic realm to the fantasmatic collective by discussing Grindr, an iPhone app that provides public space for homoerotic desire. But first, back to the time when a bookstore was public space.

RISKY BONDS

In 1988 I had come out, but I was adrift. I felt rage and sorrow and loss more often than not. I was struggling to write a dissertation in political theory without a clear sense that I would ever earn my advisors' (who were themselves bitter adversaries) approval. My topic was the evolution of educational discourse on *childhood* from Progressive Education's emphasis on democratic experience to the quantification of *risk* by test scores. Risk, I argued, singled out the Child subject, who, as a consequence of identification, became the reified object of expert intervention.

If I spoke then in the idiom that I write in now, I would explain that, after John Dewey (1916), I considered *childhood* a collective object drawn in the public mind. Dewey (1927) understood *the public* in a way that foreshadows a relational view of *the social*. Not quite an entity, and not yet a group, the collective operates in unformulated experience (Stern, 2003; Guralnik and

---

[1] I've wrestled with what to call Jessica because she is my teacher and friend. Should I retain the familiarity of Jessica or defer to the scholarly surname? I've decided to use both names in a way that, I hope, recognizes Jessica as my object and Benjamin as the subject of this article.

Simeon, 2011) where it is set to assemble in states (Harris, 2005; Hartman, 2011a) that register emergent knowledge. When people are mutually engaged in the presence of domination (much as Benjamin, 1988, described), an inchoate sense of *problems* coheres in the nascent collective. As such, Dewey considered knowledge to be dependent on social experience and social experience, in turn, to be knowable only through dependence.[2]

At the level of the individual child as at the metalevel, Dewey (1916) believed that the concepts we use to map experience only come into being in the social surround. How we construe childhood in a democracy grows from collective encounter so that we may together experience childhood. Moral development then, as Benjamin (1988) demonstrates in the individual domain, requires formulation in public space. *The Public* does not exist prior to the experience of formulating problems. Only when citizens begin to formulate a sense that negative external factors (e.g., unemployment or military inscription relative to access to higher education) are shaping experience in a deleterious way does *the Public* come into being, ultimately as the State, so that those consequences may be further addressed. Until then, the collective is held in something like a collective unconscious as a latent or "diffuse" potential. One can think of its emergent interests as collective objects that have good and bad qualities relative to the nature of an external threat.

What made Progressive Education *progressive* (as opposed to an agent of social control) was Dewey's ardent conviction that public education would iterate process-based knowledge (Ghent, 1992) so long as it emphasized democratic experience. "Democratic," in Dewey's pre-Winnicottian lexicon, referred to a potential space where learning values was experienced collectively among subjects prior to any necessary legislative choices. Democracy was, in this sense, a constant although government may be more or less democratic. Paradoxically, then, progressive educators could not know what education had in store for itself. Nor, absent the theories of State power that informed Althusser's (1971) and Bourdieu's (1977) theories of the State were progressive educators equipped to foresee how postwar public education would increasingly privatize knowledge in the interest of achievement. *Childhood*, once seen as constant potential to be iterated in experience, increasingly became associated with *risk* and education with risk management.

As I traced the transition in childhood from potential to risk and from good to bad collective object, it became clear to me that a culture of risk assessment had trounced childhood. A mutant Culture of Narcissism (Lasch, 1979) and the interpellations of educational policy (Althusser, 1971) were conflating development with achievement. I considered neoconservative screed *A Nation at Risk* (Gardner, 1983) a frontal assault on potential space: education would be reformed to become a quantity to be measured, not a quality to be experienced, with the stated aim to protect America by ensuring Junior would score well enough on the SAT to get into Harvard.[3]

Risk is a political species of bad object that manifests with the fall of public man (Sennett, 1977). As a participatory way of knowing crumbles and scrutiny moves inward from the collective to the individual, risk volleys the delinking of achievement from shared history. Experience is no longer viewed as a process but an outcome. All the while, risk frames the public mind as the sum of its parts. Risk is at once, then, a social and a psychic phenomenon where the containment of risk by the collective is off-loaded to parents with education vouchers and the

---

[2] Similar to the Japanese principle of *amae* (Taniguchi, 2012).

[3] The similarity to psychology's zeal for empirically validated treatments and the identification of "medical necessity" by insurance company "treatment managers" is strikingly evident.

sad sap child of No Child Left Behind.[4] Risk singles out subjectivity by outcomes that are achieved by choices: the child who does or doesn't perform adequately enough to confirm American Exceptionalism; the person of color who does.

As the hallmark of social responsibility shifts from participation to achievement, groups of concerned citizens individuate from the more inchoate collective armed with methodologies that identify wise choices. As the narrative of choice filters across more and more domains of public life, arguments about the public arena no longer emphasize experience or history but take the form of protecting individuals from bad choices and the people who make them. Democracy increasingly becomes defined as freedom to choose: reproductive rights, the right to marry, the right to bear weapons, and so on, until it is no longer clear what Pro-Life means (Friedman, 2012).

In the shadow of risk, mind is equipped to choose *objectively*. The subject is measured by the achievement of objectives and, thus, increasingly dehistoricized and segregated from the context (or field) that informs it: quantitative assessment, not affirmative action, becomes the obvious solution. In a sense, the neoconservative view of mind banks on a Bionian principle that gets twisted into ideology: containment by a high-achieving teacher links the symbol-searching child to something poetically American. Childhood is spared risk "by an antagonistic solidarity, the secret of a cooperative understanding, the intuition of a common destiny when confronted with the stimuli of internal and external reality" (Civitarese, 2011, p. 279).

Knowledge is cogenerated but assessed unilaterally. The high-achieving knower possesses knowledge, which trumps anything else you might say about the person's experience. Qualities of personhood are deemed secondary to an overarching ideal—American brainpower—and one can easily recognize here Jessica's warning that idealistic pupils will choose SAT prep over community service as a way to bond with their teacher.

What at first appears to be a capacity to use education to make choices freely (under the banner of risk management) may just as quickly restrict choices to sustain ideal outcomes. Alas, armed with an empirically validated curriculum, one could approach teaching children from a position without memory or desire because neutral assessment is seen as the most efficient way to structure the contents of a risky mind. History and desire are dismissed as the cumbersome accomplice of the aggrieved, as a link to the part of collective from which risk emanates. Linking to meaning is a matter of getting bad teachers and bad seed out of the way so that American intelligence may speak its mind.

Perhaps it is no surprise that the backlash against this type of technocratic, unidirectional mind-set came from burgeoning relational psychoanalysis. Risk is a social construct and knowledge a mutual construction (Hoffman, 1983; Mitchell, 1993). Similar to the Bionian precept that an individual who achieves fluidity among registers of knowledge "can apprehend reality from a multiplicity of emotionally significant viewpoints, and perhaps it is this that we call mental maturity and health" (Civitarese, 2011, p. 278), Benjamin and her colleagues sought to portray how the unconscious is neither given at birth nor achieved through internalization but evolves in constant relationship with the object. This constant, mutual recognition, by comparison to the Bionian pairing of containment with noninterference, was a political position (Gerson, 1996). Intersubjectivity theory required a critique of domination lest the containment of risk become indoctrination. Neutrality could no more locate the American poetic in an at-risk child than a nonsensical whiff of analytic reverie could manifest the patient's unconscious.

---

[4]The signature educational policy initiative of Bush 43.

SELF-ISH BONDS

In this risky context, *The Bonds of Love* (Benjamin, 1988) appeared. In hindsight, *The Bonds of Love* engages the paradoxes of subjectification (Ghent, 1992) pre Citizens United[5] and prior to efforts within relational psychoanalysis to describe a recursive engagement between psyche and society (Dimen, 2003). In the potential space that was late Cold War America, Benjamin, like Mitchell (1993), cautiously juggled two versions of self—one "multiple and discontinuous" the other "integral, continuous, and separable" (Mitchell, 1993 p. 114) to effect a kind of *Glasnost* within psychoanalysis.

Once it was plausible to admit that there could be no analyst without a patient (Hoffman, 1983; Aron, 1996), the possibility of a mutually determined *self* opened space for Benjamin to illustrate how powerfully a subject must recognize her love object as a separate center of subjectivity in order to afford her *self* an internal source of recognition. Quite profoundly, Benjamin (1988) charted these "essential tensions" (p. 25) inherent in the course of mutual recognition such that "reality is thus discovered, rather than imposed; and authentic selfhood is not absorbed from without but discovered within" (1988, p. 41). The third emerges not from reverie (Ogden, 1993) but harkening back to progressive values, through participation. Recognition is *rhythmic*, not semiotic, and equal access to participation, just like identificatory love, is unevenly realized.

Benjamin thus mapped the search to symbolize recognition for two disenfranchised one-persons at a time. Neither the master nor the slave were free, even in a position of détente, until he or she acknowledged the zero-sum game that bound them in dependence. The self-state marred by misrecognition and aggression was no longer an "isolate" to be evacuated as it was in Kleinian metapsychology and *Realpolitik*, but it was not quite yet as mutually paired as early relational theory might assume. Relations of gender difference once deconstructed, the royal road still led from identificatory love to authenticity via the achievement of subjective individuality. Benjamin aptly tracked dyadic recognition ahead of internalization in the narrative arc of thirdness, gender development, and sexual discovery (which was, to be sure, a heroic rewriting of the oedipal riddle), but where in the libidinization of the subject might we levy the lawless iterations of liminal subjectivity (Hebdige, 1979) that had begun to collect en masse in the pre-AIDS Castro (Crimp, 2002; Gonzalez, 2009; Hartman, 2009; Bersani, 2010; Bersani and Phillips, 2010), in the barrios of Central and South America (Hollander, 2008), or in the derelict casinos of Manchester and the paradise garages of New York and Ibiza?[6]

Perhaps, foiled by the Summer of Love, an exercise in object relating that celebrated "free to be you and me" at the expense of "us," psychoanalysis was forced to reconcile the interpersonal field with a culture of narcissistic object use (Lasch, 1979). Analysts looked at narcissistic barriers to intimacy without reference to the ethical subject of the collective's lure (Ricco, 2002). Recognition was still caught up in concrete struggles for equal opportunity. Facing the battle for legitimacy yet to be waged in the psychoanalytic community for acknowledgment of the relational position, the time was not ripe to fully consider the subject's collective origins. Mutual would hold sway until asymmetrical domination loosened a bit. There was, as of yet, no

---

[5]The 2010 U.S. Supreme Court decision that granted corporations the same subject status as individuals.

[6]For a discussion of a distinction that I make between groups and collectives, the latter being a more emergent, anticipatory, and energetic form of identification that, as I elaborate here, does not have a temporal structure, see Hartman (2012).

Internet with which to smash Bush 41 into smithereens. I stumbled into it by chance, or was it unconscious desire?

DISSOCIATED BONDS

This begs the question, can the cultural *habitus* that registers as gender, race, class, and so on, be understood independently of the psyche in the first place? Following on Althusser's (1971) discussion of the "obviousness" of ideology, are subject/object relations always already there in a collective unconscious but somehow lost or dissociated? During the late 20th century, experiments in liminal eroticism quickly became reified and perverse—leaving but minor traces of their aspirational origins (Masud Kahn, 1979). Rising out of the fire of collective erotic imagination, there was AIDS and loss. Indeed, it would take a long while before we might again encounter a rhythmic third (Benjamin, 2004) tweeting libidinal alpha function on vibrating iPhones from Teheran to Tel Aviv.[7]

Looking back to 1988, however, intersubjectivity theory was steeped in a very clear and present danger—the loss of dignity wrought by a one-person psychology. The repudiation of difference and the internalization of sameness as a path to differentiation was an ideological mess: "Insofar as the culture forecloses this possibility by demanding a premature entry into the Oedipal world, gender identity is formed by repudiation rather than recognition of the other" (Benjamin, 1988, p. 169). *The Bonds of Love* identified subjects—turned into objects—by unmet identificatory love. At the very moment that Reagan era education was removing the mutual from childhood, Benjamin warned, "When identificatory love is not satisfied within this context of mutual recognition—as it frequently is not for girls—it later emerges as ideal love, with wish for a vicarious substitute for one's own agency" (1988, p. 122). The Equal Rights Amendment lost. Risk, however, had a study grip on the American mind as did the priority on achievement and choice; agency submit to the American ideal of possession. The bonds of childhood circa 1988 handily destined children like Paul Ryan to rise above their circumstances and prosper: like subjects–love objects who jerk off reading Ayn Rand.

Because I was just discovering object relations theory at this time and could not deploy Jessica's insight as I would now, I had no ready language to critique the policy analyst's expertise other than to name what I now call a *collective object* a "discursive formation." Beyond the fact that this clunky Foucauldean term did not capture the subtlety of objects/subjects relations elaborated by Benjamin, it positioned me toward my colleagues in political science like a Jungian bobbing aimlessly in a sea of empirically validated treatments. I struggled to feel recognized in my department and I was distracted by coming-out and hustling to earn a living. Watching my housemate and erotic ideal wither from AIDS at 27 was more erotic bondage than any new queer could bear (Hartman, in press). I could not connect with my academic career in political science

---

[7]In an ongoing project, I illustrate how cyberspace and online time present a challenge to our traditional understanding of reality. I argue that a paradigmatic shift is taking place from a reality grounded in lost and limit to one delimited by searching. As a consequence, I argue, *the object* among other psychoanalytic objects has new contours that amass in the *bricolage* of subjectification (Lévi-Strauss, 1966; Derrida, 1978). Here, I propose a collective form of erotic recognition as in earlier work interembodiment (Hartman, 2010b) and heterotopic spaces of phantasmatic erotic bonding (Hartman, 2009). If my tribute to Jessica reads too much my own intellectual history, I hope that in my search for self, I demonstrate Benjamin's likeness too.

or tolerate my country's sordid politics. Nixon may be a reconstructed hero of the fight for Obamacare now, but back then, Nixon begat Reagan begat Bush and the war against Nicaragua was a war America was fighting against anything I could believe in. Doer and done-to complementarities were everywhere. It didn't help that on the way speeding home from Kevin's funeral a crooked highway patrolman hauled me into a kangaroo court and cleaned out my pockets in the name of Justice. I soldiered on for an academic career—until I destroyed it.

The end came quickly. A phone call to my adversarial advisor: "Done," I said. "I've had enough of your cruelty." I could no longer sustain the hope that she would be curious about my point of view. And that was that. Done. Ruined. I felt very alone, ashamed, and for years after, I worried that I had wrecked my career with a masochist's balled-up glee in the melancholic shadow of adverse recognition.

Except there was none, recognition—mutual or adverse, that is, and eventually nonrecognition becomes you for lack of anything better. Using Jessica's terms, I had internalized nonrecognition as a part of my self during the debacle of repeated failed attempts to bond. I had no one to destroy—and it seemed as if there was no one to survive my destruction—but myself. In a parallel process with the subject of my dissertation, I became my own risk: unable to use *my education* because of historical and academic bonds to sadistic objects. It wasn't until many years later that I was able to trace the history of these enigmatic bonds, ties to progressive values that met a dead witness (Gerson, 2009) in the form of my would-be sympathetic dissertation advisor. As Benjamin (1995) describes, "Aggression becomes a problem...what cannot be worked through and dissolved with the outside other is transposed into a drama of internal objects, shifting from the domain of the intersubjective into the domain of the intrapsychic" (p. 40). And so it was. Like an underachieving child whose only route to subjectification was to don the title at risk, I interpellated myself all-but-dissertation and took my shame to my analyst.

Nowadays, I look back at that abysmal time in American history and in my own development from a more empathic position. I realize that I was struggling to earn a measure of recognition that could not (for reasons I won't go into here) be afforded me by my dueling advisors *en loco parentis*—nor to me—by me as an Other in my vocation. So it was, in 1988, our culture was increasingly concerned with identifying strays and converting them to risky objects. AIDS rammed this project into the erotic unconscious faster than a train wreck. When relational psychoanalysis came to me via *The Bonds of Love* (Benjamin, 1988) at Barnes & Noble, it was a jolt of survival: a two-person take on domination that didn't single out the risk object in the moment when the bonds of neoconservative ideology registered in the aloneness of my shame.

TIMELESS BONDS

I raise the problem of risk as a way to highlight a wobbly interaction between the intrapsychic and the social domains of the unconscious in relation to dynamics of recognition and destruction. I turn now to the unconscious aspects of recognition and the role of *the ideal* in identificatory love. The risk object (and the rich-as-Romney object) is always already singled out from the collective in the form of an individual's developmental achievement. I argue that the developmental tilt (Mitchell, 1984) splices risk into the theory of intersubjectivity in so far as subjectivity registers not as access to differentiation within a timeless collective embrace but in an individual's meager attempt to substitute lost love with an ideal that humbles him.

The risk bearer emerges from the collective with singularity; failures of mutual care are still announced by individual harbingers. No *we* fantasizes about itself as a sexual group unless the risk object of identification is a *them*. Among *Us,* it is the shameful barebacker who carries the collective's libidinal collapse into individual form so that we may then group to rescue our risky brethren (Bersani, 2010; Bersani and Phillips, 2010). "Who on Earth!" we say, hoping not to be identified with the risk object. Yet, outside of time and recrimination, there is an impulse to buffer the negated subject in some way that prevents us from evacuating our risk into him or her. This collective unconscious impulse to hold difference and sameness together saves the risk object from the terror of the group.

On the question of *the social*, Benjamin recently commented, "The direction of effects is doubled: discourses into which we are interpellated, as psychoanalysts insist, have origins in specific infantile or childhood fantasies" (Benjamin, 2011b, p. 50). Consistent with her position in *Bonds of Love* (1988), she prioritized a quasi-autonomous psyche. "Collected curative fantasies," she continued, "are elaborated by each individual" (2011b, p. 51). In order to make a transition from lost ideals to timeless ones, I hope to reconcile Benjamin's manner of grounding the social subject in intrapsychic fantasy with Althusser's (1971) assertion that aspects of interpellated subjectivity have an *always already* quality of obviousness. Perhaps risky business continues to prompt us, as it did Freud, to relegate cure to the individual unconscious at the expense of common cause (Dimen, 2010).

To Benjamin's great credit, *The Bonds of Love* redrew the psychoanalytic map in such a way that Freud's priority on the individual mind need neither be retained nor scrapped. As she wrote, the intersubjective and the intrapsychic dimensions of experience "are too interdependent to be simply severed from one another" (Benjamin, 1988, p. 21). Benjamin chose to elaborate mutual recognition over classical constructs such as representation and internalization because the latter historically and theoretically overshadowed the former. When intrapsychic development is attributed priority in an unconscious that has no time, no memory, and no desire, intersubjective operations are read as time- and phase-specific achievements, and they are blanched of political coloring.

From a classical viewpoint, if and when the timeless unconscious marks social experience for meaning as in Winnicott's (1971) work on play, recognition is subsumed into development. Like all temporal qualities of the subject's psychobiography, recognition becomes a sequential marker dated by its first emergence in a developmental trajectory. This accounts for a kind of splitting, as Layton (2006) wrote, of the psychic from the social. More profoundly, it imagines the timeless bond that occurs between individuals in the collective to have no place within the atemporal unconscious.

Against this bias, Benjamin (1988) emphatically argued that recognition is a constant. Narrated in time because it unfolds along a spectrum of degrees of mutual recognition, recognition describes a place "*between interacting individuals* rather that *within the individual*" (p. 29). By virtue of occupying the space *between* rather than the space *within*, recognition is not inherently more "biographical" a feature of individual psychic structure than aspects of internalization (Schafer, 1968) or projections of primitive Phantasy posited by Kleinian object relations theory. Intersubjective theory, Benjamin explained, "permits us to distinguish two subjects recognizing each other from one subject regulating another" (1988, p. 45). Alas, recognition goes awry and individuals attempting to dominate one another becomes the "hullo object!" of temporal narrative. Such is life in afterward time. But it would be a mistake to imagine that *being in the space between* is any less an aspect of timeless *being* than phenomenological *being within*.

The stakes are particularly high for erotic life. Sexuality loses its potential to bond us energetically in fantasmatic play (Corbett, 2009) if Phantasy is the province of at-risk individuals responding to unmet needs. Contra Green's (1995) infamous critique of developmental positions in psychoanalysis, by insisting that intersubjective and classical priorities need not preclude one another as constants, Benjamin opened up relational space in an unconscious where sexuality prefigures identification as a constant.

This important move could be easily swept to the side were we to only concentrate on aspects of Benjamin's feminist critique of classical theory that deal with the risks endowed by misogyny in subjectification. Because recognition is a constant, the *always already* aspect of sexuality need neither be residual to Phantasy nor a quality of the interpersonal field imposed on something *within*. In this way, Benjamin spared relational theory from the dismissive Freudian assessment that recognition and other relational phenomena came later in development than classical operations that instantiate the unconscious.

As Stein (1998) later said of sexuality, Benjamin opened space for an intrapsychic life that is "always more than oneself" (p. 619). Recognition, again borrowing Stein's words, is "neither an event nor a dateable lived trauma, but a factor which is both more diffuse and more structural, an elemental, *primal* situation, a situation that represents the irruption of human sexuality into the vital order through fantasies evoked by the object" (p. 604). From this vantage, it's a quick step to Corbett (2009): "Look at me invade you, look at me shatter you, look at me murdering you, look at me repair you, look at me resurrect you, look at me look at you looking at me grow" (p. 229). All this looking, all this searching, all this recognition takes place in an always already that is the prerequisite to loss.

In recognizing the *always more than me,* I find me. Shared unconscious fantasy is useful insofar as it provides a vocabulary for the subject to engage the object's enigmatic excess within the fantasy that that excess beckons. Time joins the story in the form of ready-made solutions (alas, gender) that proffer alternatives to timeless bonds that could or should have been were collective erotic discovery not subsumed into risk. The normative *ideal* is a reified form of recognition, a transitional identification with the always already obvious that is necessary in an economy of "unevenly realized" development. Recognition trends to *the ideal* all the more when it is rendered autistic by the defensive operations of a self-state or commanded to know its liminal place by the State (Hartman, 2010a).

Thus, in the matrix of recognition and destruction, Benjamin (2011b) traces the heroic quality of lawlessness: "Fantasy that persecutes with its redemptive demand gives way to a more authentic piece of conversation; that moment of interaction, a piece of enacted play, begins to create an intersubjective space as an alternative to unquestioned unconscious submission and fantasy substitutes" (p. 52). Fantasy (as opposed to Phantasy) is a potentially playful space so long as *the ideal* is transitional in political time.

The resulting third, Benjamin writes, "is a deliberately created alternative to our unconscious submersion in the unquestioned realm of the [normative] ideal" (2011b, pp. 51–52). The *ideal* imposed by the always already is a normative ideal that registers unconsciously in gender and sexuality. However, such an ideal, by virtue of the risk it poses to the object, may also function as a subject. Even as Benjamin's intersubjective third brokers two individuals' unconscious encounter in a collective fantasy of the ideal—it also joins them in a lawless retreat from the normative ideal (Guralnik, 2011), hopefully in a process that deconstructs the normative ideal *habitus* rather than reproducing it (Bourdieu, 1977; Layton, 2006).

Benjamin's third domesticates the energetic would-be collective. Here Corbett's (2009) sympathetic critique of Benjamin is all the more poignant. If psychic structure singles out the *mutual* by reference to a collapsed *ideal*, recognition resurrects the subject as the object of loss. But when loss is lost, either because authenticity collapses under the weight of ideological domination or because, as a paradigmatic ontology that structures reality, it no longer holds sway, *the ideal* may be experienced as the unconscious operation that launches searching. Writes Corbett, "This early mother-child overdetermination turns us away from the fantastic construction and materialization of the body and mind beyond infancy and early childhood" (p. 217) where, in the timelessness of unconscious recognition, collective *eros* enlivens the mutually constructed subject with its fantasmatic lure.

CYBERBONDS

Now, in Reality 2.0 (Hartman, 2011b, 2012), in this moment when infinite possibilities for access to online recognition increasingly supplant loss and limit as the bellwether of subjectivity and searching becomes the predominant metaphor for knowing, might destruction and survival be a less apt conduit to mutual exchange than a collective practice of *bricolage* (Lévi-Strauss, 1966; Derrida, 1978)? Perhaps Benjamin's (2011a) current emphasis on the role of witness in spaces of collective trauma marks a transition from the emphasis of relational psychoanalysis on the individual *Bonds of Love* (Benjamin, 1988) to bondless love among lawless subjects (Guralnik and Simeon, 2011) and diasporic subjects of history's making (Rozmarin, 2010), all the while training our focus still on the reality of domination, destruction, and survival felt by the person.

The risk that cyberspace dehumanizes the subject has galvanized many psychoanalytic writers to hunker down and illuminate every evil lurking in digital time and space absent a theory of the subject that accounts for digital time and space (see Hartman, 2012, and Kieffer, 2012, for review). As I have elaborated elsewhere, the hysteria that attends cyberspace can only be read as a protest against its remarkable libidinal power. Who need be at risk so that I may be an individual subject searching among fellow subjects online? Will I know me/us when I spy *him*? Or will I sink into an addictive search for the lost ideal Other whom, I imagine, must surely be lurking out there somewhere?

For Benjamin, the subject must somehow individuate from *the ideal* represented by a like subject in order to love that object as an independent subject. This is a tricky conundrum for the new millennium. If the identificatory impulse is based in the wish to be like the father of excitement and otherness (Benjamin, 1988), libidinization into subjectivity must take place in a field marked by loss: "The boy's identificatory love for his father, his wish to be recognized as like him, is the erotic engine behind separation" (p. 106). Indeed, the quest to overcome loss forces the separation of the boy as would-be subject from homoerotic *eros* that his father (now as subjective object whatever his erotic energy) must also renounce in order to become the boy's ego-ideal. Coming-out in a struggle to identify with other men and women in recognition of a father or mother who (also) renounces homoerotic desire will then become a paradigmatic act of pseudoindividuation that inevitably looks more like submission than surrender (Ghent, 1990).

Gender melancholy (Butler, 1995) is increasingly peculiar, and I don't credit this to greater tolerance in normative discourse (which is, as Foucault, 1980, pointed out, an oxymoron) so much as the plausibility of resubjectification online (Hartman, 2012).

Autonomy is not the only solution to the riddle of oedipal individuation (Gonzalez, 2009). Mutual recognition has a social cast that, although at times problematic in its temporal peculiarity, has an enduring heft (Taniguchi, 2012). Why, for instance, does so-called gaydar always already find its erotic target in no matter what culture, class, or generation? Even in the thicket of loss that was AIDS, phone sex tapped savage desire (Hartman, 2005). And so I turn now to bonds that grind where collective recognition holds desire in constant embrace.

BONDS THAT GRIND

On the day that athletes arrived at the Olympic Village in London, the gay iPhone application Grindr crashed from overuse. As reported in the *Huffington Post* (Burra, 2012), "technicians believe the arrival of Olympic teams on Monday sparked a flood of new customers—and loss of the service in East London." Elite athletes from around the globe who dare not be sexual at home had turned to their handhelds for sex. In Reality 2.0, *eros* may be cyberfueled, but it still needs a safe place to happen. But just imagine: those athletes caught on Webcam with boners during their medal ceremonies were banging each other. They met on Grindr.

Many readers will disagree, but I am comfortable arguing that Grindr paves a kind of erotic interface that is necessary to psychological and moral development: one where the lawless self recognizes itself as an Other among others (Ricoeur, 1992) in liminal territory (Hebdige, 1979). To be sure, my perspective relies on a notion of the self as social and of sexuality as a collective endeavor. Whether one cheers for Grindr's relentless demand for erotic recognition or impugns it as a garden of seductive part-objects depends on whether one frames *eros* with a social lens or demands it remain a solo venture. Plus, one has to be willing to imagine that a person sitting at a computer or holding a smartphone moves in social space.

Consider this: a grid of faces and torsos appears on your iPhone as well as the GPS-determined proximity of every would-be paramour. No need to lurk in the crevices of cyberspace; the pocket is now your rocket. The palm now your lawless pilot, the phone now your portal: Grindr is, in 2012, where 350,000 men hunt for sex at every moment of every day. If you hear a twirly bleep while your patient is midfantasy, his phone is on and someone is Grinding him from as close as a couch away.

Is the erotic identification that occurs when one may search endlessly "ideal" or necessarily voyeuristic/exhibitionistic? Might it be "in my DNA"? This is the question my patient Darren asks constantly. The erotic thrill of seeing himself in a grid of erotizing potentials is sheer recognition. The confusing sneer that accompanied his father's admiring gloss over Darren's glistening physique after a wrestling match finds form in a quick glance at the grid of potential lovers. Darren hates and loves them in equal measure, turns that ambivalence into recognition of his own struggle to bond with his father's repressed homoerotic desire and matrimonial imprimatur, seeks refuge in a flash thought of envying me and me envying him back, smiles, and grinds away. From a more traditional psychoanalytic point of view, grinding would be the fertilizer for identificatory love rather than the soil of love itself. Narcissism is summoned to reconcile an erotic bond with the many that can only be understood as breeding ground for an attempt to find the right one (Person, 1991).

By contrast to a romanticized ego-ideal, I'm struck by what gets singled out, this daddy or that bear, the one who says yes or the one who says no, a track record that amounts to dizzying promiscuity, another failed encounter that renders the parched soil of unrequited desire more desiccated. The analyst who, like Person (1991), grants collective recognition a functional purpose but fails to see it as an atemporal structure is so easily drawn into being a policymaker: when is your nation at risk—or, more succinctly, what is the nature of your risk? When, as many psychoanalytic treatments of online desire frame the process of rapidly scrolling through profiles of potential lovers, does it become an addiction? Must the tachistoscopic scan of potential lovers' avatars be linked to a constricted capacity for fantasmatic object use (Galatzer-Levy, 2012)? The subjective object of online romance is always on the defensive.

Another patient, Tom, says, "I know full well that this is a way of playing with desire. I know full well that I put myself out there to become what others will make of me, as I do for them at the same time. The odds of hooking up are like this [he shows me an itty bitty pinch like a microphallus and we laugh]. Only when I get stuck in bringing it down to that level, like I have to make something happen... that's when some imperfection singles me out to not be desired: 'I'm too old: what is this old guy doing chasing these beautiful young men?'... and then, I do, I do take it very seriously. That's when ya get stuck there, you know, when I can't just keep searching for daddy, and I start to feel like I gotta get him or I'm a big loser!" Tom adds, "Ha! That's when it kills you! It's not about hooking up—except from time to time maybe. It's searching for daddy, not finding him," Tom continues chuckling, "that's liberating because daddy is searching for me too! It's a big ole flip fuck!" Then a sigh, "Well, not really."

We laugh again, this time more genially. Quietly, I take note that Tom is older than me and rather beautiful. I have rarely noticed his strong jaw. Tom has never before verbalized any erotic curiosity about his father (a drug addict who died before he was born) and only since joining Grindr has Tom shared playful fantasies about being the bottom that were not somehow connected to spousal duty. Our laughter is not nervous in a way that might connote anxiety about an erotic transference; the thrilling thought that we might be lovers is not canceled out either. Also, the feeling of conviviality is not evasive—as if the topic were overstimulating and unconscious fears about age and Oedipal desire were insufficiently suppressed. It feels more as if Tom and I are running in the same pack without any need to reach the finish line. I glance at the clock. Time flew by without my noticing. When I motion toward the end of the hour, there is a sense of loss as well as a smirk of mutual recognition as Tom and I each reach for our iPhones and arm our pockets.

Tom's right. Ask just about anyone who has ever grinded: the hit rate is poor. "No one expects to meet Mr. Right on Grindr," Darren tells me, also assuring me that he and Dominic are just fine (it's a vestige of an earlier time when Darren worried that his uncurbed desire might put his relationship at risk). Darren used to keep me on a wobbly pedestal, imagining that he could get more of himself by being more like me—all the while managing any chance I might retaliate for his envy by donning my risk factor as his. Lately, he refers to that phase in his treatment as a time when he felt pressured to curate his image. Every identificatory gesture was sure to be met with ridicule because Darren could not have a property of his own without the feeling of avarice. As Benjamin (2011b) wisely noted, Darren had to turn the ideal of homoerotic love into lovers of his own. But the possession of a lover and a home troubles him.

Darren, who is a fervent leftie from a large family of mostly "compassionate conservatives," blisters at any mention of Paul Ryan. The spokesman for liberty reminds Darren of an older brother whose wealth allowed him to claim the family mantel after their father died. Darren is not comfortable inhabiting a space where *rising above* is a measure of achievement. Just recently, in the session where Darren haltingly reassured me after being sought out by a young athlete on Grindr, he switched topics and told the story of a time when his father visited him at the public school in the South Bronx where Darren continued to teach even after earning his Ph.D. After class, a student approached Darren asking for help. Darren's father stood by ready to admire his son's expertise in pedagogy. "Can you leave us alone?" the at-risk girl asked Darren's father. "This isn't about my grade. I need him to help me with something important."

Darren's father recounted that story many, many times, each time with a pride that Darren couldn't quite metabolize. Were he to bask in the glow of his father's admiration, he would berate himself for confusing his father's look of solidarity with an unspoken feeling of mutual desire. Beyond that mind warp, Darren's awkward libidinal reception of a paternal gateway to something larger than himself would register in his siblings as hubris. Darren would be savaged by their envy and estranged from his father's gaze all the more. Alas, solidarity and recognition are so easily confused with idealization and vanity when mutuality is a scarce resource (Dewey, 1916).

This time around, Darren is circling back to the moment of reassuring me there was reason for me to fear him grinding, no risk. Darren doesn't need to get daddy or trade up or down from daddy as he believes his siblings have. There is no contest in that moment at the Bronx school. Solidarity with daddy, Darren has it in a "yours, mine, ours" way. The guy on Grindr, he explains, Darren has him, "that you and I love each other," he says with confidence, "I have that too." As the session ends, Darren jokes, "And—that Australian water polo player on Grindr: he's mine!".

What more often happens is that Mr. Right replaces Mr. Wrong—both of whom are me and us, all of us on Grindr at any given time. Collective objects that assemble quantitatively as *me* when I am singled out reconfigure as who *we* might be as I search. It comes as no surprise, then, that the goal of Grinding is to keep on grinding. Time is beside the point; as Jessica explains, mutual recognition is a constant. Tom often has several chats going for weeks at a time with no intention to seal the deal and no sense that time has lapsed. It is a carnival of energetic possibilities. By attracting men across the age, race, and to some extent body-type spectrum in one place, fantasy quickly broadens as more and more men recognize one another. Spin-offs of Grindr cater to more specific audiences but Grindr remains a space for "anonymous" gay men to post and peruse profiles. Anonymous is a misnomer, I think, a vestige of risk. I would be extremely surprised to meet an urban analyst who sees gay men who hasn't encountered the fantasmatic avatar that is grinding and somehow wondered, Is that *me*? With whom in the erotic collective is the analyst now joined?

Tom's lover, Ben, is slightly appalled by all this. He feels that Tom should have grown out of it by now. He and Tom have been trying to work out a way to realize desire in middle age in a relationship that has long been stymied by sexual inhibition. For Tom, Grindr is a kind of nonsexual libidinal fix. For Ben, whose history is marked by parental homoerotic betrayal, it is not so easy to swim in the chlorinated collective (Hartman, 2009) be it a woozy changing room at the pool or a Palm Pilot. So Ben, worries Tom, is a bit stiff.

Urged on by his therapist, Ben consents to allow Tom to keep his profile active but, he insists, it must be limited to a certain number of hits lest Ben risk falling into addiction. I am grateful to my supervisee, Cindy Sherbon, for helping me think this one through. Sherbon (2012) points out that the "rooms" where 12-step groups meet are always already there. Mutual recognition as the abject risk object was in the room long before any I/eye stepped into it and saw itself (Stern, 2004) and it will be there long after I have moved on. The formulation of desire as my excess is but an emblem of the normative ideal of individuation from risk. We are all in this together.

Tom remarks that perhaps he and Ben should get married. They have been together for many years and, as it becomes time to figure out what sexuality looks like in "the Glass Coffin" (Hartman, in press), marriage would supply the "ballast" necessary to contain Ben's anxiety that Tom and Ben have lost their potency—hence Tom's fascination with Grindr. Tom asks me about my marriage and whether or not I think it's worth getting married as a safeguard against erotic estrangement.

I'm a bit stopped in my tracks. I've known Tom for many years, and this may be the first time he has asked me what feels like a direct question about my subjectivity. I answer that I have married for several reasons, primarily for romance (Hartman, 2008) but also for social security. I start to drift away a bit, anxious about the disclosure and concerned, also, that my often idealized romance has lost some of its torque. Tom breaks into my daydream about careening into a stack of books with a very funny quip: "Grindr is a cocky ballast for a stiff marriage," and I return his playful volley: "The great thing about marriage is that you get to commit adultery!" We laugh and laugh knowing that each of us is a happily married gay man with an active fantasy life, something neither of us could have imagined we would ever be in the years when Jessica was writing *The Bonds of Love* but a notion held in our mind by the fallen soldiers of gay liberation (and contained for my reverie by the Gang of Four plus Kenny).

REFERENCES

Althusser, L. (1971). *Lenin and Philosophy: And Other Essays*. New York, NY: Monthly Review Press.
Aron, L. (1996). *A Meeting of Minds*. Hillsdale, NJ: Analytic Press.
Benjamin, J. (1988). *The Bonds of Love*. New York, NY: Pantheon.
———. (1995). *Like Subjects, Love Objects*. New Haven, CT: Yale University Press.
———. (2004). Beyond doer and done to: An intersubjective view of thirdness. *Psychoanalytic Quarterly*, 73, 5–46.
———. (2011a). Acknowledgement of collective trauma in light of dissociation and dehumanization. *Psychoanalytic Perspectives*, 8, 207–214.
———. (2011b). Facing reality together: Discussion of the social third. In: *With Culture in Mind: Psychoanalytic Stories*, ed. M. Dimen, New York, NY: Routledge, pp. 49–66.
Bersani, L. (2010). *Is the Rectum a Grave and Other Essays*. Chicago, IL: University of Chicago Press.
——— & Phillips, A. (2010). *Intimacies*. Chicago, IL: University of Chicago Press.
Bourdieu, P. (1977). *Outline of a Theory of Practice*. New York, NY: Cambridge University Press.
Burra, K. (2012, July 23). Grindr in London overwhelmed by gay Olympic athletes? *Huffington Post*. Retrieved from http://www.huffingtonpost.com/2012/07/23/olympic-athletes-london-grindr_n_1695173.html
Butler, J. (1995). Melancholy gender: Refused identification. *Psychoanalytic Dialogues*, 5, 165–180.
Civitarese, G. (2011). The Unconscious: Response by Giuseppe Civitarese. *International Journal of Psycho-Analysis*, 92, 277–280.
Corbett, K. (2009). *Boyhoods*. New Haven, CT: Yale University Press.
Crimp, D. (2002). *Melancholia and Moralism: Essays on AIDS and Queer Politics*. Cambridge, MA: MIT Press.
Derrida, J. (1978). Structure, sign, and play in the discourse on the human sciences. In: *Writing and Difference*, trans. ed. A. Bass. London, UK: Routledge, pp. 279–294.
Dewey, J. (1916). *Democracy and Education*. New York, NY: Dover, 2004.
———. (1927). *The Public and Its Problems*. New York, NY: Holt.
Dimen, M. (2003). *Sexuality, Intimacy, Power*. Mahwah, NJ: Analytic Press.
———. (2010). Reflections on cure, or "I/Thou/It." *Psychoanalytic Dialogues*, 20, 254–268.
———. (2011). Introduction. In: *With Culture in Mind: Analytic Stories*, ed. M. Dimen, New York, NY: Routledge, pp. 1–10.
Foucault, M. (1980). *Power/Knowledge*. New York, NY: Pantheon.

Friedman, T. (2012, October 28). Why I am Pro-Life. *The New York Times*. Retrieved from http://www.nytimes.com/2012/10/28/opinion/sunday/friedman-why-i-am-pro-life.html?_r=0

Galatzer-Levy, R. M. (2012). Obscuring desire: A special pattern of male adolescent masturbation. *Psychoanalytic Inquiry*, 32, 480–495.

Gardner, D. (1983). *A nation at risk: A report to the nation and the Secretary of Education, United States Department of Education, by the National Commission on Excellence in Education*. Washington, DC: U.S. Government Printing Office.

Gerson, S. (1996). Neutrality, resistance and self-disclosure in an intersubjective psychoanalysis. *Psychoanalytic Dialogues*, 6, 623–645.

———. (2009). When the third is dead: Mourning and witnessing in the aftermath of the Holocaust. *International Journal of Psycho-Analysis*, 90, 1341–1357.

Ghent, E. (1990). Masochism, submission, surrender: Masochism as a perversion of surrender. *Contemporary Psychoanalysis*, 26, 108–136.

———. (1992). Process and paradox. *Psychoanalytic Dialogues*, 2, 135–159.

Gonzalez, F. (2009). Negative Oedipus redux: Transfigurations of a field part one. *Ex nihilo*: Precocity and negation. Paper presented to the Psychoanalytic Institute of Northern California, San Francisco, CA, February 8.

Green, A. (1995). Has sexuality anything to do with psychoanalysis? *International Journal of Psycho-Analysis*, 76, 871–883.

Guralnik, O. (2011). Raven: Travels in reality. In: *With Culture in Mind: Psychoanalytic Stories*, ed. M. Dimen, New York, NY: Routledge, pp. 67–74.

——— & Simeon, D. (2011). Depersonalization: Standing in the spaces between recognition and interpellation. *Psychoanalytic Dialogues*, 20, 400–416.

Harris, A. (2005). *Gender as Soft Assembly*. Hillsdale, NJ: Analytic Press.

Hartman, S. (2003). Reification and the ecstasy of the Chelsea Boy. *Journal of Gay and Lesbian Psychotherapy*, 3, 169–185.

———. (2005). My savage mind: Sex in the relational unconscious. Paper presented at the spring meeting of Division 39, American Psychological Association, April, New York City.

———. (2008). We did it for romance. *Studies in Gender and Sexuality*, 9, 206–207.

———. (2009). Swimming in the chlorinated collective: Commentary on paper by Francisco Gonzalez. Paper presented to the Psychoanalytic Institute of Northern California, San Francisco, CA, February 8.

———. (2010a). *L'état c'est moi*, except when I am not: Commentary on paper by Orna Guralnik and Daphne Simeon. *Psychoanalytic Dialogues*, 20, 428–436.

———. (2010b). Ruined by pleasure: Commentary on Steven Botticelli and Jeffrey R. Guss. *Studies in Gender and Sexuality*, 11, 141–145.

———. (2011a). Darren then Harvey: The incest taboo reconsidered, the collective unconscious reprised. In: *With Culture in Mind: Psychoanalytic Stories*, ed. M. Dimen, New York, NY: Routledge, pp. 67–74.

———. (2011b). Reality 2.0: When loss is lost. *Psychoanalytic Dialogues*, 21, 468–482.

———. (2012). Cybermourning: Grief in flux from object loss to collective immortality. *Psychoanalytic Inquiry*, 32, 454–467.

———. (in press). The glass coffin: What age is desire. *Studies in Gender and Sexuality*.

Hebdige, D. (1979). *Subculture: the Meaning of Style*. London, UK: Routledge.

Hoffman, I. (1983). The patient as interpreter of the analyst's experience. *Contemporary Psychoanalysis*, 19, 389–422.

Hollander, N. C. (2008). Living danger: On not knowing what we know. *Psychoanalytic Dialogues*, 18, 690–709.

Kieffer, C. (2012). Epilogue. *Psychoanalytic Inquiry*, 32, 513–520.

Lasch, C. (1979). *The Culture of Narcissism: American Life in an Age of Diminishing Expectations*. New York, NY: Norton.

Layton, L. (2006). Attacks on linking: The unconscious pull to dissociate individuals from their social context. In: *Class and Politics: Encounters in the Clinical Setting*, eds. L. Layton, S. Gutwell, & N. Hollander, London, UK: Routledge, pp. 107–117.

Lévi-Strauss, C. (1966). *The Savage Mind*. Chicago, IL: University of Chicago Press.

Masud Kahn, M. (1979). *Alienation in Perversions*. London, UK: Karnak.

Mitchell, S. (1984). Object relations theories and the developmental tilt. *Contemporary Psychoanalysis*, 20, 473–499.

———. (1993). *Hope and Dread in Psychoanalysis*. New York, NY: Basic Books.

Ogden, T. (1993). *The Matrix of Mind: Object Relations and the Psychoanalytic Dialogue.* Lanham, MD: Rowman and Littlefield.
Person, E. S. (1991). Romantic love: At the intersection of the psyche and the cultural unconscious. *Journal of the American Psychoanalytic Association,* 39S, 383–411.
Ricco, J. (2002). *The Logic of the Lure.* Chicago, IL: University of Chicago Press.
Ricoeur, P. (1992). *Oneself as an Other.* Chicago, IL: University of Chicago Press.
Rozmarin, E. (2010). Living in the plural. In: *First Do No Harm: The Paradoxical Encounters of Psychoanalysis, Warmaking, and Resistance,* eds. A. Harris, & S. Botticelli, New York, NY: Routledge, pp. 305–326.
Schafer, R. (1968). *Aspects of Internalization.* New York, NY: International Universities Press.
Sennett, R. (1977). *The Fall of Public Man.* New York, NY: Knopf.
Sherbon, C. (2012). Addiction: In pursuit of unrequited love. Graduation paper presented to the Psychoanalytic Institute of Northern California, January.
Stein, R. (1998). The enigmatic dimension of sexual experience: The "otherness" of sexuality and primal seduction. *Psychoanalytic Quarterly,* 67, 594–625.
Stern, D. (2003). *Unformulated Experience: From Dissociation to Imagination in Psychoanalysis.* Hillsdale, NJ: Analytic Press.
———. (2004). The eye sees itself: Dissociation, enactment, and the achievement of C. *Contemporary Psychoanalysis,* 40, 197–237.
Taniguchi, K. (2012). The eroticism of the maternal: So what if everything is about the mother? *Studies in Gender and Sexuality,* 13, 123–138.
Winnicott, D. W. (1971). *Playing and Reality.* London, UK: Tavistock.

What's Love Got to Do with It? Sexuality, Shame, and the Use of the Other

Galit Atlas, Ph.D.
New York University Postdoctoral Program in Psychotherapy and Psychoanalysis

This article examines Jessica Benjamin's path-blazing feminist work on domination/submission as the foundation for later studies on sexuality and emphasizes intersubjectivity both as a philosophical model and as a clinical concept. The problem of dependency in the mother-infant relationship, the terrors and desires of the mother-baby relationship, and the intersubjective aspects of sexuality as they appear in the clinical work are discussed. The article suggests that the mother's body plays a fundamental role in the discovery of oneself and of the other and particularly in the development of the capacity for love.

Men are not gentle creatures who want to be loved, and who at the most can defend themselves if they are attacked; they are, on the contrary, creatures among whose instinctual endowments is to be reckoned a powerful share of aggressiveness [Freud, 1962, pp. 58–59].

This quote from Freud opens the introduction to *The Bonds of Love* (Benjamin, 1988), one of the most significant feminist-psychoanalytic books ever published. A woman opens our scope to the world of domination and almost naturally starts by discussing men. It can be easy to forget that until the book's release a mere 25 years ago, the psychoanalytic inquiry into domination was focused exclusively on the struggle for power that took place between fathers and sons. Benjamin defines a new problem of domination that is not based on the conflict between instinct and civilization but on the centrality of love. Obedience to the law of civilization, she reminds us, is first inspired not by fear of authority but by love of early powerful figures that demand obedience. Benjamin introduces the interplay between love and domination. She defines a problem that goes beyond aggression and civilized constraints, with origins in the bonds of love.

Unlike some early feminists' work, it seems that Benjamin insists on preserving love of men. Implicitly, she discusses dependency on and need for the appreciation of masculine qualities in a way that confronts her and the reader with shame and the cultural perceptions of "unmasculine" qualities. Dependency, after all, belongs to babies, not to liberated women and especially not to men. In opposition to that cultural trend, Benjamin takes the psychoanalytic position: domination begins with the attempt to deny dependency. The acknowledgment that we cannot magically control the other, particularly the female other who cares for us (mother), that we need the other and are dependent on her, is, ideally, the foundation for intimacy and mutual respect.

But that acknowledgment begins with recognizing shared responsibilities and the ways we project shame on each other, men on women, Western culture on the east, adults on children. We all tend to discard the unwanted "primitive" parts of ourselves, and at the same time it is difficult to not fall into a new and so common counterpolarization of feminine and masculine by elevating the oppressed or denigrate what has been overvalued. Benjamin (1988) tries to maintain the dialectical tension between tenderness and aggression, love and hate. She accomplishes this primarily by working within the psychoanalytic tradition and asking individuals to take responsibility for reflecting on their own participation in the dynamics of interpersonal relating. She asks herself as a woman to own her part in the larger dynamics that occurs between men and women. This perspective is directly related to the sense of agency women tend to lack, and although Benjamin criticizes the idealization of the masculine perspective, she doesn't maintain a split by supporting the reactive valorization of femininity. Thereby, *The Bonds of Love* describes not only the original love for early attachment figures but also the enactments of attachment and love toward the opposite sex.

Aron (1995), Layton (1998), Butler (1993), and others challenged the "convicting" gender binaries with the belief that these are culturally contingent decisions, that is, they aim to promote heterosexuality. In Benjamin's (1988) work, we are dealing with a binary pair that although isn't equally valued, still influences each other in mutual ways. Benjamin offers a dialectic for thinking about autonomy and dependency and the positions of master and slave. She recognizes the feminine and masculine as a system that impact and influence each other. But moving into a dialectic realm requires the ability to maintain the coexistence of love and aggression, destruction and recognition (see Butler, 2004), to hold in mind the oedipal and preoedipal, positive and negative oedipal, Pragmatic and Enigmatic elements (Atlas-Koch, 2012), verbal and preverbal, and so on, all intermingled and existing simultaneously. In that sense, the contribution of a feminist theory that addresses these inherent binaries is the theory's ability to shed light on the psychology of both sexes. Masculinity and femininity, as Derridians discuss, are coconstructing each other and have meaning only in their relation to one another (Benjamin, 1998; Layton, 1998). The attempt to liberate the slave opens the door for the master who was trapped in his position and paves the way for other gender and sex possibilities beyond what we have traditionaly defined as masculine and feminine.

Challenging this split requires the recognition that the master is also a slave and in a different way the slave is also a master. Referring to Georg Simmel's work, in 1926 Karen Horney used a similar terminology of the master and slave and noted that it is one of the privileges of the master that he does not have to constantly think that he is master, whereas the position of the slave is such that he can *never* forget it (Horney, 1926). Horney's point that the slave can never forget in the way the master can was true in the sense that those in different positions of power are never equivalent, and yet, in order to challenge the patriarchy of her era, she may have overstated this difference, polarizing master and slave while not appreciating, at this moment, their similarity and common dilemma. As we see in our clinical work, both master and slave might enjoy their positions and at the same time lose their freedom in different ways while unable to forget their roles. In my short review I underline Benjamin's early feminist work on domination as the foundation for later studies on male sexuality and emphasize how feminist work contributes to the development of both sexes, perceiving the master and the slave as two sides of one interlocking whole.

BONDS AND LOVE

Twenty-five years later, Benjamin's contribution to the world of feminism is almost obvious. Less obvious is the influence this thinking has had on more recent work around masculinity. I do not discuss here the history and theory of hierarchies and gender binaries but limit my discussion to the early work of Jessica Benjamin as a foundation for our later work on sexuality and especially on male sexuality, sexual excitement (Atlas-Koch and Benjamin, 2010), body needs and shame (Atlas-Koch, 2011), and I present thoughts on the ability to use the other and the confusion between use and abuse.

As mentioned, Benjamin (1988) pointed out that the psychoanalytic inquiry into domination from Freud and on was constantly formulated around the primary metaphor of the father-son oedipal struggle and opened a new way of thinking about domination. Using psychoanalytic theorizing, feminist critique, and philosophy, she defined a new problem of domination and reframed its origin. This psychological structure of domination can be traced back to the problem of dependency in the mother-infant relationship. We are no longer considering merely a father-son dynamic, as we are shifting the focus from the oedipal complex to the preoedipal, from father to mother, from drive and defenses to objects and attachment, and as we add the body to our discussion.

"Domination begins with the attempt to deny dependency," Benjamin states (1988, p. 52). In order to understand the origins of male mastery and female submission we must start by understanding the different differentiation processes of the two genders. From a masculine point of view, a girl grows up and is disappointed to find out that she is missing something: the penis. Horney (1926) was one of the first to challenge this developmental perception, pointing out the way Freud (1932) adopted the view of the little boy, who realizes girls don't have a penis. Challenging the Freudian description of that feminine break, Benjamin points to a different break, the break of identification that the *boy* experiences when he finds out he won't grow up to become his mother. Because the boy's first attachment and love object is usually the mother, a female, he identifies with her and feels himself to be like her. But there is a point when the boy realizes that he is different, that he is the different sex. This discovery requires the boy to overcome a primary identification with the mother. Unlike Freud, then, who defines the masculine identity as the primary one, Benjamin, following Stoller (1974) and Chodorow (1978), claims that the masculine identity is a secondary phenomenon, defined by separation from the mother's body and identity. The boy breaks the identification and denies the dependency on the mother as well as his need for the mother's body. This denial is an essential component of gender polarity. Dependency belongs to women only; men are not supposed to be needy or dependent. And although feminine submission can be motivated by the fear of separation from the mother and reflects the inability to express one's own desire and agency (Benjamin, 1988, p. 79), masculine anxiety is related to the return to oneness with the mother and to any profound experience of dependency. Benjamin suggests that men need to master in order to deny dependency and need.

These ideas are the foundation for Benjamin's (2004b) and our later work (Benjamin and Atlas-Koch, 2010) on the intersubjective aspects of sexuality, based on a developmental perspective. Stoller (1979) writes that one might expect to find the origins of sexual excitement, or lack thereof, concealed in the early history of a person's mental life. Exploring sexuality from this perspective allows us to depict how early intersubjective failures lead to a later inability to tolerate sexual arousal and excitement. We emphasize the ways failures of self-regulation—excess—are generally linked to failures in recognition and regulation, to arousal caused by inadequate or overwhelming responses, and to an absence of mentalization (Fonagy and Target, 1996a, b).

Our approach is based on Benjamin's early work on excess and supplements Laplanche's view with an intersubjective perspective on sexuality that also considers how excess results from both specific and structural misrecognitions and structurally from the overstimulation attendant on failures of containing by the maternal or primary caregiving others. Specifically, the intersubjective failure between mother and son, which we define as attachment trauma, is linked to Gender Trauma, when the son is caught in a personal mythology of gender identity. My patient Ben, for example, a man in his mid-30s, asks me, when I seem moved by his story, to "stop that fucking feeling," to not "dramatize things" but rather to sense without making a sensation. Ben requests that his emotional experiences remain unfelt and prefers stating that "there are worse things than these," referring to his father's death and the emotional detachment from his mother that has ensued ever since. As we explore (see Atlas-Koch and Benjamin, 2010), the therapist's feelings threaten to revive parts of the dyadic experience—a live mother with a living baby. Ben as a boy cuts off parts of himself and forbids himself to get excited by the mother, casting his gaze away from her. Any vital signs that she subsequently transmits to him are experienced as dangerous and physically disgusting as they touch upon the dangerous longing and excitement that she might evoke and the fear of being betrayed, aroused, and then dropped. Ben and other male patients describe a similar experience of feeling like an excited, humiliated boy "with an erection." They experience themselves as too needy, too dependent, and therefore not a "real man."

Our work focuses on the constant attempt to disguise need, longings for submission, and the underlying shame that is related to masculine dependency and emphasize the importance of working through the terrors and desires of the mother-baby relationship as they emerge in the transference-countertransference. Tolerance of these affects is necessary in order to develop the ability to hold excitement and stimulation without experiencing the too-much as the unbearable. For those patients, we believe, the "too-muchness" of excitement recalls the experience of being a stimulated, overwhelmed, unsoothed boy and results in a later inability to tolerate sexual arousal and excitement.

How does one solve the problem of "wanting" and the shameful needs of the mind and body? And in what circumstances might these needs become something that threatens gender identity and impacts one's sexual life? In a different paper (Atlas-Koch, 2011), I describe Danny and the way he becomes the container for his own mind. Corrigan and Gordon (1995), following Winnicott's (1949, 1951) concept of "premature ego development," defined the "mind object," when the mind is cathected as an object that omnipotently attempts to replace the caretaking environment. It is the tendency in early development to turn prematurely away from the mother and toward the mind instead. The mind then replaces the object as an adaptation to the intersubjective failure and as an attempt to solve the problem of "wanting" and the shameful needs of the mind and body. In Danny's case, we deal with the shameful longing for the maternal body and his preoccupation with women's clothing as representing remnants of the maternal skin that he is not allowed to want. The need, then, creates much shame, and women are a threat because they might expose his physical and emotional needs and longings for the mother, thereby generating the experience of excess—more tension than is felt to be pleasurable or even bearable.

My patient feels that he must always be ready so that the moment the breast arrives he can be active and gratify it by suckling from it. It's the breast who should need him and not the other way around. His fear is that a woman will find out that he needs her breast, that he wants to suckle and play with the breast, and that he lays back like a paralyzed baby in face of this longing. "It is so unmasculine," he sighs. The assumption is that a real man is not supposed to need the breast but rather to control it, and a man who experiences his desire as "needy" tends to question his masculinity. Any excitement about the other, including erotic transference, leads to anxiety and shame. With Ben, Danny, and other patients (see Leo's case; Atlas-Koch and Benjamin, 2010), one of the therapeutic achievements is to be able to recognize the female therapist as a woman and perceive themselves as men. Spontaneous play and any excitement touches humiliation and shame. We see how excitement and anxiety become indistinguishable; excitement becomes dangerous and shutdown of desire is the result.

USE AND ABUSE

One way to think about these intersubjective failures is related to the infant's use of the mother's body and hence to the full discovery of the other and of oneself. Referring to Winnicott, Benjamin distinguishes two dimensions of experience; first we relate to an object and only then can we use it. Although relating is still an internal experience that happens in the subject's mind, using the object requires the object to be an outside entity, external, independent. When the subject fails to make the transition from "relating" to "using," it means that he has not been able to place the object outside himself, to distinguish himself from his mental experience of omnipotent control (Benjamin, 1988, p. 37).

As Benjamin (1988) notes, from an intersubjective point of view, the movement to accepting the other's independence is crucial because it represents the essence of mutual recognition and a sense of connection to the other rather than omnipotence and control. It promotes the pleasure of connecting with the outside, with an other, and is part of secure attachment.

For the other to exist and be used, then, we have to differentiate the other from us. In order to be able to place the other outside, claims Winnicott (1971), we have to destroy the object that is inside, in our fantasy. Aggression and omnipotence must crash against the reality of a surviving other. We can destroy our fantasy and the object that is in our own mind, but to destroy the external object we need to act in reality and not only in our own mind. To survive the infant's aggression, the object needs to exist independently and the destruction of the internal object is necessary.

But what if there is a consistent intersubjective failure, if the object doesn't allow the infant to use it? What if the mother leaves the baby excited and doesn't satisfy the need? And for our discussion, how might that look later in life?

When the external object is not safe, the infant returns to rely only on his own mind. As described before, the mind becomes an object that replaces the real external object. The infant then has to hold on to omnipotence and control and cannot develop to using or being used in a Winnicottian way. This is an attempt to deny any need of the body and mind, which might evoke feelings of helplessness and humiliation. Here we touch the shame experienced by the fervent, excited infant, when the breast was suddenly taken away from him. The infant remains exposed, and as one of my patients describes it, "You learn that you'd better calm yourself down before you get hurt, before you realize that you're an excited idiot." When you don't trust the object, getting excited by it is too dangerous. Therefore, the infant learns to limit his excitement. Suckling and later on touching another body becomes a mechanical act filled with fear and rage and promotes the experience of exploitation. One touches another body as a way of gratifying himself, exposing without being exposed, penetrating without being penetrated, dodging the need for human contact and intimacy. Stein (2005) describes these acts as an active replacement of intimacy by a sexualized, enticing "false love," when intimacy is experienced as threatening. The domination becomes a defense against love and dependency. These patients have often been originally exploited and the love they got was immersed with hostility and toxicity. They need to cathect to their own mind, use omnipotence and control in order to feel safe, and at the same time make sure they don't get seduced to believe in another person.

From that perspective, to be able to use the other then is a developmental achievement. I find that these patients who struggle with sexual excitement are usually unable to use the therapist and are very alert about being used in an exploitative way. My patient Leo has fantasies about raping women and in many ways is worried about me raping him, abusing him, forcing him to touch me. When I speak he usually does not answer. He makes a physical movement with his head or rises to take some water. He brings food to sessions and eats and then he talks about his sex life and about the way he abuses his partner. "Her body feels like metal and I go in and out," he says, breaking her to pieces. She is a vagina and breasts and face and hands. Sex is a mechanical act filled with fear and hostility. In these cases, the patients recoil from any signs indicating that the therapist feels and might evoke overstimulating feelings. They can't have an alive object that might evoke love or excitement, and as mentioned before, ask me to stop feelings, to not revive the memory of a live connection and primitive sensory interchanges. The rage is not only a repetition of toxic object relations or as Stoller (1974), following Freud (1932), suggests, a way to turn passive into active, trauma into triumph. I believe the hostility is also a cover for vulnerability and shame and disguises the original longing.

It is not surprising to hear these patients repeatedly express the fear that I will forcefully evoke the sense of loss, that I will forcibly drive my excitement and myself into their minds in a dangerous way and then drop them. With these patients, becoming a new safe object is almost an impossible mission because any positive affect feels like a lie, like a trap. As Atlas-Koch and Benjamin (2010) describe, in these cases using the therapist's subjectivity is essential. The patient will necessarily project his vulnerability and need on the analyst and the analyst, who might feel attacked or humiliated, will tend to try and disguise her vulnerability and by doing that she will collude with the patient's original strategy.

Using the analyst's subjective experience is potentially a way to share the shame and open a new way of relating. When Leo attacks me and I realize I'm afraid of him, I feel shameful and angry. I fantasize about getting rid of him. "I don't *need* a patient like that," I think to myself. Reflecting on my own feelings, I start recognizing the ping-pong of shame and need. He doesn't need me and I don't need him. I ask myself if he pays me enough and conclude that I don't need his money, that I don't need anything he brings me. As long as I deny my feelings, I'm a reflection of his own defenses, claiming that no one can hurt me and withdrawing from attaching. Typically, I might throw the ball back to him, interpreting his vulnerability, his mother's betrayal and him as a helpless needy infant. This is too humiliating to him and he throws it back to me, dismisses and attacks me, asking me to stop these "fucking feelings." We are then trapped, both of us feeling in danger. He is unable to use anything I offer him and I can't use his mind.

But in fact in those moments, the shame belongs to both of us. It touches my own historical shame and without getting into details, I share with Leo the feelings of shame, vulnerability, and fear, and I suggest that my feelings are evoked in that specific timing as part of a process that is happening between me and him and are related to his own similar feelings. Leo sighs and then starts crying. It opens the door for him to talk about the shame we are sharing and the shame he carries with him. In that specific treatment, this was a first step toward mutual recognition and even love. Later on, our mutual ability to feel that we are attached to each other changed something fundamental in Leo's analysis and later on in his life and relationships with women.

This discussion is obviously not only about love. It's also about hate and aggression, about sex as a discrete phenomenon, about sensuality and attachment, and about vulnerability and shame. Our patients need to be able to use our minds without feeling that they are abusing us. But just as important, they need to know they bring us something meaningful, that we can use them as well.

Many of these ideas are developments of Benjamin's early and later ideas on recognition and acknowledgment. What most differentiates the present from the past and the analyst from the original caregiver is the analyst's willingness to acknowledge what was heretofore denied and take responsibility for his or her own difficulty in tolerating his or her response to the patient, notes Benjamin (2004a) following Ferenczi. In that sense, intersubjectivity is not only a philosophical model but also a clinical concept. It assumes that the analyst's emotional process promotes change and growth for both the patient and the analyst (Slavin and Kriegman, 1998). To include the analysts' subjectivity, to acknowledge his or her shame and vulnerability, frees the patient from being the only one holding that shame rather than perpetuating patriarchy and split-off shame that the patient carries for the analyst. Mutuality, responsibility and recognition, reciprocal processes, attachment, and even loosening some boundaries are part of mature love and maybe part of mature analysis, which can be seen as a cure through love.[1]

One evening, in a personal conversation, Jessica read me this poem by the Israeli poet Yehuda Amichai:[2]

> Thus have lovers preeminence above all others:
> Others may say, take my place.
> But lovers actually keep their word.
> Now I am in your place, and you in mine. You are me, I am you.
> Everything has changed; nothing has changed. Only the places.
> The others. Sometimes people argue, You're
> Just using me, you're taking advantage.
> But lovers say the very same words with joy, with passion:
> I want it, take advantage of me, I
> Want it too—use me
> Up.

And as always, we ended up with love.

REFERENCES

Aron, L. (1995). The internalized primal scene. *Psychoanalytic Dialogues*, 5, 195–238.
Atlas-Koch, G. (2011). The bad father, the sinful son and the wild ghost. *Psychoanalytic Perspectives*, 8(2), 238–251.

---

[1] From a letter from Freud to Jung, in which Freud states that "the therapy (psychoanalysis) is actually a cure through love" (as cited in Loewald, 1960, p. 255).

[2] Excerpt from "Houses (Plural); Love (Singular)" from OPEN CLOSED OPEN: Poems by Yehuda Amichai, translated from the Hebrew by Chana Bloch and Chana Kronfeld. Copyright © by Chana Bloch and Chana Kronfeld. Reprinted by permission of Houghton Mifflin Harcourt Publishing Company. All rights reserved.

———. (2012). Touch me know me: The enigma of erotic longings. Presented at Spring Division 39 of American Psychoanalytic Association, April, Santa Fe, NM.

——— & Benjamin, J. (2010). *Excited Idiot: Sexuality and Anxiety in the Therapeutic Dyad*. San Francisco, CA: IARPP.

Benjamin, J. (1988). *The Bonds of Love: Psychoanalysis, Feminism and the Problem of Domination*. New York, NY: Pantheon.

———. (1998). *The Shadow of the Other*. London, UK: Routledge.

———. (2004a). Beyond doer and done to: An intersubjective view of thirdness. *Psychoanalytic Quarterly*, 73, 5–46.

———. (2004b). Revisiting the riddle of sex. In: *Dialogues on Sexuality, Gender and Psychoanalysis*, ed. I. Matthis, London, UK: Karnac, pp. 145–172.

Butler, J. (1993). *Bodies That Matter*. London, UK: Routledge.

———. (2004). *Undoing Gender*. New York, NY: Routledge.

Chodorow, N. (1978). *The Reproduction of Mothering: Psychoanalysis and the Sociology of Gender*. Berkeley: University of California Press.

Corrigan, E. & Gordon, P. (1995). *The Mind Object: Precocity and Pathology of Self-Sufficiency*. Northvale, NJ: Aronson.

Fonagy, P. & Target, M. (1996a). Playing with reality: I. Theory of mind and the normal development of psychic reality. *International Journal of Psychoanalysis*, 77, 217–233.

———. (1996b). Playing with reality: II. The development of psychic reality from a theoretical perspective. *International Journal of Psychoanalysis*, 77, 459–479.

Freud, S. (1932). Female sexuality. *International Journal of Psycho-Analysis*, 13, 281–297.

———. (1962). *Civilization and Its Discontent*, trans. J. Strachey. New York, NY: Norton, 1962.

Horney, K. (1926). The flight from womanhood: The masculinity-complex in women, as viewed by men and by women. *International Journal of Psycho-Analysis*, 7, 324–339.

Layton, L. (1998). *Who Is That Girl? Who Is That Boy?* Northvale, NJ: Aronson.

Loewald, H. (1960). On the therapeutic action of psychoanalysis. In: *Papers on Psychoanalysis*, New Haven, CT: Yale University Press, 1980.

Slavin, M. O. & Kriegman, D. (1998). Why the analyst needs to change: Toward a theory of conflict. *Psychoanalytic Dialogues*, 8, 247–284.

Stein, R. (2005). Why perversion? *International Journal of Psycho-Analysis*, 86, 775–799.

Stoller, R. J. (1974). Hostility and mystery in perversion. *International Journal of Psycho-Analysis*, 55, 425–434.

———. (1979). *Sexual Excitement: Dynamics of Erotic Life*. New York, NY: Pantheon.

Winnicott, D. W. (1949). Mind and its relation to the psyche-soma. In: *Collected Papers*. London, UK: Hogarth, 1958, pp. 243–254.

———. (1951). Transitional objects and transitional phenomena. In: *Through Paediatrics to Psycho-Analysis: Collected Papers*. New York, NY: Brunner/Mazel, 1992, pp. 229–242.

Revisiting *The Bonds of Love*

Fran Bartkowski, Ph.D.
Rutgers University–Newark

This article is a look back at the place Jessica Benjamin's first book, *The Bonds of Love* (1988), had in my intellectual formation as a feminist and a teacher; it is also a look at the present and the ways we may imagine our futures with her work on intersubjectivity and recognition in mind.

When the e-mail call came for a contribution to this issue, I was, of course, glad to be invited to speak about Jessica Benjamin, one of our provocative thinkers, whose work I was reading closely in the late 1970s and who serendipitously became a friend when we found ourselves living in the same town. This work of retrospection was appealing—to think about precisely how *The Bonds of Love* (1988) was a text that mattered in my formation. This was first true in graduate school, then in my writing, later in my teaching, and even later informed years of conversations that took for granted Benjamin's ideas about intimate relations—these bonds of friendship, lovers, mothers, and more.

I knew when I said yes that the first thing I would need to do in order to think anew was to re-read a book well handled and marked up aplenty but long untouched on my shelf. I took it down and there was the familiar cover image of Burne-Jones's *The Baleful Head* staring up at me from my reading/coffee table for some weeks as I came to test its spine, to open and to begin to take in Benjamin's words from long ago, once again.

Our boys and her book were born in the same year, 1988, coming up on 25 years ago, but word of this book had been circulating for some years before, announced in the contributor's notes to articles by Benjamin that were circulating anywhere that feminism and psychoanalysis met up in the 1970s; those meetings were many, fraught, thrilling, and challenging. In my personal reader's history, Juliet Mitchell's *Psychoanalysis and Feminism* (1974) was the early call not to throw out the psychoanalytic baby with the feminist bathwater of the 1970s when many women could only understand Freud, that intellectual provocateur, as a patriarch whose interests were not ours. By the time Benjamin's essays and her book came along, many had come to appreciate that we might need a theory to help us understand so many phenomena from the world of culture, politics, and personal narratives in order to navigate how deeply rooted and twisted were the vines of what had been called "the unconscious," a truly dark continent. Benjamin helped shine a light on that space so as to find the cracks that would help blaze new trails. Her book opened channels that helped us to comprehend what scenarios kept us repeating, repeating, repeating... stories of love that were bound up in desires that had set anchor deep under our skin.

I can recall rather vividly how we readers of feminist theory wanted more of what the articles promised was coming in the shape of a book yet to be published, and by 1988 we had it all in covers to dwell in and contemplate.

As I returned and re-read, here are some of the questions Benjamin was aiming to address that speak back to then and forward to now:

1. How is desire anchored?
2. What do we need to understand about the dialectics of control in which we are all enmeshed?
3. What do we make of the utopian impulse driving the discourse of mutuality?
4. How do we maintain tension and ambivalence and not insist on rigid resolutions that bring an end to play in the place of desire?

These questions remain very much alive, even as my re-reading cast me back into conversations and vocabularies that have not been with me much now.

To return to Benjamin's rereading of *Story of O* this season is especially sobering when millions of readers are taking in *50 Shades of Grey*, a poorer rendering and more popular, yet still we find a character caught in the honeyed trap of female masochism that Benjamin aimed to explore, explode, respect, and rewrite. Benjamin asserted the need to comprehend intersubjectivity—those transactions that take place between subjects of desire, agency in dialogue and in conflict. This then became a site of investigation that worked out psychoanalytic theory bonded to the wishes of feminist theory with its search for women's agency in matters of love.

The 1970s and 1980s were fueled by the utopian impulses of feminist movement and theory even as feminists began to stake out positions that would come to define the divergent debates of the following decades. But that impulse drives Benjamin's book and her thoughts in her efforts to insist on mutuality through the maintenance of tensions that we retain rather than resolve into fixed ideas and positions.

The utopian was the aspect of feminist thought that I was investigating closely at the same time I first read *The Bonds of Love*. It was a heady time of manifestos and communities imagined and real: there were feminist bookstores and women's restaurants and publishing houses, carpenters, gardeners, and builders. There were lesbian feminist outposts in rural settings dotting the map of the United States where in many cases, men were not welcome; there were festivals and support groups and networks being woven into guises of cyborgs and goddesses. From our daily words to our colonized minds we were aiming to weed out patriarchy root and branch.

What was also framed under the rubric of feminist/women's studies was an interdisciplinary project staking claims to institutional intellectual life and space, which has massively and dramatically changed education, even as it has also been changed in name, in its designated objects of knowledge and in our understandings of mind, brain, body, and gender.

I venture that although for many of us outside the psychoanalytic community its modes of discourse do not remain as vital and present as they once were, we nevertheless continue to teach about intersubjectivity and recognition in many venues where new terms and debates have come to predominate. Women's studies became gender studies, which has in many places become critical sexuality studies, or lesbian, gay, bisexual, transgender (LGBT) studies; and the powerful lens of psychoanalytic understandings of relations of power moved into cultural studies, postcolonial studies, and genocide studies to name some of the more recent reframings of how we define and discern our objects of knowledge.

Benjamin's book gave us the very complex picture of how connected our personal and political narratives of daily life were to structures that we depend on—others who make the world cohere as they hold us and let us go. She gave us to contemplate what we would have to take along and carry forward as we tried to remake the world a safer place for the vulnerable among us—children, women, those not closely knit into circles of care. It should not be surprising that Benjamin's own work in the past decade has stayed with questions of mutuality and recognition but moved into a sphere as political as always and as local and global as the problems of recognition in the contested heart of the land of Palestine/Israel. This is work, writing, and advocacy that may not come dressed in feminist colors first and foremost, but it is impelled by the desires of then as she came face-to-face with the rigorous questions of domination. Although it was a question of relations of intimacy, and primarily heterosexual intimacies, Benjamin's book never fully swerved away from "the other"—and the admonition of her conclusion is one I take with me into the classroom no matter if I am actually teaching feminism, psychoanalysis, or literature of any genre—that we read for relations of power and study closely how these are negotiated even as subjects or characters bind themselves to others and make these ties "not shackles but circuits of recognition" (p. 221).

REFERENCES

Benjamin, J. (1988). *The Bonds of Love*. New York, NY: Pantheon.
Mitchell, J. (1974). *Psychoanalysis and Feminism*. New York, NY: Basic Books.

The Bonds of Love: Looking Backward

Jessica Benjamin, Ph.D.
New York University Postdoctoral Program in Psychotherapy and Psychoanalysis

In giving this brief account of the development of and influences on the book I hope to make it possible to see its location in a particular moment of not only psychoanalytic history but also the social and intellectual history of my generation. I delineate the influence of specific individuals, but more important, the way in which I was located in a number of transformational movements and disciplinary currents: the German student movement and the critical social theory it embraced, feminism and its particular way of revising psychoanalysis, infancy research and the transformations it brought to psychoanalysis, relational analysis and the changes in clinical practice. I also try to give some sense of the direction in which the book pointed me, where I see the main continuities with current thinking. Inasmuch as *The Bonds of Love* (1988) was an effort to bring together all these currents to think about a specific set of problems, it seemed right to me to mainly fill in the story of those tributaries and leave others to carry forward their own thinking about those problems in light of the present.

A BOOK IS WRITTEN IN A SPECIFIC HISTORICAL TIME

I finished the *Bonds of Love* (1988) manuscript shortly after I became pregnant with my second son, having written it in the period of 6 years after I had my first. I was on the fourth or fifth rewrite, meeting with my editor, when I joyfully recognized the telltale queasiness. I had also just completed my analytic training at New York University (NYU) Postdoctoral a year before. Although motherhood and psychoanalytic practice were central experiences in writing the book, the themes of *Bonds of Love* span an arc of 2 decades in which the discovery of both feminist and psychoanalytic thinking changed my approach to the world and my own life. At various points on this arc I could plot my engagement with, in order of discover, critical theory (aka the critical social theory of the Frankfurt school, with its twin peaks of Hegelian Marxism and Freudian thought), psychoanalysis, the insights of de Beauvoir, the practices of women's liberation, clinical psychoanalysis, and motherhood.

The beginning of *Bonds of Love* (1988) as a theoretical work I can trace back all the way to 1967, in Madison, WI, where I took to my typewriter after reading de Beauvoir. This was the outcome of a lucky moment when a few stalwart young women insisted our first women's group read *The Second Sex* (de Beauvoir, 1949) once the majority of women, having come only to "support our boys" in resisting the draft, had decamped in fear lest we create trouble with men. We remaining had the audacity to insist on the glimmer of an idea—that the oppression of women and even our very own oppression—mattered. Fired up about some common indignity we were subjected to at the time, I pounded out a manifesto on my typewriter (it was deemed helpful for girls to learn touch typing so they could work as secretaries while their husbands attended graduate school). The manifesto encapsulated my new Beauvoirian understanding of the way all famous dualisms of Western history were organized around the opposition of male and female, and all masculine sides of the polarity were valued while all feminine were devalued. The idea of split complementarities functioning along gender lines was emergent in our collective feminist consciousness; though commonplace now, such ideas felt utterly radical, risky, and exhilarating.

Although a subsequent 4 years of studying critical social theory in Frankfurt gave me the tools for developing ideas about binary oppositions, I found there no validation, no awareness of the reproduction of the binary in Freud; quite the contrary. Returning home I made the subject of my dissertation the failures of both Freud and critical theory— their implicit denial of the need for recognition, intersubjective process and the problem of paternal authority, which was fully ego syntonic for them. To write such a thesis it was necessary to return to the United States, where feminism was in full swing and I could find an unconventional home in the graduate department of sociology at NYU, where women's studies was just being introduced.

At NYU, as before in Madison, although immersed in critical theory and psychoanalysis I still turned to de Beauvoir for insight into recognition, the other, and the gender binary. So upon graduation it was not accidental I became involved in organizing an international conference on feminist theory, a tribute called The Second Sex: Thirty Years Later. The Institute for the Humanities at NYU, started by my mentor Richard Sennett, was supporting the conference and also my trip to Paris to interview de Beauvoir, which I took together with Margaret Simons, a philosophy student who was convinced that de Beauvoir, not Sartre, had developed certain key ideas about the Other. Although de Beauvoir demurred at Simons's direct questions, when I asked her whether the problem of "recognizing the Other," which was addressed in her earliest writing, *She Came to Stay* (de Beauvoir, 1943), was specifically her contribution she replied with alacrity, "Oh yes, that was my problematic!"

While organizing the tribute to de Beauvoir, I was simultaneously writing the first essay called "The Bonds of Love," bringing together the problem of recognizing the other with sexual domination. It must have seemed a strange combination of interests to someone who didn't know about the dazzling reach of Frankfurt critical theory into psychoanalysis, early socialization, Weber's critique of Western rationality, and Hegelian-Marxist theories of social domination. I met with Dan Stern to talk about doing infancy research (he was incredibly supportive and wanted to come to our reading group on Lacan's mirror stage). And at the same time I was obsessed with the work of Dinnerstein (1976) and Chodorow (1979, 1980) on the pervasive nonrecognition of the mother's subjectivity. Had I known then that I was actually capable of writing my way through the problems that were shaping up in my head, I could have been confident enough to enjoy this amazing confluence of disciplines. As it was, I felt more like a person running with bags from one airline to another in a different terminal than one with an organized itinerary.

The connection I was trying to make involved more closely linking up the de Beauvoir/Dinnerstein ideas around woman as subject to Hegel's organizing presentation in the Master and Slave chapter of *The Phenomenology of Spirit* (1807), so influential for the French existentialists. Somehow I got to feel that Winnicott was the passageway between terminals.

Having studied Hegel in Frankfurt, in turn, I had felt a shock when reading Winnicott's (1971) "Use of an Object": when I asked my friend who had studied there with me to read it, she too spontaneously remarked, "It's just like Hegel." Feeling supported in my audacious impulse to make such an unlikely connection, I proposed that surviving destruction was exactly what the slave could not do for the master who did not recognize his subjectivity. This must have led by association to *Story of O* and thence to the insight that one whose subjectivity is not realized cannot return the recognition of subject to subject, so that the master is never satisfied. This latter idea was then reinforced as I found a translation of a small article by Bataille (1976) on the master-slave dialectic, which helped complete the picture.

It turned out later that none of these links save that between Hegel and Winnicott were a stretch. For instance, it was revealed later that Dominique Aury, who wrote *Story of O* under the pen name Pauline Reage (De St. Jorre, 1994), had indeed been part of the Parisian milieu that Kojève (1969), teaching Hegel, was taking by storm. And what of the oddity that a British psychoanalyst with not the slightest hint of Hegel in his bones could arrive at a similar problematic of omnipotence? But then again imagine an entirely different outcome: an analyst who survives destruction of the object? It seems to me one of those moments that, if we are lucky enough to be exposed to genuinely different disciplines and traditions, we can recognize the homologue in two entirely unlike forms, sameness despite difference. Such bridging of difference, in my view, was exemplary of the way to not only deconstruct but also radically reconfigure oppositions that might otherwise lead to impasse.

Even with all this intellectual background, there could have been no *Bonds of Love* (1988) without the help of Manny Ghent. As my analyst, Manny not only introduced me to Winnicott, he also made the meaning of recognition poignantly clear: the vivid difference his profound attunement and understanding made in facilitating the distinction between the "internally conceived" and the "objectively perceived" object, a difference we have now come to formulate as a shift in selfstate. Manny taught me about (and later gave me an early draft of) his version of the difference between submission and surrender (Ghent, 1990), ideas that suffused what I wrote about the alienation of recognition. The idea of alienation as opposed to a pejorative view of perversion—meaning that otherwise unshareable mental anguish and emotional pain are expressed in an alienated or disguised form—was novel in psychoanalysis then (excepting Khan, and in a less explicit form in self psychology). This perspective shaped my life and work; it was one I felt in my bones: that behind the shameful, the abject, the fearful lie buried needs and longings; we do not simply structurally reject normativity—as psychoanalysts we look beneath to what cries out for our recognition.

Equally important, I felt that Manny recognized and seemed able to identify with my outsider intellect. For all the influences I shared in common with my generation, there was a perspective on those ideas that was rather uncommon—a perspective that came from growing up Red, with parents who had been until my early childhood part of a movement for social justice that in their eyes was in many ways successful though ultimately compromised (by Stalinism and other Communist tragedies). Their perspective included always seeing things through the double lens of what is and what potentially could be as well as the continual negotiation of reality in our alternative culture and the reality outside. As many in their cohort read *The God that Failed* (1949) and mulled over what went wrong with their ideal while others steadfastly hewed to the party line, my parents continued to believe not in the Communist Party as God but in human beings who could retain some agency by keeping some positive relation to ideals even when terrible miscarriages occurred in practice. For them the tragedy of European communism was weighed in the balance against the gains of the Communist participating in the labor movement, the struggle to secure rights and needs, perhaps above all the agency that people were given to act on their own behalf. My father's joy was to revisit Gallup, New Mexico, where he helped lead the miners' strike and hear from a miner's wife that of course she recognized him after 30 years, the strike was the most important event of her life. The value of giving everyone the power to transform the conditions of their own lives, to create that agency together with others, was in our family life paradoxically inseparable from the sense of trauma and persecution that came with McCarthyism. Both sides inspired me to look for a different perspective on the social struggles of my generation: one that was more psychologically introspective and emotionally in touch yet preserving the values of rejecting social conformity and oppression.

Of course this position of not throwing out the baby with the bathwater would not have been satisfying without the ability to actually analyze what goes wrong when people uncritically embrace ideals. The perspective I believed Manny shared and encouraged was that attachment to ideals could be both dangerous and redemptive, but even ideals that took form in perverse and painful expression could be redeemed by understanding the desire and aspiration that lay beneath. This idea of redemptive critique, as well as all the writing I did in relation to the problems of critical theory and feminism, were equally supported and influenced by my then husband Andy Rabinbach, who as a German intellectual historian was deeply immersed in, among others, the ideas of Walter Benjamin and Ernst Bloch that pointed in this direction.[1] And so the idea of the alienation of recognition could be used not only to analyze how domination can be linked to precious ideals but also to imagine a different, more complex path to liberation. This perspective allowed me to write *Bonds of Love* (1988) in light of what I felt were the miscarriages in feminism (as representative of radical social movements generally) and psychoanalysis while trying to redeem them both. When the conference The Second Sex: Thirty Years Later transformed itself before the organizers' chagrined eyes into a manic celebration of feminist political correctness and normativity, I turned my attention more fully to the psychoanalytic questions I was exploring in the early version of "Bonds of Love" to understand how victims can perpetuate their victimhood by becoming stuck in the complementarity of doer and done-to. As the *Ms.* magazine feminists largely followed the position of the antipornography movement, seeing themselves as victims of the sexual revolution, only a small minority were interested in that other side, the power of desire (see Snitow, Stansell, and Thompson, 1980). But of course, that was the side that favored the exploration of our psychic complexity and resistance to the traditional identification of femininity with a sacrificial motherhood an idealized view of nurturance and clean sex—it was the side of "no more nice girls." That side, of course, was the one I hoped to ground by radicalizing psychoanalysis as well.

BABIES AND BEYOND

Saving the baby while throwing out the bathwater, as I said, actually demands exacting analytic work. This is a deceptively simple admonition that leads to a distinctly complex enterprise. Part

---

[1] I have written in more detail about Andy Rabinbach's influence on my work in "Andy Rabinbach as the Inspiration for a Work of Feminist Theory" in *New German Critique* (2012).

of the work of that analysis involved, for me, life and study with real babies—the other trajectory that was so important in writing the book. Establishing within American psychoanalysis the position of infancy as well as the importance of the mother was a new enterprise in the 1980s, and the arguments in *The Bonds of Love* (1988) reflected, in part, a decade of immersion in research on infancy (and motherhood). The discovery of the interpersonally active infant—more than a bundle of disorganized drives declared unsuitable for psychoanalytic understanding by orthodox analysts of the time—constituted a kind of revolution in psychoanalytic thought. Infant capacities for social engagement and differentiation far outstripped the kinds of primitive ego actions Freud attributed to earliest life, for example, hostility to the impingement of the outside world. In particular the studies of early communication confirmed the idea of primary intersubjectivity, a position first developed by Trevarthen (1977, 1980) and then taken up with some differences by Daniel Stern (1985).

Trevarthen, it seems, read Habermas (1968) and so adopted his use of the term "intersubjectivity" for lack of a better word. My use of the idea of intersubjectivity, prior to the encounter with infancy research, was rooted in Habermas, whose book (*Erkenntnis und Interesse* [Knowledge and Human Interests]) was eagerly awaited in Frankfurt in 1968. The book explicated the move that took critical social theory from the Marxian idea of human beings as producers of their world to that of communicators. It was here I heard the term "the intersubjectivity of mutual understanding" for the first time and sat in seminars on socialization, communication theory, and George Herbert Meade. Coincidental with this paradigm shift was the German students' enthusiastic resurrection of the historical texts of a psychoanalytic pedagogy that were wiped out by the Nazis. They looked to the writings of Freud's socialist followers who set up clinics and nursery schools in Vienna and elsewhere, their imagination seized by the undertaking of radically changing childrearing and overthrowing a legacy of punitive and authoritarian parents. Hoping to repair their own personal traumas of abuse and deprivation as well as to reform an unreconstructed educational system, they set to work on creating an alternative system of early childhood education, nursery schools and kindergartens. So along with those readings of poorly mimeographed reproductions of Anna Freud, Melanie Klein, Sigrid Bernfeld, and Vera Schmidt, my first work with babies, four of them ages 13–20 months, began in 1969.

The grounding of intersubjective theory in the study of infancy represented a whole giant step beyond that perspective, of course, wrapped up as it was and long remained in Freudian drive theory. But even with the compelling change brought about by object relations and Winnicott, infancy research electrified me. What awesome possibilities it seemed to open up, is what I felt when I first encountered the work of Stern (1974a, b) and Beebe (Beebe and Stern, 1977) in 1978. Face-to-face play was the primary illustration of how mutual recognition is possible so early! Discovering Trevarthen's use of intersubjectivity and its subsequent use by Stern completed another unlikely circle between critical social theory and infancy studies. As it now seemed that all roads were leading to recognition and intersubjectivity, somehow I had to get them all on the same map.

So now it was actually possible to show how early mutual impact occurs in microanalysis, how active babies engage with mothers in a form of mutual recognition and intersubjectivity—and yet there was something missing on the map. None of the work considered the mother's subjectivity even in discussions of mutuality. All of the work I encountered was done from the standpoint of the infant, as though the mother were simply the answer, the interlocking gear, in relation to the infant's endogenous structure and needs. Her existence as a separate person was somehow subtly ignored, as if the conflict with her own needs and subjectivity were a nonissue if she was good and devoted enough. The question of what would make it possible for a parent, an adult of either sex, to give that kind of attention and devotion guided my first research question, What did mothers need to be able to do this? Dan Stern was warmly encouraging about pursuing this line of thought, and Beatrice, whom I reencountered in my 1st year of training at NYU Postdoctoral Psychology Program, gave me the chance to explore these kind of questions with the mothers in her study while I helped with the staging and coding of the Ainsworth Strange Situation, measuring infant attachment at 1 year.

The attempt to be equally preoccupied with what infants and mothers need, to hold in mind what did an infant need and what do I now as a mother need to meet my baby's needs, sprang from a tension that was defining in my generation of feminist struggle—as one sees in writings like Jane Lazarre's (1976) *The Mother Knot*. But it was to be equally crucial for the evolution of relational psychoanalysis. By embedding this tension between mother and baby within psychoanalytic theory and an understanding of complementary dynamics the effort was to make mutual recognition into a container for something much more complex, indeed the origin of so many later dilemmas of intersubjectivity: negotiating the sticky compromises and paradoxes of a dyad in which there is mutuality but asymmetry, identity of needs but conflict of needs, deep attunement but also difference. For my sensibility the profoundest inspiration of feminist theory was the search for a perspective that transcends the either/or of needs and unlocks the impasse that leads to domination—the Hegelian struggle to the death for recognition in which only one can live, the other must die—to show how there can be two subjects in one relationship, neither one subjugating the other, neither having to coerce or defend themselves from the other. In other words, I was determined to have mother and baby "live" in the same theory and so bring together feminism and the psychology of infancy.

The initial conceptual solution to this impasse was to shift from the then prevalent developmental dynamic in which a child separates from mother—shedding her, as it were—to the idea of an engagement in which there is a tension between each partner acting/impacting the other and each recognizing the other's action. A dynamic balance that so easily goes awry, that even at its best the process of mutual accommodation is characterized by conflict and more often by breakdown and restoration of recognition. This idea of breakdown and recognition is, interestingly, an idea quite similar to Tronick's (1989) rupture and repair, published in the same year. From this developmental perspective on the inevitable tension of recognition, the necessity of restoring it after breakdown, a very different view of clinical process emerges as well—but it is one I could not yet elaborate, only intuitively sense.

Tronick's (1989) formulation seemed to me a dramatic conceptual breakthrough, confirming how we could see basic patterns of all interaction in infancy and confirming the unformulated knowledge behind the idea of mutual recognition as something that necessarily breaks down. The fact that mothers and infants *benefit* from the process of recreating a state of mutual regulation after mismatching and dysregulation offers an entirely different perspective on what it means to be "good enough," to grow, to heal. Mutual accommodation and correction become the name of the game, thus giving the lie to the burdensome and arrogant idea of the analyst's interpretive truth, correct technique. In a sense, it provides the cornerstone of any theory of therapeutic enactment, any idea of moving from separation to reunion, opening up the way resilience and attachment are built on imperfect unions. It thus truly shifts the understanding of recognition versus destruction, showing that both members of the dyad, and the relationship itself—the third upon which it is based and which is its space—must survive collapse or breakdown. Of course, it is crucial to appreciate that repair, in many cases, means recognition of distress by the caregiver, the most important predictor of secure attachment in infancy (Beebe et al., 2012), and by extension by the therapist who may himself or herself have caused the pain.

MUTUALITY AND CLINICAL PRACTICE

So although *Bonds of Love* (1988) posits the possibility of mutual recognition, in fact it sees it as a precarious business. Yet somewhere along the line, it seems that a version of this concept of mutuality was transferred whole cloth to the clinical situation and taken to mean, in effect, that Benjamin believes the patient *must* recognize the therapist (Orange, 2010a, b) or that recognition is only a matter of Hegelian collision and not of maternal attunement to early needs (Benjamin, 1999; Reis, 1999). In actuality, when I wrote the book and for some time after I was a rather conventional object relations analyst influenced by self psychology as well.

Yet the issue of whether recognition was mutual did become somewhat thorny in relation to self psychology insofar as it charted empathy as a largely one-way process. Kohut's ideas of mirroring and empathy bore some resemblance to the idea of recognition, Stern and other psychoanalytic infancy researchers embraced self psychology, yet there were important differences between the two approaches. For instance, the idea of mirroring, Stern (1985) contended, was inadequate to capture the mutuality of face-to-face play, the necessary level of discrepancy between expectation and event. Even misattunement had to balance out attunement to create an element of difference (Beebe and Lachmann, 2002). However, speaking more broadly, I noted in self psychology the failure to grasp how developmentally important is the capacity to enjoyably give recognition, which evolves as one is secure that one is indeed recognized by the other. Although eventually I think self psychology found a way of coming to grips with the problem of difference and the meaning of my sense of recognition became more evident (see Orange, 2010a, b), it initially seemed to miss the idea that when the other survives destruction, this means more broadly that the other takes care of oneself and that the patient is released from enmeshment in the other's needs; the safety of nonretaliatory survival means that the uncontrollability and unpredictability of the other can become a source of joy. In my assessment the lacuna in appreciating the importance of a capacity to recognize and thus fully engage (and enjoy!) a different other subject reflected a gap in realizing how our sense of agency and power come from giving and not merely from receiving.

Although *Bonds of Love* (1988) appeared just as we were getting the relational track at NYU off the ground, and I might have thought intersubjectivity theory could be a basis for relational analysis, I had no idea what that would mean practically. I had only unformulated knowledge; we studied with analysts like Bollas and MacDougall (by far the most expansive personality in mainstream analysis), who both used their subjectivity to reflect on the process, but their way was just a beginning, a crack in the patina of orthodoxy. What it meant to practice relationally was just beginning to appear on the horizon, and I did not see myself as defining clinical theory in direct terms. I was highly aware of the way patients might fear exploitation, how forms of disclosure or demands for mutuality might interfere with the patient's need for holding of very early or disorganized selfstates, in other words, block the positive aspects of "regression" to dependency.

Thus my sense of mutuality was initially more cautious: that affect attunement and sharing of emotional states could be a basis for mutuality inasmuch as we feel a sense of mutual recognition when we attune to our babies and they "recognize" us by calming down or brightening up. Of course, this sensibility was already a departure from what was at that time called "being a real analyst," maintaining Freudian neutrality and being a blank screen. In addition to the primary intersubjectivity of attunement, state-sharing, what I would now call the rhythmic third (Aron, 2006; Benjamin, 2011), my original sense of how the analyst was recognized was primarily in terms of "survival of the object," the analyst as a subject who truly exists outside the patient's control, can take care of herself and need not be vigilantly managed or minded by the patient. I distinguished between the patient recognizing our outsideness, being a subject who acts independently and above all responsibly, from being a person, a defined fleshed-out subjectivity, which could be overstimulating or frightening.

However, I did (and do) strongly believe that this inhibition was not an exact parallel to how we needed to be as mothers or parents. Again, I took it that gratitude as a subjective experience was the intersubjective correlate of recognition, the child recognizing the parent's loving intent or action. In addition, it was very clear to me that knowing the parent's mind was something many patients felt lacking in their upbringing. Hence, I believed part of the mutual accommodation with children was more explicitly giving them the opportunity to understand their parent; knowing where she was coming from would give them more agency and strength in the relationship. Lew Aron (1996) did adapt the ideas about recognizing maternal subjectivity and mutuality in developing a clinical theory of mutual knowing in psychotherapy, stressing how the patient wants to know and get into the analyst's mind. But Aron was also careful to stress asymmetry along with mutuality, which made mutuality in practice seem less dangerous. This seemed to me, as it still does, a crucial tension; further it implies (a point I was first able to articulate in thinking through with Aron) the need to be connected to the third as a principle of interaction.

This appeared to me gradually, a decade after the book, as the idea of the third (Aron and Benjamin, 2000; Benjamin, 2004, 2011) as what we surrender to, a mutually created choreography that survives rupture and creates a sense of lawfulness. Rupture and repair could be described as a dyadic movement, an overarching process of the third that choreographs both partners. This movement creates new relational patterns or expectancies in both; in responding to these expectancies each creates recognition in self and in the other. This sense of shared expectancy can occur within an asymmetrical relation of giver and receiver of nurturance—a fact that may serve to clarify the essential point that mutual recognition is not based on identical or symmetrical experiences but rather is a relational movement that can encompass a great deal of difference or asymmetry in identities as well as complementary roles.

How mutuality works therapeutically is another story, one that required the development brought about by many other relational thinkers. Certainly the idea of rupture and repair helped to underpin the position that collisions and negotiations, now stressed by relational clinical theory (Pizer, Bromberg, Slochower), need to occur and are not simply an unavoidable by-product of our being human. The viewpoint that in some sense we are all equal, the mutual identification which rejects the idea that we are healthy people curing sick people (a delusion named by Racker, 1968) informed the new relational sensibility. Steve Mitchell (1993, 1997) embodied this sensibility and pointed the way toward learning to recognize the impact of our own subjectivity on the treatment and consciously use our own subjectivity in direct interaction. With his leadership, the project of realizing a form of mutual knowing in practice and reflecting on it theoretically was to take the decade of the 1990s. I confine myself here to saying that the idea of recognition seems to me borne out by the work of those who showed how the analyst must change (i.e., Slavin's [Slavin and Kriegman, 1998] patient, "We have to understand you to understand me!"), that the sense of badness must be contained by a We who each know the other can be hateful (Davies, 2004) or dysregulated and dissociated (Bromberg, 2006, 2011). For me, influenced by Lew Aron's reflections on this, Ferenczi's (1933) idea that the analyst must acknowledge his part of the interaction came to seem emblematic of the way in which reciprocity and mutual knowing could be healing (Benjamin, 2006).

The ideas of state sharing as well as rupture and repair seem to be the place where the study of infancy and relational analysis have met. Focusing on the role of shared states, affect regulation, and joint dissociation allowed a perspective on how to use enactments and to flesh out the insight that at some level mutual knowing is both unavoidable and desirable. The view that recognition is based in the sharing of affect states, which is in turn crucial to mutual regulation, has essentially transformed the field. The charting of recognition process in infancy spread far beyond its original domain. For me, it made possible in *Bonds of Love* (1988) an anticipation of what became a clinical theory of moving from complementarity to the third: "To transcend the experience of duality... requires a notion of mutuality and sharing... both partners are active; it is not a reversible union of opposites (a doer and a done-to). The identification with the other person occurs through the sharing of similar states. ..." (p. 48).

IDENTIFICATORY LOVE

Although I find much to expand the idea of recognition from 25 years ago, most of it seems in accord with what I think today. Reading back over *Bonds of Love* (1988) regarding gender is a very different experience, for me at least, perhaps because so much of it is an argument with theories that now have gone into the dustbin of history. Object relations theory so thoroughly outpaced sexual instinct theory that the idea that what is missing is the relationship to father rather than the phallus seems simply to have been incorporated in the dominant practice, at least in North America, where interpretations of penis envy as a "thing in itself" have become rather rare (although my German analyst in the late 1960s did believe this, much to the detriment of our relationship). However, although the outdated villain of penis envy may have been vanquished by our current thinking that anyone can have anything, and many of us want the symbolic overinclusiveness obscured by the rigidity of old oedipal theory, my "discovery" of homoerotic identificatory was an important by-product of that argument, which really remains fresh for me.

The idea that girls could only get the father's penis by having his baby felt emotionally wrong not only because I saw babies as a desideratum in their own right, as Horney (1924) argued. What felt right was that girls would want to use the father in the traditional way that was described for boys in the literature of that time: as a figure of identification who supports separation from mother, as the coming-and-going parent, as the one who represents the outside world, and so on. There were other ways to have a phallus. As a tomboy, I wanted to throw the ball the right way, which was not the girl way; as an adolescent, I wanted to challenge my father's politics and in that sense be his oedipal "son" as well as his daughter. Why shouldn't girls do what boys did?

But this quickly led to a reconstruction of what was then in the literature about the boy's pre-oedipal love of the father as well, starting with Freud. There appeared to be something in this love quite different from oedipal love, which was based on the strict separation of being and having and thus on the taboo of having the like object—the separation that institutes heterosexuality. I felt sorry for my Freudian instructor who told us how his toddler boy came running to greet him at the door as he came out of the elevator crying, "Out, out!" and thought the boy wanted to be left alone (stuck Inside where he had been all day) with mother—I was pretty sure that, like my toddler boy, he had wanted his father to take him Outside.

What is intelligible as desire itself would be other than what Freud assumed in describing the love object. Certainly this early father love did not jibe with the idea of the negative oedipal, being as the mother is to the father. I came up with the not so euphonious term "identificatory love," a homoerotic love, meaning love of what is seen as or wished to be "like." This relation of mirroring, twinning, subject-to-subject desire for recognition and love of the "like subject" would differ from the oedipal love of the other (whoever it might be, same or opposite sex, whatever felt like that otherness). I still see this powerful desire, which I think matches up with what Ken Corbett (2009) has noted in his little boy patients, who seem to be focused not on wanting Mommy but to be big and strong and bigger and stronger than someone whose power they respect.

These thoughts began with an early draft of "Woman's Desire," which started by asking why women seemed preoccupied with the language of autonomy rather than desire, why unlike men self-assertion appeared not to be equated with being the subject who says (like the rapprochement boy), "I want that!" It seemed that for boys, homoerotic identificatory love formed the sense of oneself as subject of desire. But this identificatory love requires recognition in return, the father who says, "I can see myself in you, recognize your desire as my desire." What happened to girls? Did they miss this personally or was it simply not culturally available?

In the years since I've noted the continuous appearance of this identificatory love in the transference as a homoerotic (whether with same or opposite gender) desire or longing for recognition, which is often missed because it is in fact not the same as conventionally conceived transference love. Among other ways it differs from that erotic transference is that we believe it is possible, nay necessary, to meet the need for mirroring, for mutual idealization and recognition, to empower and share in the development of joyful grandiosity and to counter the past, often traumatizing deflation and shame of feeling not big, not powerful, of having been helpless to gain the attention and recognition of the outside parent. And for a long time, the homoerotic identificatory needs were missed in the transference: despite self psychology having openly embraced everyone's need for idealization and mirroring it missed its gender and erotic aspects; on the other hand there were constant catastrophes in Freudian analyses as the need for mirroring and mutual idealization was denigrated along with homosexuality, the need for recognition missed, as the analyst tried to retain the phallic position of knowledge as power.

But how does this notion of identificatory love of the father remain relevant for understanding masculinity once we affirm (or rather once I restate what I am often rebuked for—not emphasizing the obvious explicitly enough) that the figure of attachment and separation excitement need not be so split; that mothers can be exciting as well as safe; that fathers can nurture; and that—at a social cost to be sure—boys can be girly, girls boyish, moms dads, dads moms, and everybody everything (or nothing) while anatomy and destiny too can be reversed?

In short, when we incorporate the ideas that have been expanded by queer theory, what is left of identificatory love?

Identificatory love, I think, still gives powerful meaning to the idea that being recognized in one's loving desire to be like the other is as crucial as being safely attached to the source of goodness. Rejection of that need for recognition can be withering and crippling.* When what was traditionally the paternal figure, the exciting separation figure, is unavailable, disdainful, shaming, belittling, rivalrous—whether because frightened of his own erotic feeling for the child (boy or girl)or envious of the baby's gratifications with mother—this rejection intensifies the split between being mom's baby and dad's son/daughter. The rejection of this need for identificatory love in girls also poisons the well of desire and subjectivity and leads to a submissive form of ideal love in both women and men, both clinically (read some old cases and see how much the opportunity to recognize identificatory love was missed!) and in and out of the transference. The dearly missed Ruth Stein (2010) argued that the trauma of his father's contemptuous rejection led Mohammed Ata to his self-immolating ideal love of God the father and his violent assertion of the power to destroy others. In traditional culture, paternal contempt for the little boy's bond to the mother generated the dissociated but powerfully spoiling patriarchal denigration of woman. The ensuing exaggeration of the oedipal split between being and having is a marker of the fault line of gender, which it does more than merely regulate; it produces perverse and destructive forms of desire in the futile effort to escape its shameful clutches.

Judith Butler (1995), in her idea of gender melancholia, showed how identificatory love was perverted into the boy/man's thought "I never loved him, I never lost him"; he wouldn't be caught dead being what one wants to have/possess. But my focus here is on the terrible consequences of frustrating the (as it were) premelancholic, primary identification as an emotional tie—a major part of the love that was "never lost."

Everything that came after *Bonds of Love* (1988), written in the crucible of the 1990s, reflected a much greater sense of that instability, overinclusiveness, and mix-and-match relation to gender (as reflected in the later writings of Aron, Bassin, Dimen, Goldner, Harris, and Layton, among others). The idea I took from Fast (1984) that the overinclusiveness of the preoedipal needs to be renounced seemed self-evidently wrong and gave way to the idea of a postoedipal phase in which gender becomes unconventional and transitional (Benjamin, 1995). Yet the oedipal structures and rigidity remain alive in the culture—as contemporary political battles to retain rights we achieved in the 1970s make clear. The oedipal structure includes Freud's ambiguous equation of femininity with passivity—a real appearance, in other words one that gets embodied in the culture even when we no longer see it in terms of lacking the reified phallus. What if, as Freud's own story suggests, the repudiation of homoerotic identificatory love between fathers and boys was constitutive of the fear of passivity, the repudiation of identification with the mother and the projective creation of the feminine? Speaking structurally, what if fear of as well as shameful need for the father underlies fear/hatred of woman? What if men's traumatic relationship to passivity, as originally codified in psychoanalysis, is only now being questioned and reconsidered? These were questions I was able to take up 10 years later in deconstructing Freud's view of femininity as the "daughter position" (Benjamin, 1998). As mindful as we need to be of the extreme asynchrony of different parts of contemporary society, I believe we still need to review and deconstruct Freud's theory as a credible reflection of patriarchy whose fragmented and unstable persistence continues to define many of our political woes.

THE BONDS OF LOVE, REVISITED

PSYCHOANALYSIS (OR ITS OBJECT) NEVER LOSES ITS COOL OR ITS HOT

Psychoanalysis, even its antiquated form, just cannot seem to lose its relevance. As if we needed any proof of the persistence of patriarchy, passivity and submission are not gone from the discourse of the feminine. Is *Story of O* still relevant? According to Katie Roiphe in *Newsweek* (2012) the new fascination with sadomasochism is merely a matter of enjoyment, albeit perplexing to feminists. Why, she ponders and asks researchers (alas, no psychoanalysts) is *Fifty Shades of Grey,* far more poorly written than *Story of O*, a bestseller among young mothers and executives? Because they want to surrender control, lose themselves. Feminist theory is purportedly flummoxed by this phenomenon or that of the highly popular show "Girls," with its male sadist character who directs the actual director, Lena/Hanna, to be his slave. It is incumbent upon us to note that although something has changed to allow this on television, not enough has changed to allow lesbian sadomasochism, which was a movement in the 1980s, to be worthy of Roiphe's mention. And so we must also sadly note that in popular culture, the heterosexual trope of male activity, female passivity is still untouched by queer theory's hits to the reigning discourse of anatomical destiny. How is it possible to have ignored that vast outpouring of feminist theorizing liberated from the moralizing constructions of the 1980s in whose shadow I wrote about sadomasochism? In actuality, we psychoanalytic feminists are armed to the teeth with dangerous theory and outfitted to the nines with our explanations—we just can't get a date with mainstream media.

There are, now that successive generations of feminist thought have come into their own, more contradictions now than the simple controversy about "pornography or heterosexuality, good or bad?" that defined the narrow milieu of the 1980s. On the one side the academic importance of queer theory, of understanding gender as a regulatory discourse and as performance, on the other side the compelling social fact that the more gender is cut up, the more it hydralike multiplies. This multiplication suggests that the components of masculinity and femininity are far more malleable than supposed, but this malleability does not trump, rather cooperates with, the need for socially mediated bodily intelligibility, which often revivifies traditional gender meanings within new combinations. In the private clinic and in public expression, psychocultural structures and contents, though shifting, remain oddly recognizable, make selves intelligible, and remain embedded in our collective mind as our history. As myth and kinetics they offer a language of what we can have and be, our traumas and our desires, our losses and longings. I quoted Foucault as saying power not only represses, it "produces things, it induces pleasure, forms knowledge, produces discourse" (Foucault, 1980, p. 119.) Whereas the focus on regulation and prohibition offers insight into shame, the focus on gender as shaping powerful versions of "this is me" or "is this me?" opens up the contents of desire and longing—contents that are in some sense historically transmitted and perhaps partially alien to the self that embodies them.

In *Bonds of Love* (1988) I defended the possibility of sadomasochism as play, rather than as simple domination, against the then prevailing heterosexual feminist discourse. I saw this play as an incarnation of the historically shaped imagining of desire that could be either concrete or symbolic, shutting down or liberating. The language psychoanalysis invented to open up those contents originally was so organized by the oedipal binary as to be punitive, but the postoedipal world of play can still make great use of psychoanalytic language to break free of the punitive, to unlock desire produced in a world of subjects who are at least partially knowable to each other. This is all the more true when we use psychoanalysis "with culture in mind," with a grasp of social interpellation (Dimen, 2011). Resisting the split between identificatory love and object love, reconfiguring the meaning of subjects and objects, is part of resisting normativity and regulation in the name of producing something other. That something might be called overinclusiveness, multiplicity, or queerness, but what matters to me is its preservation of emotional aliveness and recognition in the face of pain and shame.

Knowing, recognition, finding ways to identify and share feeling without shame... all of these allow us to step into a world of others in which bodies meet and are "carriers" of emotion. *Story of O*, read by my cohort in 1967 shortly after de Beauvoir, made intelligible to me many permutations of desire that only found cultural expression years later. But, with its subtext of Hegelian thought, it also allowed me to elaborate the idea of the split complementarity, that is, of a dynamic system in which each partner's embodiment of one side (sadist, masochist; doer, done-to) depends on the other. This idea of doer and done-to became central in my later understanding of clinical impasses, relationships of perpetrator and victims, as well as symmetrical relations in which each person feels done-to, each person feels in the right, each afraid of being blamed.

In closing, I can only celebrate the cunning of history in bringing these most disparate and unlikely metaphorical systems into collision and conjunction at one time: Hegelian Marxism, critical social theory, psychoanalysis, feminism, infancy research, relational analysis, and yes the fiction of sadomasochism. I'm grateful so much more has been added in the last 25 years that continues to amplify the collisions and transforms theory and practice both in psychoanalysis and feminist thought. I'm grateful for the loving and critical support of all who have participated in thinking and writing with me, who have contributed to this issue of *Studies in Gender and Sexuality*, as well as all who will go on to do something different, related or opposed. Let the show go on....

REFERENCES

Aron, L. (1996). *A Meeting of Minds: Mutuality in Psychoanalysis*. Hillsdale, NJ: Analytic Press.

———. (2006). Analytic impasse and the third. *International Journal of Psycho-Analysis*, 87, 344–368.

——— & Benjamin, J. (1999). Intersubjectivity and the struggle to think. Paper presented at Spring Division 39 of American Psychoanalytic Association, April New York, NY.

Bataille, G. (1976). Hemingway in the light of Hegel. *Semiotext(e)*, 2(2), 12–22.

———, Lachmann, F., Markese, S., & Bahrick, L. (2012). On the origins of disorganized attachment and internal working models: Paper I. A dyadic systems approach. *Psychoanalytic Dialogues*, 22, 53–272.

Beebe, B. & Lachmann, F. (2002). *Infancy Research and Adult Treatment*. Hillsdale, NJ: Analytic Press.

——— & Stern, D. (1977). Engagement-disengagement and early object experiences. In: *Communicative Structures and Psychic Structures*, eds. N. Freedman & S. Grand, New York, NY: Plenum, pp. 35–55.

Benjamin, J. (1988). *The Bonds of Love: Psychoanalysis, Feminism, and the Problem of Domination*. New York, NY: Pantheon.

———. (1995). *Like Subjects, Love Objects: Essays on Recognition and Sexual Difference*. New Haven, CT: Yale University Press.

———. (1998). *Shadow of the Other*. New York, NY, and London, UK: Routledge.

———. (1999). A note on the dialectic: Commentary on paper by Bruce E. Reis. *Psychoanalytic Dialogues*, 9, 395–400.

———. (2004). Beyond doer and done to: An intersubjective view of thirdness. *Psychoanalytic Quarterly*, 63, 5–46.

———. (2006). Our appointment in Thebes: Analytic acknowledgment of failures and injuries. Lecture presented at IARPP, January, Boston, MA.

———. (2011). Afterword: Beyond doer and done-to. In: *Relational Psychoanalysis: Vol. 4. Expansion of Theory*, eds. L. Aron, & A. Harris, New York, NY: Routledge, pp. 124–130.

———. (2012). Andy Rabinbach as the inspiration for a work of feminist theory. *New German Critique*, 117, 5–8.

Bromberg, P. (2006). *Awakening the Dreamer: Clinical Journeys*. Mahwah, NJ: Analytic Press.

———. (2011). *The Shadow of the Tsunami and the Growth of the Relational Mind*. New York, NY: Routledge.

Butler, J. (1995). Melancholy gender: Refused identification. *Psychoanalytic Dialogues*, 5, 165–180.

Chodorow, N. (1978). *The Reproduction of Mothering: Psychoanalysis and the Sociology of Gender*. Berkeley: University of California Press.

———. (1979). Gender, relations and difference in psychoanalytic perspective. In: *Feminism and Psychoanalytic Theory*. New Haven, CT: Yale University Press, 1989.

Corbett, K. (2009). *Boyhoods*. New Haven, CT: Yale University Press.

Davies, J. (2004). Whose bad objects are we anyway? Repetition and our elusive love affair with evil. *Psychoanalytic Dialogues*, 14, 711–732.

de Beauvoir, S. (1943). *She Came to Stay*. Cleveland, OH: World Publishing Company, 1954.

———. (1949). *The Second Sex*. New York, NY: Knopf, 1952.

De St. Jorre, J. (1994, August 1). The unmasking of O. *The New Yorker*, pp. 42–46.

Dimen, M. (2011). *With Culture in Mind: Psychoanalytic Stories*. New York, NY: Routledge.

Dinnerstein, D. (1976). *The Mermaid and the Minotaur*. New York, NY: Harper & Row.

Fast, I. (1984). *Gender Identity: A Differentiation Model*. Hillsdale NJ: Analytic Press.

Ferenczi, S. (1933). Confusion of tongues between adults and the child. In: *Final Contributions to the Problems and Methods of Psychoanalysis*. London, UK: Karnac, 1980, pp. 156–167.

Foucault, M. (1980). *Power/Knowledge: Selected Interviews*, ed. C. Gordon. New York, NY: Pantheon.

Ghent, E. (1990). Masochism, submission, surrender. *Contemporary Psychoanalysis*, 26, 169–211.

Habermas, J. (1968). *Knowledge and Human Interests*. Boston, MA: Beacon Press, 1971.

Hegel, G. W. F. (1807). *Phenomenologie des Geistes* [The Phenomenology of the Spirit]. Hamburg, Germany: Felix Meiner, 1952.

Horney, K. (1924). On the genesis of the castration complex in women. In: *Feminine Psychology*. New York, NY: Norton, 1967.

Kojève, A. (1969). *Introduction to the Reading of Hegel*. New York, NY: Basic Books.

Lazarre, J. (1976). *The Mother Knot*. Boston, MA: Beacon.

Mitchell, S. (1993). *Hope and Dread in Psychoanalysis*. New York, NY: Basic Books.

———. (1997). *Influence and Autonomy in Psychoanalysis*. Hillsdale, NJ: Analytic Press.

Orange, D. (2010a). Recognition as: Intersubjective vulnerability in the psychoanalytic dialogue. *International Journal of Self-Psychology*, 5, 227–243.

———. (2010b). Revisiting mutual recognition: Responding to Ringstrom, Benjamin and Slavin. *International Journal of Self-Psychology*, 5, 293–306.

Racker, H. (1968). *Transference and Countertransference*. London, UK: Karnac, 1982.

Reis, B. (1999). Thomas Ogden's phenomenological turn. *Psychoanalytic Dialogues*, 9, 371–395.

Roiphe, K. (2012, April 16). The fantasy life of working women: Why surrender is a feminist dream. *Newsweek*.

Slavin, M. & Kriegman, D. (1998). Why the analyst needs to change. *Psychoanalytic Dialogues*, 8, 247–285.

Snitow, A., Stansell, D. & Thompson, S. (1980). *Powers of Desire: The Politics of Sexuality*. New York, NY: Monthly Review Press.

Stein, R. (2010). *For Love of the Father: A Psychoanalytic Study of Religious Terrorism*. Stanford, CA: Stanford University Press.

Stern, D. (1974a). The goal and structure of mother-infant play. *The Journal of American Academy of Child Psychiatry*, 13, 402–421.

———. (1974b). Mother and infant at play: The dyadic interaction involving facial, vocal and gaze behavior. In: *The Effect of the Infant on Its Caregiver*, eds. M. Lewis & L. Rosenblum, New York, NY: Wiley, pp. 187–201.

———. (1985). *The Interpersonal World of the Infant*. New York, NY: Basic Books.

Trevarthen, C. (1977). Descriptive analyses of infant communicative behavior. In: *Studies in Mother-Infant Interaction*, ed. H. R. Schaffer, London, UK: Academic Press, pp. 227–270.

———. (1980). Communication and cooperation in early infancy: A description of primary intersubjectivity. In: *Before Speech: The Beginning of Interpersonal Communication*, ed. M. Bullowa, New York, NY: Cambridge University Press, pp. 216–242.

Tronick, E. (1989). Emotions and emotional communication in infants. *American Psychologist*, 44, 112–119.

Winnicott, D. W. (1971). The use of an object and relating through identifications. In: *Playing and Reality*. London, UK: Tavistock.

The Benjamin Chreode

Uri Hadar, Ph.D.
Tel Aviv University

This article describes the development of Benjamin's ideas and discusses them critically on a theoretical level by comparing them with Lacan's ideas. I argue that Benjamin's and Lacan's theoretical formulations start from the same tradition of continental philosophy but develop in different directions. I follow the track of such concepts as *intersubjectivity, domination, thirdness*, and others and take the notion of thirdness from the clinical to the social domain. I then describe in some detail a series of workshops for Palestinians and Israelis—the Mutual Acknowledgment Project—that try to promote reconciliation by processing the deepest injuries that trouble the two communities. Analysis of the project gives rise to some insights regarding the third in its social action.

INTRODUCTION

The British developmental biologist C. H. Waddington (1957) coined the term "chreode" to designate a path along which a particular gene pool may develop. The idea he wanted to convey was that virtually identical gene pools may develop into very different phenotypes due to the different trajectories that they follow. When the same genetic material follows one route, it may end up as one organ, say, a nose, whereas when it follows a different route, it may end up as a different organ, an ear, for instance. In this article, I employ this notion of chreode as a metaphor in order to describe the specificity of the trajectory that Benjamin's work has taken since the publication of *The Bonds of Love* (BoL; Benjamin, 1988), a trajectory that started with such notions as *intersubjectivity, domination,* and *recognition* and then continued with the concepts of, for instance, *thirdness, injury,* and *mutual acknowledgment*. In the course of this development, the practical domains to which her theory applied widened from the primary focus on therapeutic psychoanalysis and the gendering of dyadic relations to group relationships, especially as they are enacted by ethnic groups.

The theoretical and practical implications of the Benjamin chreode, I feel, come out with particular clarity when compared with another view that started with a very similar theoretical "gene pool," so to speak, but worked its way toward a different theoretical site. I refer here to Lacan's view, especially as it applies to intersubjectivity. Unlike Benjamin's view, Lacan's does not simply affiliate with the term "intersubjective" despite the fact that during the 1950s Lacan used it many times and with reference to different aspects of his theory or teaching, as he liked to call it (see the following). Later, Lacan (1960a) objected to some uses of the term in psychoanalysis, especially as they apply to transference interpretations. Still, in this article, I set out from the idea that Benjamin's and Lacan's views began with similar theoretical "genes," consisting of the phenomenological and dialectical ideas of continental European philosophy with its concepts of subjectivity and what it means to be a subject. I refer here primarily, but not exclusively, to intersubjectivity as articulated in the Hegelian master-slave dialectic, namely, to the dynamics whereby one consciousness is dependent on the recognition of another's in order to constitute subjectivity. Consequently, I argue, there are some remarkable issues on which Lacan's and Benjamin's theories resemble each other, notably regarding the notion of thirdness but also regarding intersubjectivity as well as their respective critiques of the biological tradition in psychoanalysis. Both attempt to found psychoanalysis on methods that are gleaned from the humanities and the social sciences rather than from empirical science and biology.

Benjamin's and Lacan's views of intersubjectivity, despite being similar in some ways, are, however, also crucially different in some other ways, and accordingly each developed ideas that are clearly missing in the other. In this article, I focus on Benjamin's extension of her ideas about the (psycho-)logic of intersubjective *domination* and its undoing in therapy and social activism. Benjamin sets out from the dyadic logic of the development of subjectivity in the face of strong forces of domination; she then extends it to the logic of (ethnic) groups that are bound together by a common fate, so to speak. In the course of articulating these extensions, Benjamin addresses social issues generally and issues of postcolonial theory in particular. This allows Benjamin to analyze the mutual dependencies of victim and perpetrator at various sites of conflict, including Germany, New Zealand, and former Yugoslavia. However, in this article I only elaborate upon her ideas regarding the Israeli-Palestinian conflict and the formative role, on group level, of the experience of injury, including the loss of life and home. From this, I discuss the particular practice emanating from Benjamin's analysis of ethnic dependencies, notably those pertaining to mutual acknowledgment in the Israeli-Palestinian arena. This is of particular importance to me because, unlike some other, excellent analysts of the postcolonial situation, Benjamin manages to think through and apply her work as a practice of enlarging and enriching interethnic relations even prior to conflict resolution on the political level. To my mind, such a process offers a major step forward in terms of interethnic relations, both prior to and after the political resolution of the conflict.

By way of illustrating the aforementioned ideas, I describe in some detail a project that Benjamin initiated and led during 2004–2010 and in which I was directly involved. The project, which we called The Mutual Acknowledgment Project, gathered together mental health workers from different ethnic groups and subgroups: West Bank Palestinians, Israeli Palestinians, Israeli Jews, and people from the rest of the world ("internationals") who had experience in situations of ethnic conflict. The project comprised a series of meetings in different group formats in which participants tried to talk with each other in ways that were expressive of their own injuries on the one hand and cognizant of having inflicted injuries on the other. In my discussion, I do not attempt to give a comprehensive account of the project—this would require a separate and elaborate effort in its own right. Rather, I describe and discuss episodes in which we experienced a particular kind of thirdness, which is, to my mind, immensely important in understanding the Palestinian-Israeli situation as well as for gaining a grasp of a particular and unusual form that thirdness can take. I start, however, with the more theoretical aspect of Benjamin's work.

THE INTERSUBJECTIVE IN BENJAMIN AND LACAN

The intersubjective nature of Benjamin's theory is clear to the point of self-evidence, not only because she has elaborated her theory under this heading, already before BoL, but also because her approach has been recognized as paradigmatic, even exemplary, among intersubjective approaches to psychoanalysis. Yet, I take a brief pause to spell out this aspect of her theory in order to show the sense in which later developments could be seen as realizations of particular potentialities. In BoL, Benjamin introduces the notion of the intersubjective with the following words:

> From the study of the self who suffers the lack of recognition, as well as the new perspective of the active, social infant who can respond to and differentiate others, emerges what I call the *intersubjective view*. The intersubjective view maintains that the individual grows in and through the relationship to other subjects. Most important, this perspective observes that the other whom the self meets is also a self, a subject in his or her own right. It assumes that we are able and need to recognize the other subject as different and yet alike. . . . Thus the idea of intersubjectivity reorients the conception of the psychic world from the subject's relation to its object toward a subject meeting another subject [Benjamin, 1988, pp. 19–20].

I stress, at this point, for reasons that will become increasingly significant, that the subject, in this view, is not positioned in a symmetrical relation to another subject because even here the subject is oriented toward an external entity, as in object relations. The difference with object relations lies in the fact that this other entity's subjectivity needs to be addressed and recognized in order to allow the development of one's own subject positioning. This does not mean, in my understanding, that subjecthood is established in relation to somebody whose subjectivity has the same order of vitality as does the subjectivity of oneself. There is, and probably has to be, an asymmetry between subject and other, but the subjectivity of the other has not been adequately considered in psychoanalysis insofar as it is constitutive of the subjectivity of the self. This is the prime novelty of Benjamin's formulations.

The asymmetry of the relation of subject to other—subjecthoodwise—is not surprising considering that its origin is in Hegel's master-slave dialectic. Thus, already in BoL, Benjamin (1988) writes, "The conflict between the assertion of self and the need for the other was articulated long before modern psychology began to explore the development of self. Hegel analyzed the core of this problem in his discussion of the struggle between 'the independence and dependence of self consciousness' and its culmination in the master-slave relationship. He showed how the self's wish for absolute independence clashes with the self's need for recognition" (p. 3). In this respect, Benjamin says, Freud's position is comparable to Hegel's: the subject only needs the other to confirm his or her own independence (or rather, his or her position as a subject, as someone whose claim to autonomy is recognized). From her intersubjective perspective, by contrast, Benjamin sees the subject as someone who may well gain from a less instrumental pursuit of the other's recognition. Indeed the subject stands to lose from being unable to adopt such a position. This "less instrumental" attitude requires that both subjects understand and act toward a two-way process of recognition of the value and nature of the other's subjectivity. Although the ability to perceive and respond to the subjectivity of the other appears very early in life, in Benjamin's view, and is probably inborn, the engagement in offering and receiving recognition, and its mutual regulation, needs to be understood and cultivated if its psychological potential is to be realized. "In this sense, notwithstanding the inequality between parent and child, recognition must be mutual and allow for the assertion of each self. Thus I stress that mutual recognition, including the child's ability to recognize the mother as a person in her own right, is as significant a developmental goal as separation. Hence the need for a theory that understands how the capacity for mutuality evolves, a theory based on the premise that from the beginning there are (at least) two subjects" (Benjamin, 1988, p. 24).

And this is where things may go wrong. Rather than offering and receiving recognition with joy, people may engage in manipulating the other's needs, in denying, foreclosing, or totally negating the other's subjectivity. What we have here is not only aggression on the part of the individual but also an inherent cognitive difficulty: "The reciprocal relationship between self and other can be compared with the optical illusion in which the figure and ground are constantly changing their relation even as their outline remains clearly distinct—as in Escher's birds, which appear to fly in both directions. What makes his drawing visually difficult is parallel to what makes the idea of self-other reciprocity conceptually difficult: the drawing asks us to look two ways simultaneously, quite in opposition to our usual sequential orientation" (Benjamin, 1988, pp. 25–26). Yet, seeing things in a two-way fashion and acting accordingly (by both offering and receiving recognition) is necessary if we are to avoid the need to secure the other's recognition in aggressive ways. "The primary consequence of the inability to reconcile dependence with independence, then, is the transformation of the need for the other into domination of him" (Benjamin, 1988, p. 26). This, according to Benjamin, is what Freud, like Hegel, conceived of as the natural state of the human psyche, which can only be reined in by social constraints. However, this essentially one-sided view of subjectivity underestimates the mental abilities we all have and constitutes human morality in an inherently negative field of fear. This is psychologically restrictive and morally pessimistic.

Unlike in Benjamin's theory, intersubjectivity in Lacan is problematic. During the 1950s, he often referred to intersubjectivity as an aspect of his own theory and some early formulations about this matter are almost Benjaminian. Thus, in his 1951 conference lecture he wrote, "What must be understood about psychoanalytic experience is that it proceeds entirely in this subject-to-subject relationship, which means that it preserves a dimension that is irreducible to any psychology considered to be the objectification of certain of an individual's properties" (Lacan, 1951, p. 176). This conceptualization of the psychoanalytic process is not limited to the overt need for speech-based communication but extends to unconscious processes. For example, in his 1955 seminar on Poe's story "The Purloined Letter," Lacan's initial and strongest point consisted of showing that repetition compulsion, which is usually conceived of as an entirely intrapsychic phenomenon, is in fact enacted in an intersubjective fashion, placing subjects in predictable positions in relation to each other. Lacan wrote, "What interests me today is the way in which the subjects, owing to their displacement, relay each other in the course of the intersubjective repetition." And then, "Having thus established the intersubjective module of the action that repeats, we must now indicate in it a repetition automatism in the sense that interests us in Freud's work" (Lacan, 1955, p. 10). Lacan continued to use intersubjectivity by reference to the manner in which language recreates positions among the subjects that are connected by it and even insisted that this is the original sense of transference, which later came to be used only in its more limited sense, to refer to repetition within the analytic situation: "For in the *Traumdeutung*, it is in terms of such a function [displacement] that the term *Uebertragung*, or transference, which later will give its name to the mainspring of the intersubjective link between analyst and analysand, is introduced" (Lacan, 1957, p. 434). However, soon afterward, in his designated seminar on transference, Lacan adopted the more usual sense of the term as it applies to the analytic process and set himself up against its construal as intersubjective, namely, as a subject-to-subject relation.

> The doctor and the patient—as we are told—this famous relationship which gets people so excited, are they going to become intersubjective and who is going to do it best? Perhaps, but one can say that in this sense both one and the other take precautions; "He is telling me this for his own comfort or to please me?" thinks the one; "Is he trying to trick me?", thinks the other. Even the shepherd-shepherdess relationship, if it engages in this way, is badly engaged. It is condemned, if it remains there, to end up with nothing. This is precisely why these two relationships, doctor-patient, shepherd-shepherdess, must at all costs be different to diplomatic negotiation and the ambush [Lacan, 1960a].

From around 1960 on, Lacan hardly ever again used the term intersubjective in describing his own approach. We can see that he steered clear of intersubjectivity in precisely the pivotal direction to which Benjamin took it (transference phenomena). To understand this, one has to appreciate that, like Freud, Lacan saw the asymmetric master-slave dynamics as an existential necessity rather than a cultural or historical contingency. Thus, he writes,

> From the conflict between Master and Slave, he [Hegel] deduced the entire subjective and objective progress of our history, revealing in its crises and syntheses the highest forms of the status of the person in the West. . . . Here the natural individual is regarded as nil, since the human subject is nothing, in effect, before the absolute Master that death is for him. The satisfaction of human desire is possible only when mediated by the other's desire and labor. While it is the recognition of man by man that is at stake in the conflict between Master and Slave, this recognition is based on a radical negation of natural values, whether expressed in the master's sterile tyranny or in work's productive tyranny [Lacan, 1948, p. 99].

Here Lacan articulates the inherent asymmetry that emerges in the subject's relation to otherness, any otherness, whether personal or not: wherever subjectivity comes into being, it carries the trace of its existential other, namely, of death, and consequently it marks a position of subservience. This roughly defines the role of culture as a guardian of subjectivity, as the only scene that allows the subject to escape the tyranny of otherness. The dynamics of the subject is always away from the natural, from the biological, which constitutes another convergence between Benjamin and Lacan: both are wary of the ability of biological concepts to explain subjecthood or the subject. In the words of Benjamin, "The original challenge for interpersonal and object relations theories was to eliminate the notion of a biological drive underpinning destructiveness and yet find a place for the destructive and reality-negating forces in mental life. My exposition of the crisis of the self is meant, in part, to answer this challenge. If we want to claim that relations with others are essential to the self, then we cannot help but acknowledge aggression as a necessary moment of psychic life" (Benjamin, 1995, p. 45). Lacan held very similar views on these matters on which, however, I do not elaborate here because they are somewhat tangential to the line of thought that I wish to develop in this article.

DIVERGENCES: POWER AND LANGUAGE

If we compare Benjamin's and Lacan's approaches, each can be seen to hold a certain perspective that is central to the development of their respective theories but is relatively absent from the other's theory. In the case of Benjamin, the related perspective is that of power and power relations, especially as it applies to interpersonal domination, whether strictly dyadic or social. Domination in Benjamin's theory takes many forms and shapes: it can be directly created between two people who are emotionally engaged with each other or apply at the social levels of gender relations (Benjamin, 1988) and, later in her work, interethnic relations (Benjamin, 2006). Summing up her ideas about domination in the most general terms, Benjamin writes,

> Domination does not repress the desire for recognition; rather, it enlists and transforms it. Beginning in the breakdown of tension between self and other, domination proceeds through the alternate paths of identifying with or submitting to powerful others who personify the fantasy of omnipotence. For the person who takes this route to establishing his own power, there is an absence where the other should be [Benjamin, 1988, p. 219].

Later, already in the context of interethnic hostility, Benjamin further stresses the coproduction of power relations even in cases of domination:

> When recognition breaks down...the complementary structure takes over, in which dependency becomes coercive such that each person's action defines the other's reaction; both parties are drawn into the orbit of the other's escalating reactivity and impasse is created. Based on internal splitting, ejecting responsibility into the other in the form of blame, a structure of mutual accusation takes hold where neither party can truly recognize the pain or the struggles of the other. Even though the relationship is asymmetrical—even when one side has power over the other—each side has the symmetrical experience of being helpless to change it. In this sense, complementary relations are characterized by loss of agency and responsibility [Benjamin, 2006, p. 7].

Lacan, by distinction, does not consider power relations at all and is entirely reticent with regard to sensibilities that originate in this perspective. The reason for this is twofold: first, Lacan accepts the master-slave dialectic as the basic logic of intersubjectivity. This asymmetry, for him, is not something that one can transcend or balance but something that one can learn to use in positioning himself or herself as a subject. Second, Lacan does not incorporate a psychology of the intentional mind and, continuing a libertine tradition, bases his ethics on notions of freedom and the subversion of limits. He does so comprehensively, from the most fundamental levels of pleasure to the most abstract realms of thought, and articulates this in detail in his seminar The Ethics of Psychoanalysis (Lacan, 1959). Lacan (1963) also argues that the libertine and the conservative share a view of morality that always holds the law at its epicenter but that they position themselves on opposite sides of the law. As a result, Lacan's theory can be read in both a conservative as well as a radical mode, both of which options have been taken up by followers, but this only accentuates the degree to which his theory disregards interpersonal power relations generally and domination in particular.

As a result, Lacan received some critical comments from critics such as Jameson (1977) and Butler (1997). In articulating what could have been a Benjaminian critique of Lacan, Butler wrote the following:

> To underscore the abuses of power as real, not the creation or fantasy of the subject, power is often cast as unequivocally external to the subject, something imposed against the subject's will. But if the very production of the subject and the formation of that will are the consequences of a primary subordination, then the vulnerability of the subject to a power not of its own making is unavoidable. That vulnerability qualifies the subject as an exploitable kind of being. If one is to oppose the abuses

of power (which is not the same as opposing power itself), it seems wise to consider in what our vulnerability to that abuse consists. That subjects are constituted in primary vulnerability does not exonerate the abuses they suffer; on the contrary, it makes all the more clear how fundamental the vulnerability can be [Butler, 1997, p. 20].

Jameson (1977) also noted Lacan's utter disregard for issues of domination and contrasted it to the writing of such thinkers as Fanon and Foucault. Jameson argued that thinkers in the Hegelian master-slave tradition can be divided into those who care for issues of power relations and domination and those who do not. By contrast to Lacan, Jameson cited a range of works that articulate the postcolonial critique of psychoanalysis and Marxism, starting with Sartre and continuing with Fanon and Foucault: "This approach—the reading of cultural phenomena in terms of otherness—derives from the dialectic of the relationship to the Other in Sartre's Being and Nothingness, and beyond that, from the Hegelian account of the Master and the Slave in the Phenomenology. It is a dialectic which seemed to lay the basis for an aggressive critique of the relations of domination" (Jameson, 1977, p. 379). Benjamin's approach clearly articulates such a "reading of phenomena in terms of otherness" but, in her early writings, she anchored this reading primarily in clinical phenomena. Nevertheless, as we see later, she also extended it to cultural phenomena at large, including gender relations and the relationships between ethnic groups.

Lacan, for his part, also articulated a dimension of psychoanalytic thought that is absent from Benjamin, namely, the generative role of language and speech in constituting the subject. For Lacan (e.g., 1960b), language and speech are at the heart of subjectivity. By contrast to Descartes, who considered *thinking* the basic tenet of being a subject, Lacan thought that *speaking* plays this role. Indeed, he called our species "the speaking being." The main difference between thought and speech, in this regard, is that speech is a more exterior property than thought, more intersubjective. As a result, subjectivity in Lacan turns more toward external agencies—toward otherness—than in Descartes and, indeed, more than in most other psychoanalytic approaches. Of course Benjamin, in this respect, was on the same side as Lacan: for her subjectivity is also dependent on (the recognition of) an external agency, namely, another subject. Nevertheless, there is an important difference here because for Lacan the external agency is not always a person as such—either subject or object. The prime external agency that in Lacan's view determines subjectivity qua language is what he called the signifier, namely, the set of rules that governs signification in language and language-like systems. Only by recognizing these rules—a prime objective in therapy—can a person hope to attain and develop her subjecthood. Moreover, for Lacan the equation of *otherness* with another subject means to imprison the subject in a relatively limited system of signification that he called the Imaginary, namely, a system that is governed by projections, introjections, and identifications instead of the rules of syntax, which are much more productive, so to speak. In this respect, society behaves like language in being rule-governed (although Lacan called the rules in the context of society *the Law*). Together, the systems of language and society, which are both intentional systems (though not the products of individual intentions), form what Lacan called the *Symbolic register*. For Lacan, by remaining blind to the constitutive role of language and social rules, the subject remains locked in the Imaginary world of projections and identifications.

In Benjamin, by contrast to Lacan, the constitutive function of language and speech is virtually absent. Although she considers parts of the Symbolic—the parts appertaining to social processes—she never treats language as an object of psychoanalytic investigation in its own right. This difference has considerable consequences with regard to analytic practice: Lacan often bases his interpretation of the patient's speech on investigating the words he or she uses and the etymological ramifications of particular lexical choices, an aspect of interpretation that is virtually absent from Benjamin's illustrations. These clinical aspects, though, may be differentially valued by different practitioners; not everyone is appreciative of linguistic analyses in the session. However, with regard to theory, the lack of consideration for linguistic phenomena becomes noticeable in Benjamin's development of the notion of thirdness. To start with, in the philosophical tradition of both Europe and the Americas, thirdness relies fairly much on the analysis of language and language-type functions in shaping the mind, on one hand, and social institutions, on the other. Benjamin does not always connect to this tradition. Also, to my mind, Benjamin's thirdness is unstable in its autonomy with regard to dyadic processes. Sometimes it needs to be concretely embodied in a third agency, as in the case of ethnic conflict (see later). At the same time, thirdness purports to be an essentially dyadic dynamics (the mutual recognition of the subjectivity of the other). By distinction, for Lacan, the externality of language and the law always precede dyadic intentions, so the third is always available for adoption by interested parties. Let me examine this in some detail.

THIRDNESS

In both Benjamin and Lacan, as indeed throughout the history of 20th-century philosophy, thirdness refers to the extension of the subject-object *relation* into a mode of being or, in more subtle formulations, a mode of experiencing. Generally speaking, if we take subject as a first and object as a second—to indicate the phenomenological asymmetry between the two—then thirdness refers to a mode of being that is *neither and both* subject-object. In 20th-century philosophy, this notion of thirdness was understood as the kind of being that is embodied in *language and cultural phenomena*, as can easily be seen in the work of such pioneers of this idea as Charles Peirce (1960), Roland Barthes (1977), or Karl Popper (1978). This is particularly apparent in Popper's translucent definition: "By world 3 I mean the world of the products of the human mind, such as languages; tales and stories and religious myths; scientific conjectures or theories, and mathematical constructions; songs and symphonies; paintings and sculptures. But also aeroplanes and airports and other feats of engineering" (Popper, 1978, p. 144). Although this definition effectively refers to the objectified realm of the third, that is, its manifestations in observable phenomena, its illustrative value lies in bringing out with special clarity the positioning of the third between object and subject, between the domain of intentionality and that of things (or the world of *das Ding*, as Kant called it, emphasizing its inner logic rather than its factuality). Of course, both Benjamin and Lacan emphasize the psychological antecedents of the kind of productions described by Popper or, for that matter, by Peirce, who should probably be credited with first using the term "third" for these purposes. For both Lacan and Benjamin, the third is not symmetrical between subject and object, the way it is for Popper, for example. Rather, the third is an extension of the subject and of subjectivity, but whereas for Lacan this extension is toward the other as Other, the Other as an impersonal representation of otherness, for Benjamin the third is always directed toward a particular, personal other. This is one way in which for Benjamin otherness is constitutive of a psychological reality inasmuch as it is a carrier of subjectivity.

Probably the first construal by Lacan of the manner in which mental function involves three different modes of establishing subjectivity appears during the intersubjective, early period of his theorizing, in the seminar on Poe's story "The Purloined Letter" (Lacan, 1955), which I have already quoted as promoting an intersubjective model. Here Lacan describes thirdness as an order of representation that is aware of its own principle of representation. Because the principle only emerges post hoc, something in signification always remains hidden, so that one does not need to hide a meaning in order for some meaning to remain hidden and vice versa: even the most hidden meanings leave traces that can be used to uncover their principle. This dual dynamics constitutes the unconscious for Lacan. In his words,

> Thus, [we can identify] three moments, ordering three glances, sustained by three subjects, incarnated in each case by different people. The first is based on a glance that sees nothing: the King and then the police. The second is based on a glance which sees that the first sees nothing and deceives itself into thereby believing to be covered what it hides: the Queen and then the Minister. The third is based on a glance which sees that the first two glances leave what must be hidden uncovered to whomever would seize it: the Minister and finally Dupin [Lacan, 1955, p. 10].

Lacan articulates here, after Peirce (1960), what I noted in a recent paper (Hadar, 2010), namely, that the third is tied up with a first and a second in an increasing order of complexity. The first "sees" the world along a single line of view that is determined by his own desire; the second sees two-dimensionally: being aware of the blindness of the first in addition to his own desire. The third sees not only the former two views but also the logic of the system as a whole, the logic of the symbolic order, namely, the manner in which it is informed by a principle of representation, a principle for constructing representational entities.

In another construal, which is more easily associated with the usual understanding of Lacan, he describes the third as the role of the father in the family scene:

> In the first and most Utopian situation, the child finds in the gift of food the gift of love which he desires. The breast and the maternal response can then become symbols of something else. The child enters the symbolic world and can accept the unfolding of the signifying chain. The oral relation as absorption can then be abandoned and the subject evolves in the direction of normal growth. For this to happen, the mother must have taken on board her own castration. A *third* term, the father, must be present for the mother. Only then what she seeks in the child will not be some kind of erotogenic satisfaction which makes of the child the equivalent of the phallus, but a relation in which as mother she is also the wife of the father [Lacan, 1961, p. 232].

Interestingly, here thirdness is not in relation to the primary first, the child, but in relation to the mother, who, by letting this third take its place in relation to her, by making place for this third, allows the child to develop his or her symbolic abilities. This, in fact, is not unlike Benjamin's idea, when she writes that "the mother or primary parent must create that space [of thirdness] by being able to hold in tension her subjectivity/desire/awareness and the needs of the child" (Benjamin, 2004, p. 13). In both cases the mother creates the space for the third in her relatedness to the child, but for Lacan she does so by inviting in the father—a third agency—whereas for Benjamin she does so by insisting on being a subject herself (with the child).

On the whole, with Lacan, the modes of subject positioning (first, second, and third) are overdetermined by different factors such as the mental orders, the linguistic system of personal pronouns, and mental forms of intentionality. Thus, first, second, and third inform, respectively, the Real, Imaginary, and Symbolic at the same time that they are influenced by first, second, and third persons in their linguistic functions; they are also enacted by child, mother, and father in the family scene. Of course, subject positioning may manifest in a single person as modes of intentionality (as in desiring, interacting, and making decisions); they may act to shape dyadic intercourses as patterns of communication (say, touching, acting together, and conversing), but they ultimately represent a three-person logic (Hadar, 2010). In that sense, there is an unbridgeable gap between Lacan's third and Benjamin's third, for whom it is a two-person phenomenon.

Benjamin starts her discussion of thirdness by contrasting her view to a host of other approaches—including that of Lacan (whom she recognizes as the one who initiated the use of this concept in psychoanalysis): "The concept of the third means a wide variety of things to different thinkers, and has been used to refer to the profession, the community, the theory one works with—anything one holds in mind that creates another point of reference outside the dyad" (Benjamin, 2004, p. 7). By contrast, she writes, "I think in terms of thirdness as a quality or experience of intersubjective relatedness that has as its correlate a certain kind of internal mental space; it is closely related to Winnicott's idea of potential or transitional space" (p. 7). In elaboration, Benjamin writes, "thirdness is the intersubjective mental space that facilitates or results from surrender" (p. 8). Here "surrender" represents the balanced position between the active and the passive attitude to the other, suggesting the experiential manner in which one may position herself between subject and object. "I take this to mean that surrender requires a third, that we follow some principle or process that mediates between self and other" (Benjamin, 2004, p. 8). Despite the clarity of its definition, thirdness cannot be fully appreciated without contrasting it to the split complementarity of doer-done to, of active and passive. The two are not only contradictory but also the need for thirdness arises from split complementarity in the first place. "Considering the causes and remedies for the breakdown of recognition ... and the way in which breakdown and renewal alternate in the psychoanalytic process ... led me to formulate the contrast between the twoness of complementarity and the potential space of thirdness" (Benjamin, 2004, p. 9). Analysis, of course, aims specifically at the creation of thirdness as a space of healing. In analysis,

> We surrender to the principle of reciprocal influence in interaction, which makes possible both responsible action and freely given recognition. This action is what allows the outside, different other to come into view. ... It opens the space of thirdness, enabling us to negotiate differences and to connect. The experience of surviving breakdown into complementarity, or twoness, and subsequently of communicating and restoring dialogue—each person surviving for the other—is crucial to therapeutic action. From it emerges a more advanced form of thirdness, based on what we might call the *symbolic* or *interpersonal* third [Benjamin, 2004, p. 11].

Thirdness, then, develops as a response to the threats that face mutual recognition, namely, the threats to two-way recognition of the subjectivity of the other. Thirdness is, in a way, the antidote to split complementarity but, as such, it is predicated upon split complementarity in a far-reaching manner. Thus, on the whole, it seems, the form that thirdness takes depends on how much splitting it needs to counter. In the most benign situation, the existence of values that drive the subject toward the other are sufficient to effectively combat regression to split complementarity—this form is the moral third or the symbolic third. It is defined by Benjamin (2004) as "the ability to maintain internal awareness, to sustain the tension of difference between my needs and yours while still being attuned to you" (p. 13). In functioning adults, this form of thirdness is the most accessible and can usually be trusted to be achievable in regular analytic contexts. However, when split complementarity involves persistent hostility and threatens with outright violence, thirdness must be enacted by a third person. In her clinical vignettes, Benjamin often illustrates how the therapist enacts the third, first in a one-way manner, which later may allow the patients to develop their own thirdness within the space that has been created for them (and with them) by the therapist.

The prime difference, in my mind, between Lacan's and Benjamin's third lies in its respective mode of existence (or, as Lacan would probably have preferred, ex-sistence, to indicate the manner in which thirdness is always in some way external to the subjective realities of those who enact it). For Lacan, thirdness appears in the Other in the first place in the form of language and the symbolic order. As such, its existence does not depend on the subject's recognition: it is always already in place. For Benjamin, although it is never only emergent, without its coenactment in the dyad the third is empty, a mere potentiality. For both of them, the prime task of the analyst is the promotion of thirdness, but for Lacan the analyst functions as a third in the first place, structurally, as it were, for better and for worse. It is the analyst's task to allow the patient to connect to this thirdness, but the analyst should not act from any other place, definitely not from the place of the Imaginary Second, a position from which she or he would create a threat to the patient's subjectivity. For Benjamin, the third forms a shared domain, and even in its primary form, as the coordination of rhythm between infant and mother, it does not exist outside the realm of shared intentionalities. Thus, even when the analyst endeavors to develop the space of the third and secure it, she or he still cannot do this on her own. The analyst can act initially in an asymmetrical symbolic reality, but without the patient's participation thirdness will collapse.

Nevertheless, when it comes to group processes, as in ethnic conflicts, where split complementarity seems "intractable," it becomes necessary for the third to be enacted by a separate entity, an embodied entity. Here, Benjamin's position, inspired by Lacan's writing in the first place, aligns even closer with his view of thirdness. However, Benjamin, unlike Lacan, and probably reflecting their differential concerns for issues of power and domination, has developed her thoughts specifically so as to suit group processes and group work. I now discuss this work because I view it as particularly important in the development of psychoanalytic ideas. Because most readers may not have a firsthand experience with this, let me start out by describing a group project initiated by Benjamin, where Israelis, Palestinians, and Internationals joined in the frame of a workshop to work through conflicted emotionality and hostile constructions of the other (henceforth, The Mutual Acknowledgment Project). Thereafter, I briefly discuss the theoretical nuance of thirdness that emerges from the consideration of the Israeli-Palestinian conflict.

THE MUTUAL ACKNOWLEDGMENT PROJECT

Benjamin initiated the Mutual Acknowledgment Project in January 2004 while she was visiting Israel to attend a conference of Faculty for Israeli and Palestinian Peace (FFIPP). She took the opportunity of the conference and a tour of the occupied Palestinian territories, organized by FFIPP, to get into touch with Dr. Eyad al-Sarraj, psychiatrist and president of the Gaza Community Mental Health Program, an organization that has run mental health services in the Gaza Strip since 1990. Sarraj, like Benjamin, had been dwelling for years on issues concerning the split and paranoid conditioning of both Palestinians and Jews in a reality marked by colonial oppression. He was preoccupied with the question of how to escape such conditioning and replace it with different patterns of communication that may allow Jews and Palestinians to cooperate in resisting the occupation. It was Sarraj's belief that such cooperation might act as the main lever toward ending the Israeli occupation and reaching a just political settlement. Being Benjamin's host during this visit, as well as an old acquaintance of Dr. Sarraj, I too was involved, somewhat as a bystander, in these initial steps. Benjamin and Sarraj found they had much in common in the way they saw things and they prepared an outline for a series of workshops dedicated to an innovative way of processing the group traumas of both Israelis and Palestinians. This involved an open and daring approach to mutual hostility and prejudice as well as to difficult encounters with the other, allowing also for the expression of guilt and shame or, by distinction, of desire for a different kind of coexistence between Israelis and Palestinians, a more caring one.

The planning of the project also included other psychotherapists working in the Israeli and Palestinian communities—the latter, both from within Israel and from the occupied territories—who had experience in work with groups. This team wrote a project proposal that joined together Benjamin's theories about the third with models of group dynamics, structurally in the spirit of the Tavistock model (Miller and Rice, 1967), although in a fairly liberal application, and dynamically in the spirit of Foulkes's (1968) theories. This model offers the frame for intensive work by creating various subgroup formations within the larger group of participants. The model requires that participants spend a few days together in an environment that allows group discussion in diverse formats, including accommodation and meals, which is a cost-intensive setup requiring adequate funding.

Given that the dynamics of this process was difficult to anticipate, although hard feelings were obviously going to be vented, the initial vision of the project was that of a learning experience involving mental health professionals who were well versed in dealing with complex emotions. The idea was to develop routines that could eventually be widely practiced with the Israeli and Palestinian populations at large but that would initially be worked out in detail through a preliminary process with only mental health professionals. Ultimately, only this phase was completed due to the lack of funds and even that in a reduced format from the one that the planning team originally envisaged.

I cannot here go into a comprehensive description of any of the issues listed earlier. Instead, I present and discuss a number of vignettes that, in my mind, illustrate the complexity of the function of the third in the project. I believe that the project offers some novel lessons about the manner in which thirdness occurs in group processes and maybe also in individuals. All of my vignettes narrate events in which thirdness was not enacted by the Internationals but rather by the Israeli Palestinians. In that sense, they illustrate strongly Benjamin's view that thirdness can and should develop as a part of the dyadic dynamics that seeks mutual recognition. Yet, I argue, this kind of thirdness builds upon split complementarity at the same time that it transcends complementarity. Let me present the illustrations first and then discuss what seem to me their theoretical and practical implications for thirdness in working through the Israeli-Palestinian conflict.

During a 4-day workshop in Aqaba (May 2008), on the 1st day, after the long general assembly that opened the workshop, one of the afternoon's small group discussions was conducted on an ethnic basis: Jews, Palestinians, and Internationals each met separately. As we—Israeli Jews—were just sitting down to start the session, two of the Israeli Palestinians surprised us by joining in. When asked about their presence in the Jewish group, they reported that their group had met during lunch break and decided to split up, with participants choosing to join either the group of West Bank Palestinians or the Israeli Jews. They told us that they had made this decision in order to express the split identity with which they have to live. Once the Palestinians offered their initial explanation, the following exchange ensued (I recapture the discussion sketchily, as best as I can from memory):

Jew: Yes, but this is not a meeting of Israelis as such, but a meeting of Israeli Jews.
Palestinian: Of course, I know. That's why I am here.
Jew: But you're not Jewish.
Palestinian: I am. I am not only Jewish, I am Palestinian too—but I am Jewish as well. That's why we split up and some of us went to the meeting of the West Bank people.
Jew: So you are Jewish just because you say so? Does it seem such a subjective business to you?
Palestinian: "Do you want to check my grandmother's identity papers then? Or find out how many of the *mitsvot* I actually keep?
Jew: No. I just want to understand in what sense you are Jewish.
Palestinian: Hebrew is half my mother tongue, I studied the Bible from when I was 6 and Bialik when 7. Sometimes I awake from a nightmare in which I am chased by a German soldier—is that not enough?

It was—and the Palestinians stayed in the Jewish group and participated fully through that day. During the following days, though, Israeli Palestinians acted as a free-floating ethnic group in every possible way: as a separate formation, as Israelis, and as Palestinians. These choices, these performative moves, symbolic and concrete at one and the same time are, in my mind, remarkable in the way they transcend the distinction between split complementarity and thirdness. Clearly, in the way that these moves forced Jewish Israelis to open up their group identity so as to include Palestinians, they created the third within the Israeli group between Jews and Palestinians. Indeed, the Jewish participants experienced this event as formative in its mediating influence in the following days. Yet, the vehicle for this function was enacted by stretching split complementarity to its limits. The Israeli Palestinians did not claim thirdness. Rather, they claimed a split identity, but by enacting it in the way they did they effectively functioned as third on both moral and interpersonal levels. Indeed, in the most intense event that took place the following day, Israeli Palestinians again functioned as third. So let me describe this in some detail.

At the end of the 1st day of the Aqaba workshop, which passed in good spirits, some of both the Jewish and the Palestinian participants felt that things were going too smoothly, too pleasantly, in a way that failed to reflect the antagonistic nature of the group traumas. They felt that the positive atmosphere concealed underlying, unvoiced hostilities. This unrest largely informed the dynamics of the 2nd day, which started off with small group meetings. The plenary assembled in the afternoon, and it was here, at some point, that one of the Jewish participants—I refer to him as A—expressed the earlier mentioned discomfort with things passing so smoothly in spite of the often difficult subject matter that had been brought up during the previous day's plenary. A added that he felt uncomfortable with the fact that some of the Palestinians, especially one West Bank participant, let me call her S, spoke about resisting the occupation without clarifying that they do not support violence. This, he said, to his mind, reflected the asymmetry in commitment between the Jews and Palestinians, and he believed it would be appropriate if the Palestinians asserted their opposition to violence. S was very angry and responded pointedly: "We've heard a lot, here, about Israeli violence," she said, "but none of us demanded a statement from the Israelis about their opposition to violence. All of the Israeli participants served in the army and some of them still do reservist duty. If there's anyone who should worry about violence it's the Palestinians, not the Israelis. And still none of us approached the Jews with a demand for statements. Violence is not my way—on the contrary, my way is to practice medicine—but resisting the occupation is our human right and I shall not voice my reservations about the method that some of my compatriots have chosen, even if it is not what I opt for." A too responded with intensity, saying that he was not ready to talk with someone who, by remaining silent, effectively supports violence directed against Israelis. Another Jewish participant commented that doing military service does not automatically mark a person as violent toward Palestinians. Most Israeli workshop participants, though former soldiers, devote much of their time to the struggle for Palestinian rights. The debate became heated as a deep rift began to emerge. Many of the Israeli Jews responded by supporting the Palestinian woman's words, or more precisely, they supported her desperate stance facing the demands that were being made by A with the support of a couple of other Jewish participants. There was no prearranged activity for the rest of the evening, but most conversations, in pairs or small groups, seemed to relate to that afternoon's clash. The coordinating committee discussed the incident at length. We wondered whether just 1 day—the last day of discussions—would suffice to prevent the collapse of participants' readiness to join together in group processes. It was at this point that the Israeli Palestinians, who among us had most dialogue experience, assured us—the organizing team—that this type of crisis of confidence occurs as a general pattern of dialogue groups and usually affords the continuation of talk on a more profound level. Indeed, this was how it turned out to be in Aqaba on the 3rd day. Here, the Israeli Palestinians acted as a containing third in a manner that could not have been paralleled by the Internationals precisely because of their external position, their lack of specific experience in Israeli-Palestinian dialogue. It is also important to note that the containing margins that the Israeli Palestinians had with regard to group processes were afforded, to my mind, not only due to their prior experience but also due to their split identifications. They did not identify with any of the polarized positions that were at the center of the anguish of the confrontational session.

A number of the project's meetings were held in Beit Jallah, just north of Bethlehem, in the absence of the Internationals, with only Israeli Jews and Palestinians. Of these, I wish to tell about one especially powerful meeting that was held 3 months after Israel's military attack on Gaza, at the end of 2008 and the beginning of 2009. The meeting took place in April 2009 and was marked by the very hard feelings of all participants in the aftermath of the attack on Gaza. Nevertheless everybody showed up for this meeting and everybody spoke their minds. The meeting was facilitated by a psychologist who coordinated the West Bank group and by me in my role as the coordinator of the Jewish-Israeli group. We started with a number of the West Bank participants lashing out at the Jewish Israelis about the atrocities of the Israeli attack on Gaza. The Israelis, although clearly identifying with the rage and the horror of the Palestinians, also became increasingly distressed at being addressed as the Israeli aggressors although they spent the period of the attack in demonstrations against it, often exposing themselves to aggressive acts by the militant Israeli majority as well as to alienation in their social milieu. They tried to communicate these experiences to their Palestinian friends but to no avail. The West Bank speakers went on in the same angry, accusatory mode. At one point, after more than half an hour of this, two Israeli Palestinians asked to speak. They turned to their West Bank friends and said that they did not travel for 5 long hours, from remote northern parts of Israel, in order to hear speeches about Israeli atrocities. Everyone in the meeting, they said, knew exactly what happened in Gaza. Everybody did their best to protest against it while it was going on. They asked to hear where each of us found ourselves with regard to our own cross-ethnic relationships. They wanted to know if people could extract themselves from fear and anger and maintain communication that preserved our humanity and expressed our commonality. They expressed anger at the blaming tone of the West Bank speakers while also underlining their identification with the horror. They said, however, that the suffering of the Gazans should not be annexed or coopted by anyone. These interventions markedly affected the discussion: the tone changed and people narrated their experience during the attack on Gaza. It was not easy to be there, it was quite harrowing and very tense, but people listened to each other. My own sense was that a commonality of values was regaining ground among participants. Again, I feel that only the Israeli Palestinians could have assumed the very specific role they did, appealing to the West Bank participants and allowing more quiet voices to be heard from within this group. Only they were in the position to bring about change in the tone of the discussion and lead us to the reestablishment of a sense of comradeship.

Israeli Palestinians, as a group in its own right, are often left out in the negotiations about the future of the region. My lesson from our acknowledgment experience is that this is a serious mistake: no one is better placed to act as third in this conflict. It might well be that a more active and marked involvement of Israeli Palestinians in the Oslo process could have prevented some of the major errors that appeared in the accord itself or in the processes that brought about the remarkable bankruptcy of the so-called peace process. This issue, however, pertinent as it might be on some levels, is outside the scope of this article.

THE THIRD IN THE ISRAELI-PALESTINIAN CONFLICT

The frame of this article does not allow a detailed investigation of the relationships between forms of subjectivity that characterize individuals and those that characterize groups. Clearly, the mapping of one onto the other is not trivial, but group dynamics and mind dynamics tend to develop along parallel itineraries. This parallelism probably comes about as a result of intricate, two-way influences between group and individual. In the direction of individual-to-group, we have a large body of theory and data since the early writings of Freud (1922), on the role of identifications in group processes, and later a range of thoughts from Bion (1961) to Miller and Rice (1967). The result of this work is a large body of observations on the manner in which groups behave like individual minds, complete with trauma, projections, and a political unconscious (Samuels, 1993).

The pressures of parallelism in the direction of group-to-individual should probably be conceptualized as processes of replication—"interpellations," as they have come to be called in continental philosophy and the social sciences (Dimen, 2011). In fact, as I noted recently (Hadar, 2011), even a basic notion of individual psychology such as the Oedipus complex may be grasped as the interpellation of family dynamics into an individual psyche. Yet, we always remain with the issue of scale: in groups the unconscious is less accessible, changes are slower, and the enactment of conflicts may more readily translate into violence and trauma. As a mere result of scale issues, group processes are more susceptible to splitting and conflicts are more difficult to resolve. They may continue over decades and centuries with their either-or logic. Either victim or perpetrator, the worst forms of split complementarity. In the case of the group, this logic becomes even more rigid because the individual must take responsibility for deeds that she may not have done. The need emanates from belonging to the specific identity group:

> The problem of witnessing and providing recognition is thus immeasurably more difficult when it comes to acknowledging the harm one has caused, in one's role as bystander or passive accomplice to the perpetrator group: to say "my flesh and blood did this to you." It includes the problem of forgiving oneself enough to apologize to and recognize the outcry of the other. The threat to one's identity, one's narrative of one's own suffering and struggles posed by acknowledging that one has done harm can be unbelievably great [Benjamin, 2006, p. 16].[1]

The difficulty of creating thirdness may become even greater due to a particular past experience of being let down by all of those who could have acted as third. "For those who feel entirely abandoned by the world, left to suffer with complete indifference, there is no such third and there is no way out of powerlessness except to reverse it" (Benjamin, 2006, p. 6). This seems to be the case with Israeli Jews. In such a reality, the healing efforts of psychologists, Benjamin's included, must center on countering the effects of the interpellation of conflict by working with individuals and small groups. "What kind of group experience, collective embodiment of the moral third, would I need in order to neither collapse nor retaliate in the face of suffering the direct impact of evil action? And how do we truthfully recognize our traumatic, fear driven or hateful parts, rather than suppressing them in the effort to be good?" (Benjamin, 2006, p. 5). Due to the pressures of splitting generated by the group trauma, even here, with small groups, thirdness can only reestablish its function when it is taken up by a body that is clearly external to the conflicting sides. "The higher the trauma-based hyper-arousal and the greater the sense of threat, the more the complementary positions sharpen and mutual accusation takes over—unless there are lawful structures or third forces in place to hold that common knowledge and allow recovery from reactivity" (Benjamin, 2006, p. 8). Also, "in the space of the third— the position of the witness—it is apparent that A and B [the conflicting sides] are co-determining and co-determined, part of a dynamic with a life of its own. But this can be observed only from a third outside the system, not within it" (p. 8). And then "it is for this reason that the literal third—the witness—is essential to help the return to the principle of the third" (Benjamin, 2006, p. 27). Even then, thirdness needs to be eventually established in the dyadic domain in order to serve recognition and promote reconciliation. "The challenge is to hear and respond to the pain of the other *when we ourselves are in some sense responsible,* or identified with those who are responsible, for causing it" (Benjamin, 2006, p. 16).

From the aforementioned emerges the paradigm that Benjamin envisages for reconciliation work generally and in the Israeli-Palestinian arena in particular: first, the sides need to be convinced to gather together in a space that is safe by being relatively isolated from the ongoing hostilities in the related communities as well as by the presence of a group of persons who do not belong to or who are identified with one of the sides, a group that initially undertakes the function of the third. It is not clear how the people or parties in conflict can be convinced

---

[1] References to the 2006 paper by Benjamin are based on an unpublished version typed in a 12-point font and spanning 29 pages..

to undertake such a step. I reckon this is an educational task in which the benefits of reconciliation need to be conveyed as clearly and seriously as possible. As we witnessed in the acknowledgment project, this first step can be extremely difficult. In fact, most Palestinians from the occupied territories will not agree to engage in any reconciliation project with Israeli Jews in the present situation of Israeli occupation, settlement, and oppression, and on the part of the Jewish Israeli population, too, only a very small minority is willing to think in terms of mutual acknowledgment. Second, the participants need to be allowed to vent their hard feelings regarding the other side and express their sense of hurt and injury. At the initial stage of this mutual engagement, the agreed-upon rules of discussion must allow each side to express its grievances. This may require the containing participation of a third group acting as third by offering recognition of injury to both sides. The next step is one in which the sides need to own up to the fact that they have inflicted injuries on the other side, that they have been the cause of suffering for persons from the other side. In order to achieve this, one side must be ready to "go first," to be the first to acknowledge that they, their people, have caused much suffering to the other side. At this stage, it makes psychological sense that the stronger side should go first, although much depends on the individual participants in the process. Finally, the two sides need to articulate their commonalities, similarities, and readiness to take up a common fate rather than maintain a phantasy of a homogeneous existence, free of ethnic or any other otherness.

I think it is clear that all of the aforementioned characteristics informed the Mutual Acknowledgment Project.

CONCLUSION

When I take a bird's-eye view of the Benjamin chreode, one feature of it stands out especially forcefully and that is its ethical nature. This does not inhere in any claim on Benjamin's part to know what needs to be done—Kant's "practical reason," the realm of morality—but rather in her epistemology (Kant's "pure reason" or the realm of truth). Unlike many other psychoanalytic writers, Benjamin does not speak about "mechanisms" or "dynamisms"; rather, her statements about psychoanalytic process always involve intentionality and responsibility. Nothing that is of psychoanalytic interest happens without them. This is at the heart of being a subject that, in turn, is at the heart of psychoanalysis. This ethical core appears in the analysis of every interactive episode, whether in an analytic setting or other. Moreover, it emerges with regard to any agency, agency as such. By way of conclusion, let me mention some agencies with which Benjamin engaged in some detail. I shall omit here the agency of the patient, despite the fact that, in psychoanalysis, it best represents the place of the subject and subjectivity; Lacan, for example, always refers to the patient as "the subject." Yet, because in the history of psychoanalysis most theoretical attention has already been turned toward the agency of the patient, let me comment briefly on some of the other agencies with which Benjamin has dealt in her writings, namely, those of the author, the analyst, and the witness.

The ethical positioning of the aforementioned agencies reflects in the view that they neither are nor should be neutral with regard to their object, be it the object of writing, treatment, or observation. These three agencies are all of an "authorial" nature in the sense that they exercise their freedom to relate or not to relate to their object; their object is always of choice. Nevertheless, or perhaps because of it, in their ethical core, these agencies position themselves close to their object matter, almost as a part of it. To reiterate, this close positioning occurs neither because some mental mechanism draws them into the scene nor because of something like repetition compulsion but because of the sense that they cannot afford the moral luxury of remaining outside of the scene. They are called upon to participate, to have a mind. *In all three instances, the ethical nature of their attitude reflects in a movement between the second and third agental positions.* I think Benjamin beautifully illustrates the movement of the analyst between these two, whereas the position of first is articulated and enacted by the analysand. In a recent paper (Hadar, 2010) I argued that, in transference, the analysand superimposes these two positions on each other. The intentional and skilled transition of the analyst between them allows the patient to construct these agental positions as separate in a seemingly paradoxical manner, by subtle juxtaposition. The important thing is that, on the part of the analyst, this transition encapsulates an ethical stance: the duality of involvement and transcendence. And the therapeutic effect of analysis emerges from this ethical positioning no less than from the particularity of interpretation. The very experience of "transcendent involvement," so to speak, is therapeutic in its own right. Of course, other things—feelings, insights, interpersonal involvements—also affect the analytic process no less than this basic (ethical) positioning, but the enormous vitality of the setting probably resides in its ethical nature.

Similar things can be said about historical witnessing: its reparatory power resides in the readiness of the witness to move between second and third positions. In my understanding, this is what Benjamin tried to do in the acknowledgment project: create a domain of transition. It is not the (reparatory) business of the witness to uphold an objective, consistently third position. I think that any attempt to act as a "pure" third, to be objective about the situation, will sooner or later put the witness into a moralistic stance and thus destroy his or her ethical positioning. In the words of Ullman (2006), to act as witness, the subject needs to take risk, to open herself or himself to the possibility of being hurt. In a similar way, it is not the business of the witness to take sides, to act as a supportive second, to second one of the sides. Neither is it the (reparatory) business of the witness to mediate between the sides. His or her most powerful effect is through incessant movement between positions: not taking either of the positions of the conflicting sides but not putting herself or himself quite above them either. The witness is invested in the situation but makes the ethical effort to recognize and acknowledge the other subjectivities that are involved in the conflict.

This particular ethics of psychoanalysis, like the ethics of other analogous social enterprises, does not originate extraneously in a professional code of conduct but rather in the very practice (and attitude) of facilitating the subjectivity of the other. In psychoanalysis it informs the very setting as it may do in other social contexts that aim to facilitate subjectivities other than that of the facilitating agency. I think this is the case with the setting of mutual acknowledgment. By laying the ground for this ethical understanding, the Benjamin chreode opens a whole dimension of applied psychoanalysis.

REFERENCES

Barthes, R. (1977). *The Third Meaning: Image-Music-Text*. New York, NY: Noonday Press.
Benjamin, J. (1988). *The Bonds of Love: Psychoanalysis, Feminism and the Problem of Domination*. New York, NY: Pantheon Books.
———. (1995). Recognition and destruction: An outline of intersubjectivity. In: *Like Subjects, Love Objects: Essays on Recognition and Sexual Difference*, New Haven, CT: Yale University Press, pp. 27–48.

———. (2004). Beyond doer and done to: An intersubjective view of thirdness. *Psychoanalytic Quarterly*, 73, 5–46.

———. (2006). Mutual injury and mutual acknowledgement: Lecture in honor of Andrew Samuels. World in Transition Conference, London, UK, October.

Bion, W. R. (1961). *Experiences in Groups*. London, UK: Tavistock.

Butler, J. (1997). *The Psychic Life of Power: Theories in Subjection*. Stanford, CA: Stanford University Press.

Dimen, M. (2011). *With Culture in Mind*. New York, NY: Routledge.

Foulkes, S. H. (1968). On interpretation in group analysis. *International Journal of Group Psychotherapy*, 18, 432–434.

Freud, S. (1922). Group psychology and the analysis of the ego. *Standard Edition, 18*. London, UK: Hogarth Press, 1955, pp. 67–143.

Hadar, U. (2010). A three-person perspective on the transference. *Psychoanalytic Psychology*, 27, 296–318.

———. (2011). The hermeneutic underpinning of ethnic brutality: The Jewish Israeli case. *Psychotherapy and Politics International*, 9, 20–28.

Jameson, F. (1977). Imaginary and symbolic in Lacan: Marxism, psychoanalytic criticism and the problem of the subject. *Yale French Studies*, 55/56, 338–395.

Lacan, J. (1948). Aggressiveness in psychoanalysis. In: *Ecrits*, New York, NY: Norton, 2006, pp. 82–101.

———. (1951). *Presentation on transference*. In: *Ecrits*, New York, NY: Norton, 2006, pp. 176–188.

———. (1955). Seminar on "The Purloined Letter." In: *Ecrits*, New York, NY: Norton, 2006, pp. 6–50.

———. (1957). The instance of the letter in the unconscious or reason since Freud. In: *Ecrits*, New York, NY: Norton, 2006, pp. 412–441.

———. (1959). *The seminars of Jacques Lacan, Book VII: The ethics of psychoanalysis*. New York, NY: Norton, 1992.

———. (1960a). *The seminars of Jacques Lacan, Book VIII: Transference*. London, UK: Karnac, 2002.

———. (1960b). The subversion of the subject and the dialectic of desire in the Freudian unconscious. In: *Ecrits*, New York, NY: Norton, 2006, pp. 771–702.

———. (1961). *The seminars of Jacque Lacan, Book IX: Identification*. Web circulation, 2005.

———. (1963). Kant with Sade. In: *Ecrits*, New York, NY: Norton, 2006, pp. 645–668.

Miller, E. & Rice, K. (1967). *Systems of organisation*. London, UK: Tavistock.

Peirce, C. S. (1960). *Collected papers of Charles Sanders Peirce, Volumes V and VI*. Cambridge, MA: Harvard University Press.

Popper, K. (1978). Three worlds. The Tanner Lecture on Human Values, April, University of Michigan, Ann Arbor, MI. Retrieved from http://www.tannerlectures.utah.edu/lectures/documents/popper80.pdf

Samuels, A. (1993). *The political psyche*. London, UK: Routledge.

Ullman, C. (2006). Bearing witness: Across the barriers in society and in the clinic. *Psychoanalytic Dialogues*, 16, 181–198.

Waddington, C. H. (1957). *The strategy of the genes*. London, UK: Allen & Unwin.

The Cat Ate Our Tongue—But We Got It Back: Benjamin's Journey From Domination to Surrender

Boaz Shalgi, Ph.D.
Bar Ilan University, Tel Aviv University, and the Winnicott Center

This article attempts to interpret the evolution of the concept of intersubjectivity in Jessica Benjamin's work as a movement from *probing into domination*, through *probing into recognition*, to *probing into surrender*. After a short discussion of Benjamin's concept of domination, the article illustrates the way Benjamin's concept of intersubjectivity shifted, with the development of her thought, from mutual recognition of separate subjects to recognition of our basic interpenetrating creation and entwinement. Through a discussion of Hegel's philosophy a case is made that the evolution from an ontological stance that gives precedence to the subjective dimension of experience to an ontology which sees subjectivity, intersubjectivity, and objectivity as three essential dimensions of every human experience lies at the core of Benjamin's evolving concepts of intersubjectivity. A clinical vignette serves to illustrate the difference between domination, mutual recognition, and surrender.

Jessica Benjamin's corpus can be looked upon as comprised of three major phases. *The Bonds of Love,* Benjamin's (1988) first seminal contribution, which is being celebrated in this issue, can be viewed as a *probing into domination*. In the introduction to *The Bonds of Love* Benjamin confronts the reader with the question that, in my opinion, voices her own passionate motivation to write this book, as quoted from Dostoyevsky's Christ in *The Grand Inquisitor:* "Why has a free act of love been transformed into a practice of submission?" (Benjamin 1988, p. 5). The inquisitor's answer echoes through the different discussions and points of entry to that question, which comprise the book: "People do not want freedom and truth, which only causes deprivation and suffering; they want miracles, mystery, and authority. The pain that accompanies compliance is preferable to the pain that attends freedom" (Benjamin 1988, p. 5). This might not be easy to digest, yet it immediately brings up an important question: What is that "pain that attends freedom"? What is the truth that people try so hard to avoid (or, as Bion so humanly and somewhat ironically puts it, "Patients hate having feelings at all..." [1987, p. 183]). According to *The Bonds of Love,* it is the truth of their "helpless fate" (1988, p. 52), of their dependence on an other who is not part of their inner psyche and even can be somewhat indifferent to their subjective experience and needs. This dependence, though it entails the seeds of real mutuality and freedom, stands in such an acute contradiction to the self's seemingly most fundamental need for assertion and recognition, that it coerces the subject into two opposite solutions: domination or submission. Notwithstanding the vast differences between these solutions, the basic paradigm that lies at their core is the subject-object paradigm, which is the paradigm that "bonds the love."

The subject-object paradigm lies at the core of Freudian psychoanalysis: here is a subject, full of desires and wishes, and here is objectivity: the reality principle, other, father, mother. In Freudian epistemology, as was the Zeitgeist of his time, the objective dimension of human experience and existence was clearly prioritized over the subjective dimension (and over the intersubjective one). Under such weltanschauung, the human task seems to be twofold: first, the subject needs to recognize that his or her own subjectivity cannot serve as the route to fulfilling himself and his desires because the "objective" world around him simply won't let it happen. The child realizes that in order to let himself be fulfilled, he must adapt his needs to reality. Yet this kind of solution, as one can feel while reading *the Bonds of Love,* is not sufficient because it does not fuel the subject with enough power to fulfill his innermost need for self-assertion. So here comes the next step: if, on the one hand, I realize that objectivity precedes my subjectivity, and, on the other hand, I need to assert my subjectivity, why not try to equate my subjectivity with the objective? Both in children's development (as Benjamin shows so eloquently in "The Oedipal Riddle"; 1988, pp. 183–219) and in social processes, the subject tries to assert his subjectivity as the objective reality and thus dominate reality and the other's subjectivity. Thus, when we look closer at the subject-object paradigm, we find that the terms might be a bit misleading. It is not that I am the subject (representative of subjectivity) and you (the mother, the other) are the object (representative of objectivity) but that I, as subject, can determine *objectively* that my subjectivity precedes yours. What I negate is not your right to feel or think—but your right to hold these thoughts and feelings valid, to bring them forth, to demand their actual realization, to ask my subjectivity to take yours into consideration. The subject-object paradigm does not mean, as sometimes can be understood, that I "objectified" your subjectivity. Was I to do so—from a philosophical and sociological point of view that gives preference and precedence to the objective dimension of existence—I would be giving priority to your experiences, needs, and thoughts over mine. So what I do is something else. I enlist the objective dimension to my need for domination and determine, "objectively," that my subjectivity is of a higher value than yours because mine is an "objective subjectivity" and yours is nothing but an inferior "subjective subjectivity." My views, feelings, opinions, and experiences are in accord with reality. Yours are merely an "opinion" or a "feeling." So actually, the process that takes place here is not one in which I "objectify" you but that I "subjectify" you—rendering you an empty subject, devoid of objectivity, and me a "real subject"—fueled with objectivity. In terms of the cultural representation of genders, this will mean that masculine subjectivity is reality—an "objective subjectivity," and feminine subjectivity is "nothing but" subjective subjectivity, thus inferior to the male power of reality.

This formulation seems, at first glance, culturally offensive, developmentally primitive, and based on an omnipotent way of experiencing the self and the outer world. Indeed it is. Yet, from a different angle, the attempt to derive objectivity out of subjectivity (i.e., the only Punctum Archimedis on which objectivity can stand is subjectivity) is long-rooted in the Western philosophical discussion, starting with Descartes' (1637) "Cogito Ergo Sum." The outcome of Descartes' (methodological) doubt was that the only direct knowledge that one has is the knowledge of his or her own mind, his own subjectivity. If this is so, subjectivity is the only ground on which we can build knowledge regarding externality in general and regarding others' minds in particular. As Donald Davidson (2001) put it, "From the time of Descartes, most epistemology has been based on first person knowledge. According to the usual story, we must begin with what is most certain: knowledge of our own sensations and thoughts. In one way or another we progress, if we can, to knowledge of an objective external world. There is then the final, tenuous, step to knowledge of other minds" (p. xvii). Yet, this kind of epistemology, which gives precedence to subjectivity and tries to ground objectivity and intersubjectivity on the foundation of subjectivity, is bound, as has been shown again and again in the philosophical corpus, to face some critical problems. If we derive objectivity, and intersubjectivity, from subjectivity, we are bound to be left with no "real" objectivity as an independent dimension of existence and with no ground for intersubjectivity. Such are, for example, the problem of representationalism (how do I know that the images inside my mind correspond to what they claim to represent outside my mind because I have no "objective platform" on which to stand and measure the correspondence), the problem of alterity (how can I know anything outside my own mind), and other philosophical mines. As Richard Rorty (1979) put it, "Nothing counts as justification unless by reference to what we already accept, and there is no way to get outside our beliefs and our language so as to find some test" (p. 178). Or, in Donald Davidson's (2001) words, "We can't get out of our skins to find out what is causing the internal happening of which we are aware" (p. 144). Thus, as many philosophers show during the 19th and 20th centuries, the only way to emerge from these problems is to present an epistemology that holds together, in one way or another, the three basic dimensions of human existence and experience: objectivity, subjectivity, and intersubjectivity. To use Davidson's words again, "All propositional thoughts... whether of the inner or of the outer, requires possession of the concept of objective truth, and this concept is accessible only to those creatures in communication with others. Third person knowledge—knowledge of other minds—is thus essential to all other knowledge. ...Thus the acquisition of knowledge is not based on a progression from the subjective to the objective: *it emerges holistically, and is interpersonal from the start*" (p. xvii; italics added).

Thus, the precedence for the subjective dimension of experience, which serves as the philosophical matrix for the subject-object paradigm as described earlier, does not, at the end, draw objectivity, or intersubjectivity, nearer to the subject's existence and experience but cuts him or her off from external reality and from his fellow subjects. In Hegel's (1807) terms (and we go much deeper into Hegel's philosophy shortly), the lord, though dominating the slave, is disconnected from nature. In Benjamin's psychoanalytic view, the dominant male subject gains independence and rules, as it seems, objective reality at the expense of losing the most human connection with his preoedipal mother/other and with his innermost self. Benjamin (1988) quotes Loewald: "[There is] a growing awareness of the force of validity of another striving, that of symbiosis, fusion, merging..." and continues in her own language: "The validation of this striving... opens a place in the reality principle for bodily continuity with an other; it includes the intersubjective experience of recognition and all the emotional elements that go into appreciating, caring for, touching, and responding to an other" (p. 177). As long as intersubjectivity is excluded from the way people encounter each other, reality, and themselves and as long as, both in the subject's mind and in the philosophical discourse, subjective becomes objective and domination is the major force that shapes intrapsychic and interpersonal dramas, people are bound to live in a hollow, empty world without real sense of themselves and of their fellow subjects. Intersubjectivity is imperative, and the first step, according to Benjamin, to encounter intersubjectivity is recognizing each other's subjectivity. Thus our focus shifts from *probing into domination* to *probing into recognition.* Though the concept of mutual recognition is a major discussion in *The Bonds of Love,* in my view, the full contribution of this concept reveals itself in Benjamin's next seminal book (1995), *Like Subjects, Love Objects,* and especially in its first (now classic) chapter: "Recognition and Destruction: An Outline of Intersubjectivity."

Turning the psychoanalytic lamplight toward the issue of recognition entails, at the outset, a major change in the basic paradigm of relatedness: the subject-object paradigm should make way to subject-subject paradigm, or, in Benjamin's (1995) formulation, "where object was, subject should be" (p. 29). However, as Benjamin writes, a question regarding the essence and implications of that change arises: "Once we have acknowledged that the object makes an important contribution to the life of the subject, what is added by deciding to call this object another subject?" (1995, p. 29). Drawing on Winnicott's (1969) famous and most valuable presentation of "object relating" versus "object usage," Benjamin anchors the way a child relates to reality in his or her developmental shift from seeing the other as an object to seeing the other as a subject: reality is no longer experienced as "Ananke, [who] has been a strict educator and has made much out of us" (Freud, 1917, p. 355) or as "a detour to wish fulfillment" (Benjamin, 1995, p. 41) but as a part of the pleasure principle: "It is a continuation under more complex conditions of the infant's original fascination with and love of what is outside, her appreciation of difference and novelty" (p. 41). The other's alterity, now, is not (only) a threat to the subject's existence but (also) an opportunity for encountering the new, for expansion of the self and for validation of the self through the other. Seeing the other as subject means that I can acknowledge our similarity as well as our difference and that I can take pleasure in sharing my mind with a mind outside myself—a mind that for me is objective and for itself is subjective (has its own feelings, perspectives, and thoughts). With such a mind I can experience "the *pleasure* of the evolving relationships with a partner from whom one knows how to elicit a response, but whose responses are not entirely predictable and assimilable to internal fantasy" (1995, pp. 31–32). The apex of the difference between the subject-object relations and the subject-subject relations is the acceptance, appreciation, and acknowledgment of the other's difference and alterity, an appreciation that in turn makes the similarity and sharing of minds much more meaningful and enjoyable: "The difference in form makes the elements of similarity or sharing clear" (1995, p. 34), and the parents and infant can take pleasure in contacting the other's mind.

Nonetheless, while reading "Recognition and Destruction," one realizes that not only has the human relatedness paradigm changed but also that the basic human need has been reconceptualized. Domination, the seemingly holy grail of "bonds of love," seems empty without the other's recognition of my existence, will, thoughts, wishes, and emotions. No lesser than the human wish to make his or her subjectivity objective and to use his newly created (apparent) superiority to dominate the other is the human need to relate to his fellow subject and to ask for her recognition. However, this becomes even more complicated because we are still operating under the basic assumption that the *first* motivation which underlies my turning to you for recognition is not my appreciation of your existence and subjectivity but my realization regarding my own unfortunate limitations, limitations that render me incapable of providing myself with my first and foremost need—to feel myself as a subject, as an independent agent of my life. Here lies what Benjamin famously refers to as the paradox of recognition: "In the very moment of realizing our own independent will, we are dependent on another to recognize it" (1995, pp. 36–37). This paradox might lead not to emergence from the problem of domination but to a reversal of domination: "This complementarity does not dissolve omnipotence, but shifts it from one partner to the other" (Benjamin 1999, p. 194).

Particularly noteworthy is that the paradox of recognition starts with the subject's intrapsychic contradiction. I *need* to feel myself as having my own will, my own value, my own existence as a subject. Yet, I *need you* to recognize me as such. So what I *need* is to coerce you to recognize me. But if I do that, I deny you of your own subjectivity. Because the recognition I need is from a "like subject" (who I know to have his or her own point of view and whose point of view I value no less than my own), I *need* to make sure that I will perceive you as a subject, so, I *need* to recognize you as a subject. This goes back to an act of domination—the subject asserts his own need and will and regards any otherness as part of his own inner psychic system. Yet, by doing so, the subject cancels his fellow as a subject, as having his own independent and distinct subjectivity. Thus, the first subject's need for recognition is compromised because the recognition he needs *is* recognition of or from a subject, that is, recognition that comes from an other. Only recognition from a truly independent and separate subject—a subject who, in Winnicott's (1969) terms is "being used"—has any real value, holding the promise of pulling the self out of its solipsistic "bubble."

Here, again, it seems that we encounter not merely a psychoanalytic problem, or even a sociological or cultural one, but an ontological problem—which is quite similar to the one that started to emerge earlier on in our discussion regarding domination, that is, the problem of giving precedence to one dimension of existence—subjectivity—over the other. The quest for mutual recognition is a quest for intersubjectivity, yet, perhaps without really acknowledging it, this might simultaneously entail cutting off the branch we are trying to sit on because *the precedence is still given to subjectivity*. The ontological stance that lies at the core of the paradox of recognition is that *first* we are distinct subjects, with wills, needs, and wishes (like the need for recognition), and *then* we turn to each other to fulfill our needs. First we live in the subjective dimension, and then we turn to intersubjectivity. It seems that we are trying to derive intersubjectivity from subjectivity only to realize that in such an epistemology we cannot extricate ourselves from the prison of the isolated mind. As in the discussion of the problem of domination, in which we realize that precedence to subjectivity will render the subject isolated, empty, and hollow, so, here too, we see that if we try to achieve mutual recognition when we take a subjective point of view—the subject's need for recognition—we are left with a torn subject, a subject who tries to emerge from his or her own mind and experience to enjoy the pleasure of alterity only to find himself locked in his own mind, his own needs, his own subjectivity. Thus, the emergence from the paradox of recognition (deriving intersubjectivity from subjectivity), similar to the emergence from the problem of domination (deriving objectivity from subjectivity), must include a dialectical interplay between all three dimensions of existence: subjectivity, intersubjectivity and objectivity.

The movement from a stance that gives precedence to one dimension over the other to a stance that positions all three dimensions of existence in dialectical tension can take many forms. One form of this movement can be seen when comparing Benjamin's (1995) use of Hegel's philosophy in "Recognition and Destruction" with a more comprehensive reading of Hegel's conception of mutual recognition, one that looks at his lordship-bondage schema as a part of the human consciousness's evolution and development as presented in his "Phenomenology of Mind" (1807). After briefly describing these two interpretations of Hegel's contribution, I try to make the case that the way Hegel posits the human subjects as recognizing each other not out of struggle and coercion, but out of the very movement and development of human consciousness, serves as the matrix from which Benjamin's (2004a) third evolutional step, which I refer to as *probing into surrender* (as presented most beautifully in *Beyond Doer and Done to: An Intersubjective View of Thirdness*), can take place.

In "Recognition and Destruction" Benjamin (1995) presents what she believes to be the core of Hegel's important chapter on "The Independence and Dependence of Self-Consciousness: Lordship and Bondage" (Hegel, 1807, pp. 229–240), which is "the self's wish for absolute independence conflicts with the self's need for recognition" (1995, p. 36). This formulation indeed relies on Hegel's dialectic of mutual recognition as described in this chapter, or, more accurately, on one of Hegel's major commentators, Alexander Kojeve's (1934), interpretation of it. The need of the consciousness for absolute independence, as Benjamin (1995) interprets Hegel, clashes with its need for recognition. On the one hand, human consciousness strives to subdue any otherness and to assert itself as totally independent. On the other hand, such total independence—the consciousness of a lord, in Hegel's terms—has to be recognized as such by the consciousness of the (dominated) other—the consciousness of a slave. Human consciousness emerges through a struggle with another human consciousness in an attempt to dominate and control it, but while doing so it realizes that it needs the other as independent and existing in its own right, that is, as equal to itself. Realizing that, consciousness is "forced" to give up its domination of the other and create relations of mutual recognition with the other. Thus, the "natural" drive of consciousness, Benjamin interprets Hegel, is to achieve recognition of the other through domination and control. In this "natural" position, the human encounter necessitates one of two alternatives: submission or struggle. Only one consciousness can create reality; the other has to be created by it. There is no space for co-creation of a reality, which is mutually constructed. However, consciousness realizes that in this state of affairs winning means losing the very possibility for recognition and thus recognizes the other. As we saw earlier, this is clearly a stand that gives precedence (both a precedence in time and an ontological precedence) to subjectivity, a precedence that can't help us move beyond the problem of complementarity and the paradox of recognition.

Yet this description of Hegel's method might, in my opinion, miss out on a far richer contribution of Hegel's perspective. The conceptualization of mutual recognition, as presented in that monumental chapter "The Independence and Dependence of Self-Consciousness: Lordship and Bondage" is only one part of Hegel's (1807) systematic philosophical investigation of the development of consciousness. In order to realize the full scope and depth of Hegel's concept of intersubjectivity, and in order for his potential contribution to move beyond the paradox of recognition, beyond the precedence of subjectivity, and in order for the movement from probing of domination to probing of surrender to be fulfilled, a more inclusive study of Hegel's thought is needed. This study will suggest that recognizing the other as a subject is not motivated solely by the need to be recognized by him or her but is part of the necessary process by which consciousness evolves toward existing in all its "Moments."[1] In order to present this argument, we have to turn now, for a while, to a closer examination of Hegel's (1807) "journey of consciousness" as it unfolds throughout his *Phenomenology of Mind*.

---

[1] In Hegel's terminology, Moments are those aspects of existence that cannot gain their full meaning unless they are standing in dialectical tension with each other in which each preserves, negates, and elevates the other.

In Hegel's system, the development of consciousness and its movement toward a position of mutual recognition and acknowledgment is revealed and discovered via the ontological discussion of the nature of existence and the epistemological problem of the human ability to know and recognize and is derived from these fundamental investigations. One major motivation of Hegel's philosophy is to mend the rift between the realm of theoretical thinking and ideas, on the one hand, and the realm of actual experience on the other, and to bring together the abstract and conceptual dimensions of things with their actual-apparent dimension. *The Phenomenology of Mind* (1807) is a breathtaking description of how consciousness evolves through four forms, or modes, of knowledge: sense-certainty (sinnlicheGewiβheit), perception (Wahrnehmung), understanding (Verstand), and self-consciousness (Selbstbewuβtsein). According to Hegel's method, progress from one mode to another occurs as a result of inherent contradictions in the former mode. The very negation of one mode of knowledge is inherent in that mode itself; in Hegel's terms, this is its immanent otherness. By this process the former mode shapes and constructs the next, higher one, which is constituted as a synthesis of the former's positive existence and its inner negation or opposition. Moreover, Hegel's philosophy is one of dialectic relations: relations between consciousness and apparent reality, which seems to be located outside it; between one consciousness and another; between different facets of consciousness itself. In dialectic relations, the negating encounter is a process of re-creating what existed before it yet could never exist without it.

Hegel (1807) sees every object as being composed of two modes of existence, or two Moments: the Moment of *plurality* and the Moment of *universality* or *unity*. The plurality Moment is both perceived and validated in the first mode of knowledge, that of sense-certainty. In this mode of knowledge the subject knows the object as it appears at a certain point in time in his or her sense-impressions (and of course there are many such appearances). Thus, by sensing and grasping the variety of appearances, the subject validates the plurality Moment of the object's existence.

Beyond the different manifestations and appearances that the subject perceives minute by minute, the object has another Moment of existence, a universal or united Moment, which enables all those appearances to exist as manifestations of one and the same object. The subject gains knowledge of the unity Moment when he or she examines the specific appearances that confront him in the sense-certainty mode of knowledge. From his examination of what seems to be sense-data, the subject realizes that he does not perceive this data directly and immediately but through *mediating* factors like the "here" and the "now." Thus, a thorough examination of what is being perceived reveals that it is not the immediate sense impression the subject perceives but another layer, more general and universal. These mediating factors, concepts, or notions, which appear to be, by this stage of the investigation, the true "object" of what the consciousness perceives, Hegel (1807) calls "the Universal" (Das Allgemeine). He gives a simple example: Through my senses, I see that now it is nighttime. The truth of my perception, therefore, is "night." In order to prove this truth, Hegel suggests, let us write it on a piece of paper: "A truth cannot lose anything by being written down" (p. 151). Yet, if we later look at what we wrote, say, at noontime, we will see that it is false. The true content of what we perceive is not "I perceive night" but "I perceive the Now." From that vantage point, what we actually perceive is not nighttime but "now-time," the Now. The mediating concept "Now" includes the immediate truth—"night," as well as its negation—"not night." Thus, the "Now" is not an immediate sense-impression but a general concept, a Universal that holds together and unites changing specific appearances.[2] In this process, consciousness moves toward a higher mode of knowledge, that of perception: "The Universal is therefore in point of fact the truth of sense-certainty, the true content of sense-experience" (p. 152).

These two Moments are seemingly in contradiction. The specific manifestation/appearance negates, it would seem, the universal concept, and the universal concept similarly seems to negate the specific appearance. But this negation is a dialectical negation because although these two Moments negate each other, they are also enabled and preserved by each other. Manifestation, the actual existence (i.e., appearance), unless it co-exists with the unity mode, would remain scattered, afloat, without order and connecting laws, and thus, in Hegel's (1807) opinion, it would vanish. On the other hand the Universal, the unitary Moment, unless it is actually expressed in its plurality and variety of appearances, remains empty, a mere illusion.

What then is the factor, the substance, that holds these Moments in this dialectical relation? Hegel's (1807) answer—and here we are moving to the next stage of the consciousness's development—is that it is none other than the human consciousness which recognizes them. Passing through the different modes of knowledge, that of sense-certainty, which recognizes the plurality Moment, and that of perception, which recognizes the unity Moment, consciousness reaches its next developmental achievement, that is, the stage that Hegel calls understanding, which is the human ability—or "force", in Hegel's terminology—to recognize the co-existence of these two Moments. It is to the human subject, then, that Hegel's system assigns the crucial and imperative task of recognizing the total and complete essence of every being. This is one of the most revolutionary thoughts in the history of Western philosophy: the replacement of the ontological transcendent as the validating force of existence by the human subject itself. The function of confirmation or validation, which was previously fulfilled by a transcendent being, becomes in Hegel's philosophy the task of the human consciousness. And, if the human consciousness is the force that provides validation and recognition of the full Moments of every being, the only way that the subject's consciousness itself can be recognized in its own full Moments is by the recognition and validation of its fellow subject's consciousness. Thus, the mutual validation and recognition of the human consciousness is not an "agreement of recognition" but *an essential and fundamental part of the ontological and epistemological state of affairs, of what the world is, what constitutes it, and of how the human subject comes to know the world, other human subjects, and himself or herself.*

Let us, therefore, carefully examine this multilayered process, starting with an examination of the plurality Moment. What is the plurality mode/facet/Moment of being of consciousness? Does it "belong" to consciousness itself? We have seen before that the plurality Moment of every being is its multiple appearances as they manifest themselves through the encounter with the subject who perceives them in the first mode of knowledge, that of sense-certainty. This plurality Moment of consciousness is nothing but the way in which it exists in its variety of appearances, which are created, shaped, and constructed through its encounters with the others who perceive it. The plurality Moment, thus, exists both as a part of consciousness itself and as always created and maintained within the encounter with the other. My multiplicity facet is a part of me, of the other, and of our encounter. *Hence, the other's recognition of that facet of mine is a result of the sheer fact that through our encounter we create and are being created by each other.* One consciousness recognizes the multiplicity facet of its fellow consciousness

---

[2]Hegel (1807) presents a similar discourse regarding the mediating concept "Here."

not by standing before one another and recognizing it but simply because they touch and connect, because they mutually create and shape each other. Thus, when I recognize the other, this also involves recognizing the plurality Moment of myself as it arises through my encounter with the other. In the same way, when the other recognizes me, he or she does not only recognize a being that is outside him—that is, me—but he also recognizes a Moment of his own, his multiplicity facet, his plurality Moment.

This significantly changes the depiction of what is going on in the process of mutual recognition. The fundamental position of subjects who are involved in this process is not *Recognize me* (a position that leads to the paradox of recognition) but *You are also a part of me and I am also a part of you—let us recognize that*. When one consciousness validates another consciousness, it does not validate a consciousness that is merely outside it but one that is both external and internal to it. When the infant, for example, "demands" his or her mother's recognition, the mother is also the infant himself because his encounter with her, the way in which she sees him, experiences him, the way he sees and experiences himself through her, are a facet of himself, his plurality Moment, whose absence would reify the human being into a tautological recognition-receiving-subject. The intersubjectivity of mutual recognition is not a social contract between subjects who need recognition but an inevitable and direct derivative of the essence of being, the essence of human consciousness, and the essence of the way in which consciousness knows and recognizes every being, including its fellow consciousness and itself.

Yet, if mutual recognition of consciousnesses were based only on the kind of recognition that belongs to the sense-certainty mode of knowledge, that is, recognition of consciousness in the multiple appearances of the other's consciousness, people's consciousnesses would merge with each other, and they would be locked in an infinite process of mutual co-creation. However, when consciousnesses come face-to-face with each other they are also recognizing the unity Moment of each other. The unity Moment is the form of existence that persists beyond the variety of appearances and beyond the multiple specific ways in which it is being perceived by other subjects. So when we recognize the unity Moment of each other, we mutually recognize not only that we are co-creating each other but also that we are *not* co-creating each other, that we have a unity Moment, that we each exist beyond the specific shape that we have just created through our encounter. But at the same time that the unity Moment is "mine" and "yours," it is also always "ours" because like any other being, a subject's Moment of unity (as also occurring in the Moment of plurality) exists first and foremost within mutual recognition. *My independent (unity) existence is not a quality of mine, which you have to recognize (and vice versa) but most fundamentally a quality of the relations.* Here we can really appreciate the profoundness of Hegel's (1807) conceptualization: Things (objects, other consciousnesses) are not merely "outside" the subject or "inside" the subject but are always a constitutive part of him or her and his fellow subject, of him and the outer world. Thus "I am a subject," "You are a subject," and "We are subjects who create each other" are not contradictions but different facets of the fundamental ontological structure, which is based on the existence of every being in both its Moments, consciousness as recognizing and holding these Moments for every being and human subjects as recognizing and holding full existence for the other.

While this recognition of the other holds together both our intersubjective and subjective dimension, it also contains within itself the objective dimension of existence. When I recognize the unity and independent facet of the other subject, I recognize, first, him or her being a subject (i.e., being a self-consciousness that, as such, validates existence and otherness). Yet, when I recognize that facet of the other subject that exists beyond any contingent perception of the other, and even beyond self-perception, I actually recognize the objective validity of it, that which stands-before (German: Gegenstand) or is-put-before (Latin: ob-ject) me or any otherness. The objective dimension of standing-outside-of or standing-before does not disappear in this multifaceted mutual recognition but is both preserved in it and a condition for it. Thus the relationship between human subjects, which inherently and necessarily encompasses subjectivity and intersubjectivity, includes objectivity as well: we are constantly objects and subjects to each other and validate for each other the objective dimension of our being as subjects. Thus Hegel's (1807) ontological and epistemological investigation evolves, systematically and dialectically, into positing the three dimensions of existence: subjectivity, intersubjectivity, and objectivity—which are so important in keeping the relations between subjects valid and meaningful—as constituting, creating, and preserving each other.

The act of recognition, then, is not an active one of giving or taking. Recognition is not something that subjects do or don't do. It is something that inherently belongs to the existence of people, to the way their minds get to know the world in which they live in, their others and themselves. The fact that human consciousnesses create, validate, and maintain each other is neither a question of domination nor a question of voluntary or involuntary recognition. It is simply what is going on. What we really should be looking at, then, is not the way we try to dominate each other and not the way we struggle for recognition but rather the way in which we enable this natural process of evolving to take place, or, in Benjamin's terms, the way we "surrender to the dyadic mental state" (2007, p. 678). Thus we move from *probing into recognition* to *probing into surrender*.

Emmanuel Ghent's concept of surrender, as Benjamin states, was the "inspiration" to *Beyond Doer and Done to: An Intersubjective View of Thirdness* (2004a). This paper, in my opinion, is the prominent representation of what I consider her third step into intersubjectivity: probing into surrender. "In my thinking," Benjamin writes, "the term 'surrender' refers to a certain letting go of the self... being able to sustain connectedness to the other's mind while accepting his separateness and difference. Surrender implies freedom from any intent to control or coerce" (2004a, p. 8). The main "Shibboleth" of Ghent's concept of surrender is that we are mutually entwined, that "everything is in flux, which means that everything, living or not, is interactive" (Ghent, 1995, p. 481) and that the basic human need is to expand and liberate the self through surrendering to the new and the unknown that lies in the heart of the people's basic mutual penetration and encounter.[3] This, as Ghent (1990) quotes from the Amae psychology, is "the freedom to bond" rather than the more common Western-fueled dominant concept of "freedom from bondage" (p. 114). We can look at Hegel's (1807) multilayered formulation regarding the human consciousnesses in their mutual validation of their two Moments as a philosophical systematic explication of surrender in which both consciousnesses realize and validate to the other and to itself their entwinement and their difference. Hegel's formulations present us with the way in which human subjects create each other while, *within this intersubjective creation, they also* validate their independent subjectivity and the objective dimension of each other and of their relationships. Consciousnesses, thus, do not have to recognize each other but to acknowledge their utter multilayered mutual creation. They have to

---

[3]Later on in his writings, Ghent refers to that basic human need as the "centrifugal motivational system" (2001, p. 26).

surrender to it. "The crucial point," writes Benjamin, "[is] that surrender is not *to* someone... [but] letting go into *being* with them" (2004a, p. 8), and Ghent writes, "Surrender... happens. It cannot be made to happen" (1990, p. 111).

In *Beyond Doer and Done to: An Intersubjective View of Thirdness,* Benjamin (2004a) presents two complementary notions that together form the matrix of intersubjectivity: the "one in the third" and the "third in the one." The "one in the third" represents the experience of oneness, the "principle of affective resonance or union" (2004a, p. 17). It is basically the experience that we share each other's mind—we find resonance in each other's thoughts and feelings, we feel a shared rhythmicity, we create each other's experiences. It is a "mutual accommodation, which entails not limitation, but a hard-wired pull to get the two organisms into alignment, to mirror, match, or be in synch" (2004a, p. 17). It is an experience of "attuned play resembles musical improvisation, in which both partners follow a structure or pattern that both of them simultaneously create and surrender to... [this] co-created third has the transitional quality of being both invented and discovered" (2004a, p. 18). On the other hand, the "third in the one" represents the principle of differentiation, a difference that lies within the intersubjective creation. This is in accord with Winnicott's well-known description, according to which "the mother is looking at the baby, and what she looks like is *related* to what she sees there" (Winnicott, 1967, p. 112; emphasis added). As Bruce Reis (2004, p. 364) interprets (following Ogden, 1994) the emphasis on "*related* to what she sees there" and not "is what she sees there" or "is a creation of what she sees there" indicates that the mother's distinctive subjectivity is already included in the most archaic form of relating. "For Winnicott," writes Reis, "mirroring is a relationship of relative sameness, therefore of relative difference" (p. 364). In Hegel's (1807) terms, the "third in the one" represents the consciousnesses' mutual validation of their unitary Moment, that Moment which stands beyond the multiple appearances and holds their distinct experience and existence. In Benjamin's terms, it is "the ability... to sustain the tension of difference between my needs and yours while still being attuned to you" (2004a, p. 13). This moral or symbolic third is what gives the baby the assurance that while the mother is sharing his or her experience, she has her own internal psyche, which can stay (relatively) calm when he is in the torment of his distress simply because she went through these kinds of situations before and she knows he will calm down later on. It is what gives the patient the comfort in knowing that even in the heat of the most co-created, subjugating-mutually-constructed enactment, his therapist is still responsible for what is going on simply because it is his role, duty, and profession. It is what serves as the royal road out of the "hall-of-mirrors" (Benjamin, 2004b, p. 747) and assures that in the midst of what Harold Searles (1961) refers to as "the symbiotic phase" (p. 459), the analyst's mind is still the mind of the analyst, and this is so regarding the patient's mind also. The dialectical holding of both "the-one-in-the-third" experience of sameness (within difference) and "the-third-in-the-one" experience of difference (within sameness) creates the more total Hegelian meeting of consciousnesses in which they hold within their relation both Moments, that of plurality and that of unity, both experiences, that of mutual entwinement and penetration (I can feel myself inside your mentality and feel you inside mine) at the same time so that, through our meeting, we can feel our differences and alterity.

This thirdness is not something that we have to recognize. It is something that is there or will be there if we don't try, with too much effort, to prevent it (through the fear-driven "ever-ready look-alike" of surrender, submission, which *is* a creation of domination). "The third is that to which we surrender, and thirdness is the intersubjective mental space that facilitates or results from surrender" (Benjamin, 2004a, p. 8). Here intersubjectivity is no longer limited to mutual recognition but is the way people are essentially mutually penetrating each other while staying the same, influencing and being influenced while maintaining their different minds, and are in an ongoing interactive flux of mutual creation. Winnicott (1945) claims that the way the hungry/ ruthless baby and the feeding/holding mother meet is by "living an experience together," an idea that Ogden (2001) sees as one that "shaped the second fifty years of analytic thought" (p. 226) and explains, "'*live an experience together*'—what makes the phrase remarkable is the unexpected word 'live.' The mother and child do not 'take part in,' 'share,' 'participate in,' or 'enter into' an experience together: they live an experience together" (pp. 226–227). This mutual surrender to "the shared, co-created third" (Benjamin, 2006, p. 384) is not recognition of the other's independent subjectivity but is rather recognition of, and surrendering to, this basic intersubjective creation, or, in Benjamin's words, "We surrender to the principle of reciprocal influence in interaction" (2004a, p. 11). While recognition under the more constricted interpretation of Hegel's (1807) thought is recognition of the other (out of the need to be recognized, which leads to the paradox of recognition), recognition under the broader interpretation of Hegel's thought is not recognition of *someone* (being me or the other) but recognition of "our...mutual influence [which] allows us to create [and *live*] thirdness together" (2004a, p. 8). In order to emerge from the complementarity problem we do not have to recognize our equal ontological status (we are both valid subjects) but our basic penetrability and entwinement. We surrender to ourselves and to each other; we surrender to the other in me and to myself in the other; we surrender to the way life is being lived within each of us and both of us, to the way we infuse ourselves in life.

DAN

Dan and I have been working together for many years. He is a young man, extremely talented, who experiences life in a very intense, anxious though exciting way. When he was first referred to me he suffered from great anxieties regarding almost everything he did or thought, especially regarding sex and relationships with women. During the years of therapy he made tremendous progress in his life and could easily sustain a job, take different courses on a variety of areas of interest, and maintain long-term relationships with women. Yet, those relationships were remarkably characterized by his need to dominate his girlfriend both sexually and in daily life. It must be said, though, that Dan is an extremely sensitive and compassionate man, and when he encounters the damage that his need to control and dominate his girlfriends causes them, he is filled with sincere tormenting guilt. This is sometimes a kind of Catch-22 because the guilt and remorse he feels frequently serves as a reason to renew control. He then demands that his girlfriends not react in a way that will make him feel guilty and anxious because they "should know by now how sensitive he is." Of course, being so intelligent and self-aware, he soon recognizes the paradox and again feels awful with himself. His domination needs are clearly connected with the character of his father, a loving and highly appreciated man, though a man who goes through life, from Dan's perspective, in a manner of "my way or no way." Dan sees his father as very manly and successful and at the same time feels that his father sees him as weak, childish, and overemotional.

There is, however, another reason for his domination needs and behavior. Being a very talented man, Dan often succeeds where many other people don't stand a chance, and he knows that. Thus, although he can sometimes feel as if reality is something he can't really handle, at other times he seems to conquer it in no time. From time to time, it seems that Dan refuses to accept the natural limitations of reality, trying again and again "to have the cake whole and eat it."

During the years that Dan and I have been working together we have developed a strong and deep relationship. He seems to think very highly of me and feels strongly connected. I feel very close to him, very much appreciate his brave and fierce way of experiencing life and greatly enjoy working with him. When we talk to each other, it seems sometimes that we really feel that we were made of the same stuff, yet other times we feel that we are mutually misunderstanding each other, that the other is distorting what we think and mean, and ultimately that a wide abyss stands open between us.

There is a lot to tell, of course, about our common journey, yet for the purpose of this article I focus on one event that took place in the 6th year of our work. At that time, Dan was sent by his company to the United States. We decided to continue our appointments over the phone. We had a regular 2-hr session once a week, at a time that was convenient to me, yet, considering the time difference between Israel and the United States, not so easy for him. During the year that he was away, I left my rented office and moved my clinic to my new home. This, of course, was not a simple transition for most of my patients and had to be worked out in many ways with each of them. Dan knew about my moving, and we sometimes talked about how he imagined me talking to him from the old and familiar office, while I was actually sitting in a different office, unknown to him, and about how strange it would be for him, upon his return, to meet me in a different place.

The new clinic was, as mentioned, at my home, where my family and I raise and love a well-tempered and beautiful cat, which we had for about two years. When I moved my clinic to my home I did not recall, though I knew it very well, that Dan was allergic to cats. I knew it very well because his parents had taken in a cat a few years before. Dan was furious about it (with great justification, one could say) and significantly reduced his visits to his parents' home.

Act 1: Domination

So here we sit, on two sides of the ocean, in one of our telephone conversations. Dan is telling me about a few incidents that took place between him and his new girlfriend, all having to do with his attempts to dominate and control her. He is indeed in a very demanding mood, and when I try to talk with him about the possibility that he may be acting with his present girlfriend in a way that is similar to past instances, and that this might backfire very soon, he gets angry and insists that I am the one looking at the situation through "the old glasses" and that I have it all wrong.

Suddenly, the cat, which sometimes hangs around outside my office door, meows. Dan stops the conversation and asks, "Do you have a cat in your new house?"

"Yes, I do," came the automatic reply. I didn't take a moment to reflect either on the automatic question or on the automatic answer.

"So how will I be able to come to your house when I return?" (This was about two months before his return to Israel).

"Well," I said, "I don't know... I am sorry, Dan, I did not think about it when I moved."

Listening to what I was saying, it seemed to me that my words might be interpreted as meaning that if *I had thought* about it, I would not have moved my office. Because (a) this was not true and (b) it seemed to me the wrong message to convey to Dan, I added something like, "Not that I could have done something about it. ..."

"So what are you saying?" Dan sounded confused and a bit irritated.

"I don't know. We will have to think ... to find a solution."

For a few minutes the conversation went back to the topics we had been talking about before, but then Dan said, "I am not comfortable with the way we sort of closed the issue of the cat. I don't feel that you really respect the severity of the issue." (He was right.) "It really is a big problem. Our conversations are one of the most important things in my life and you know it very well. You should not have a cat in your house. How can you have a cat? I can't believe it. ..."

I was probably still trying not to delve into the oncoming enactment. "Well, Dan, perhaps you're right, perhaps I didn't consider the difficulty with the seriousness I should have, but I just don't have a solution at the moment, and I think maybe we should give it some time."

"I don't think so. It makes me very nervous. We should find a solution. I can't believe you have a cat ... I don't know what to do ... maybe we should meet at a coffee shop?" He sounded totally serious. I was surprised to see that he really meant it. He knows the therapeutic boundaries very well. He should know better than that. He should know that I can't meet him in a coffee shop!

"Don't you think you are taking the issue a little bit too far?" I found myself saying.

"So what do you suggest? I can't go to a place where there is a cat. You know that. You can't do that. You should find a way. ..."

"What are you saying, Dan? Do you really think I should get rid of the cat?"

"Why are you saying it like I am being insane for even thinking about it?"

I didn't know what to say. I found it impossible to even think about moving the cat out of the house, and I felt angry and disappointed that Dan had even raised the possibility: Did he really think that I should get rid of the family cat, to which my family and I feel deeply connected, because he is allergic?

Dan went on: "Oh, this is unfair. It sounds as if I am asking you to hurt your family for me; it isn't fair to put it that way."

Silence. I was really amazed at what I saw as his unreasonable (even outrageous) demand. I was reminded of one night, only a few weeks before, when the cat got lost for a few hours and we were very scared. I felt that I was encountering the demanding, controlling Dan whom I very often heard about but hardly met directly. Both my instinctive reaction (you will not do that to me and you will not make me feel bad about it) and my therapeutic self (it is a good chance to work on his adamant refusal to accept reality's limitations [a glancing thought: objective reality? justified reality? my reality?]) told me I should try and show him how far he had gone with his need to drive the world to correspond with his own desires.

Up until that moment in the session, I believed, Dan and I were essentially revolving through the issue of domination. We were not only trying to dominate each other but also trying to dominate reality by making the subjective objective. "Dan," I said in my mind, "your expectations do not meet any standard of common sense. Reality says that it is unreasonable to ask me to get rid of the cat." If I could read Dan's mind at that moment, it would probably go something like this: "He knows I am allergic. It is not reasonable to prefer a cat over a patient, a longtime patient (a beloved patient?). I am sure that every decent therapist would not favor a cat over his professional duty." We were both tremendously lonely at that moment.

Act 2: Mutual Recognition

I believe that out of that loneliness emerged the first shift in my thinking about what was going on at that moment. Without being aware of it, I didn't want to feel so alone and bad with Dan. I didn't like the icy heat that was mounting between us. We were used to a well-established stream of mutual warmth and appreciation, even when we were in the midst of an argument or a dispute. I was probably longing to bring this Dan-Boaz matrix back from the momentary abyss it fell into. I wanted me back. I wanted him back. Of course, none of these feelings consolidated into a conscious thought. I believe that Dan was feeling quite similar.

"Okay," I said. "I suppose you are right. We should talk about it now. Perhaps I did not realize how serious this is."

"I didn't appreciate the way you dismissed my coffee shop idea. It seems that you aren't open to any solution other than me 'getting over it.' I don't think that's fair."

"But Dan, you know, somehow, that you are asking for something I can't do. Of course, there is a problem, and we will have to find a way to deal with it, but you know that a father cannot say to his children that he is evicting their pet. ..."

"I am not sure that I ever asked for that. I feel that you drove me to say that. I just felt that you were taking it all too lightly. Perhaps I went too far with it."

"I think that I reacted too hastily. I know that this is a big issue for you. You know, moving my office home is a big issue for both of us, and we didn't really have the chance to work it through. Perhaps we are starting now. Perhaps this is our way to start approaching it."

"Was it hard for you, moving your clinic home?" asked Dan.

"It wasn't simple. I guess it will be quite strange for you when you come here for the first time. ..."

The conversation went on, while each of us was trying to understand the other's feelings and point of view at that moment, keeping an open mind. It is not difficult for us to do because we really love and respect each other. Dan could pay attention to what he was really feeling about the new office, about my not asking his "permission" to move, about the cat that awaited him near my office. He could share these feelings with me and feel that I could see him and appreciate his feelings, worries, and concerns. I felt that I had found a place inside for him, whereas he found in himself a place to hear me and consider my thoughts regarding what was going on between us. The heat subsided. Each of us felt recognized again as a good, reasonable, lovable subject. We no doubt regained our mutual recognition. Twenty minutes ago, we were both filled with isolation and anger. We desperately needed each other's recognition. We definitely knew how to elicit it from one another, how to give it to each other. It seemed that we were safe again. The subject-subject mutual recognition—"Recognize me, so I can recognize you!"—had saved the day.

Yet, I was suddenly feeling so sad.

Act 3: Surrender

I felt I had sold him short. I felt that he had been feeling something that we had managed to ignore. Perhaps because it was so easy for us to regain our mutual warmth and respect, we both agreed to give up something important, something that we had felt, something that was there and that we couldn't bear. The feeling of ease that pervaded the conversation felt too convenient, too fast, too comforting. There was a truth there, hovering around, that for a moment was breaking through, erupting through our mutual love and respect, and then was evaded and sent back to its safe dissociated Gulag. The simple and painful fact was that I hadn't thought about him. I knew very well that for Dan a cat was a big issue, both physically (he was allergic, for God's sake!) and emotionally (his parents bringing a cat home, probably saying to themselves—so Dan suspected, even though these words were never spoken—that he is exaggerating, that his allergy is part of him "making a drama out of everything"). I knew all that and I moved my office home *without even thinking for a moment* that it would be a problem for him. The simple fact was that I was so busy with my own concerns that I simply forgot about him. And there was another truth here, related but much more immediate, that when our current argument regarding the cat started, I was so concerned with my love for my children (who loved the cat dearly), I simply couldn't and wouldn't think about Dan's feelings and needs. The fact that I was so sensitive about my moving and about the cat issue, along with Dan's sometimes very annoying need for domination, drove us to a very sad and irritating fact: as much as I cared about him, as much as we felt connected, I could put all that aside when, for a while, my life and my energies were taken to other places. I could never forget about someone who was *really* a part of my life, someone I was *really connected* to (member of my family, a close friend) the way I forgot about Dan. Maybe for some of my readers that "emotional truth" sounds obvious. Maybe for others it sounds awful. For me, at that moment, it felt shameful, harmful, and so, so sad.

All these thoughts, you may imagine, took some time, during which Dan went back to talking about his girlfriend. I interrupted him and told him something about what I felt at that moment. I don't recall the exact words. I told him that I thought we should, for a moment, go back to the cat issue because it was not a cat issue, it was an issue that concerned our relationship. I told him that what emerged very strongly was that I had forgotten about something that was very important to him. I said that I felt bad not only because I had forgotten about him but also because it was made very clear that I *can* forget about him, that our relationship, as much as it was close and important, was professional. I listened to myself while talking. I asked myself whether I sounded vindictive (well, dude, here is reality!), guilty, shameful.

There was silence after I finished talking. I could imagine Dan trying to digest. I could hear his breath. Then he said, and these *are* the exact words, "I know that what you say is true. I don't know what to say. It hurts like hell. I can't stand it. I prefer not to talk about it." Yet, his tone told me that he was certainly struggling now, and would keep struggling for some time, with all the pain, shame, loss and anger that this "simple" yet so awful truth held within it.

I believe that the intersubjective encounter that occurred at that moment was much more than mutual recognition. I felt that Dan's emotional experiences were penetrating me. I felt that I created Dan's experience. I felt that we both, at that moment, lived in a shared reality, in a mutually created reality, which included our loving and appreciating relationship, its cruel limitations, and the pain that those limitations aroused in both of us. The emotional truth that I encountered, that Dan encountered, wasn't created by me or by Dan. It was, no doubt, created by his subjectivity (for example, his anxieties, his need for domination, his generous and warm character); my subjectivity (my giving of myself during all those years, attuning my self-states to his so many times, letting myself be created by his ways of thinking and experiencing; my outrageous ability to forget about him); our mutual co-created "intersubjective dream-space" (Ogden, 1997, p. 152) in which all those conscious and unconscious feelings were created, shaped, and reshaped by each other again and again; and, of course, some objective ruthless facts: I had a cat, he was allergic to cats; one day we will stop seeing each other; he pays for our relationship; and so on. We created that shared reality, we bumped into it, almost crashing. Mutual recognition—you see my point of view, I see yours; you recognize my feelings, I recognize yours; we will gain our subjective sense of sanity through our intersubjectivity—was not enough here. In order to really emerge from that complementary Doer-Done to see-saw (Benjamin, 2009) we had to realize that co-created reality, to allow ourselves to feel it, to feel it as our own, as a "personal O" (Grotstein, 2000, pp. 286–287) as created by those three dimensions of human existence—subjectivity, intersubjectivity, objectivity—and to let this emotional reality be created again and again, thus resuscitating it from dissociation. We had to mutually surrender to it. I am not sure who "went first" (Benjamin, 2004a, p. 33) here. I think that in the surrender domain, there is not always someone who goes first, maybe only someone who first articulates the mutual surrender that takes place.

Two months later, Dan came back to Israel. Of course, we scheduled a meeting. In those months, neither of us raised the cat issue again. I was eagerly waiting to see him. I missed him a great deal. I arranged a 20-min break in my schedule before our meeting, closed the cat in a room as far as possible from the room that served as my clinic, and cleaned the office as much as I could, trying to make it as free as possible from the cat's hair and smell (I learned a little before about cat allergy and found out that it is mainly the cat's hair and smell that cause the allergic reaction). I did not know then that Dan arrived early to the session and hung around my (new for him) house, waiting for his appointment, perhaps learning the new surroundings.

When he came in, after giving each other a warm hug, we sat down, getting used to seeing each other again and getting used to the new setting. The first thing Dan said was, "I saw you through the window, cleaning the office. I understood exactly why. Thank you." We looked into each other. In the excitement of that moment of "reunion," these words were filled with love and with pain. We both remembered clearly how hard it was to feel that we were so connected yet that this connection had very cruel limitations. I was reminded of Eigen's sentence: "In every life there is more catastrophe than one can handle" (1996, p. 133) and his "definition" of sorts of the therapeutic endeavor: "to go through devastating times...breaking bread together, the bread of catastrophe...to break catastrophe together and metabolize bits at a time" (p. 134). In a very similar vein, I believe, Benjamin (2007) wrote, "Maybe there is grace. Maybe surrender is possible...yet...what a costly struggle it really entails" (p. 666).

At that moment it was almost tolerable.

REFERENCES

Benjamin, J. (1988). *The Bonds of Love: Psychoanalysis, Feminism, and the Problem of Domination.* New York, NY: Pantheon Books.

———. (1995). *Like Subjects, Love Objects: Essays on Recognition and Sexual Differences.* New Haven, CT: Yale University Press.

———. (1999). Afterword. In: *Relational Psychoanalysis: The Emergence of a Tradition,* eds. S. Mitchell & L. Aron. Hillsdale, NJ: Analytic Press, pp. 201–209.

———. (2004a). Beyond doer and done to: An intersubjective view of thirdness. *Psychoanalytic Quarterly,* 73, 5–46.

———. (2004b). Escape from the hall of mirrors: Commentary on a paper by Jody Messler Davies. *Psychoanalytic Dialogues,* 14, 743–753.

———. (2006). Crash: What we do when we cannot touch: Commentary on a paper by Meira Likierman. *Psychoanalytic Dialogues,* 16, 377–385.

———. (2007). A review of Awakening the Dreamer: Clinical Journeys by Philip M. Bromberg. *Contemporary Psychoanalysis,* 43, 666–680.

———. (2009). A relational psychoanalysis perspective on the necessity of acknowledging failure in order to restore the facilitating and containing features of the intersubjective relationship (the shared third). *International Journal of Psychoanalysis*, 90, 441–450.

Bion, W. R. (1987). Clinical seminars. In: *Clinical Seminars and Others Works*, ed. F. Bion. London, UK: Karnac Books, pp. 1–141.

Davidson, D. (2001). *Subjective, Intersubjective, Objective*. Oxford, UK: Clarendon Press.

Descartes, R. (1637). *Discourse on Method*. New York, NY: The Liberal Arts Books, 1960.

Eigen, M. (1996). *Psychic Deadness*. London, UK: Karnac Books.

Freud, S. (1917). Introductory lectures on psycho-analysis: Part III. General theory of the neurosis. *Standard Edition*, 16. London, UK: Hogarth Press, 1961, pp. 243–463.

Ghent, E. (1990). Masochism, submission, surrender: Masochism as a perversion of surrender. *Contemporary Psychoanalysis*, 26, 108–136.

———. (1995). Interaction in the psychoanalysis situation. *Psychoanalytic Dialogues*, 5, 470–491.

———. (2001). Need, paradox, and surrender: Commentary on paper by Adam Philips. *Psychoanalytic Dialogues*, 11, 23–41.

Grotstein, J. (2000). *Who Is the Dreamer Who Dreams the Dream? A Study of Psychic Presence*. London, UK: Analytic Press.

Hegel, G. W. F. (1807). *The Phenomenology of Mind*. London, UK: Allen & Unwin, 1949.

Kojeve, A. (1934). *Introduction to the Reading of Hegel*. New York, NY: Basic Books, 1969.

Ogden, T. H. (1994). *Subject of Analysis*. London, UK: Karnac Books.

———. (1997). *Reverie and Interpretation: Sensing Something Human*. London, UK: Karnac Books.

———. (2001). *Conversations at the Frontier of Dreaming*. London, UK: Karnac Books.

Reis, B. (2004). You are requested to close the eyes. *Psychoanalytic Dialogues*, 14, 349–371.

Rorty, R. (1979). *Philosophy and the Mirror of Nature*. Princeton, NJ: Princeton University Press.

Searles, H. (1961). Anxiety concerning change, as seen in the psychotherapy of schizophrenic patients—with particular reference to the sense of personal identity. In: *Collected Papers on Schizophrenia and Related Subjects*. London, UK: Karnac Books, 1965, pp. 443–465.

Winnicott, D. W. (1945). Primitive emotional development. In: *Through Paediatrics to Psychoanalysis*. London, UK: Karnac Books, 1958, pp. 145–156.

———. (1967). Mirror-role of mother and family in child development. In: *Playing and Reality*. New York, NY: Basic Books, 1971, pp. 111–118.

———. (1969). The use of an object and relating through identification. In: *Playing and Reality*. New York, NY: Basic Books, 1971, pp. 86–94.

Intersubjectivity and French Psychoanalysis: A Misunderstanding?

Régine Waintrater, Ph.D.
Paris 7-Diderot University

French psychoanalysts harbor many misconceptions about the relational movement, which they tend to confuse with the object-relations school. Indeed, the latter has never been popular in France, mainly due to the influence of Jacques Lacan. The French believe that these trends have transformed psychoanalysis into a kind of psychology, more concerned with psychotherapeutic techniques than with metapsychology. Anglo-Saxon empiricism is considered responsible for a theoretical dispersion that French psychoanalysts, who advocate a unified theoretical approach, see as endangering the very foundations of psychoanalysis. Their criticism focuses mainly on the idea that the American conception favors interaction and meaning over the unconscious and infantile sexuality. The notions of intersubjectivity, mutual recognition, and negotiation are met with distrust; as a result, the French analytic community remains largely ignorant of theoretical developments in the relational and intersubjective feminist schools of thought.

Intersubjectivity, feminism, and gender studies are viewed by French psychoanalysts with some degree of mistrust, as a confusing muddle with no clear direction. Several reasons explain this state of affairs.

The first is quite prosaic: very few English-language psychoanalytic works have been translated into French. Some translations exist of works that were first published far from recently: as a result, French readers have been given a rather anachronistic view of English-language psychoanalysis. This continues to be true today despite the recent publication of new works in translation. The French understanding of Anglo-Saxon psychoanalysis is limited to the object-relations school and Ego psychology, and the result is a deep misunderstanding of what can generally be called American psychoanalysis. Two books, recently published in France, illustrate this fact. The first is a small book on American psychoanalysis published in a popular series that provides readers with basic information on a wide variety of subjects (Tessier, 2005). The book offers a synthetic overview of the history of psychoanalytic thought in the United States, and about one third, or 40 or so small pages, are devoted to contemporary psychoanalysis. In so few pages, it is no wonder the different schools of thought—the relational school, the intersubjectivist school, the neuroscientific approach, and cognitivism—seem like a package deal. Despite the author's rigorous approach, such a vast topic cannot be addressed in such a short volume without sacrificing detail and nuance, which are the object of very specialized scientific publications in the United States.

The same can be said about the special issue devoted in 2000 to this subject by the respectable *Revue Française de Psychanalyse* of the Paris Psychoanalytical Society. Its title—"Controverses américaines dans la psychanalyse" ("American Controversies in Psychoanalysis")—sounded promising (Durieux & Fine, 2000) But what a disappointment! The authors repeat the idea that American psychoanalysis is a deviation from Freudian orthodoxy, a deviation best described as a rejection of the drive theory in favor of a theory of relations, globally represented by the intersubjective school. The most well-known (to the French) theoretician of this group is Owen Renik, whose works on self-disclosure have generated passionate debate (Renik, 1995, 1996). The views expressed in this issue are typical of the French understanding of American psychoanalysis: feminism and gender studies are ignored. Indeed, with the exception of Stoller, whose work was translated several years ago, French psychoanalytic thought has never acknowledged these trends. Feminism and gender studies are considered to belong to the fields of sociology and political philosophy, foreign to psychoanalytic practice and therefore unconcerned by the debate. Thus, Judith Butler is viewed as a political philosopher and despite their revolutionary aspects, her ideas are not perceived as threatening to psychoanalytic theory or practice (see Butler and David-Ménard, 2009). On the other hand, Jessica Benjamin, whose work directly concerns psychoanalysis, is largely unknown among French readers, although a French translation of *The Bonds of Love* was published 20 years ago (Benjamin, 1988). This makes it difficult, if not impossible, to describe how the French view her work. Instead, I try to briefly explain this resistance and describe the position of French psychoanalysis today regarding these issues.

THE DEFENSE OF METAPSYCHOLOGY

In an article of the aforementioned review, French psychoanalyst Christine Anzieu-Premmereur—who lives in New York—describes the radical direction taken by classical psychoanalysis in the United States (Anzieu-Premmereur, 2000). She speaks of a deep misunderstanding between both countries. This article, which also has a historic intent, highlights what she believes are the major transformations, that is, the fact that sexuality is no longer the central reference, and the criticism of the economic point of view, considered too biological. Once again, we have the statement of an absolute conflict between two theories, one based on the drives and the other on the notions of meaning and goal. French analysts react with perplexity, if not astonishment, to such ideas as the relative nature of interpretation, the primacy of the here and now, and the deconstruction of authority, especially the analyst's. In the French view, such ideas reflect an ideological tendency, close to cultural relativism; they mark the end of the specificity of psychoanalysis, reduced to a branch of psychology. Once again, Anglo-Saxon empiricism and the French tradition of highly speculative thought are at odds: in the country of Foucault, Derrida, and Lyotard, psychoanalysis remains opposed to any kind of social constructivism. The French view the effort of American psychoanalysts to rethink psychoanalysis from a postmodern perspective as the demise of psychoanalysis, the ruin of the edifice of Freudian metapsychology.

The idea of a subjectivity born of the encounter with the Other contradicts the notion of a sexual unconscious; infantile sexuality disappears and is replaced by a wider use of the notion of attachment. A watered-down unconscious, or even no unconscious at all: this is how intersubjective theories are perceived in France. For French psychoanalysts, the indomitable force of transference and of the drives cannot be reduced to a transaction between two persons: intersubjectivity and the entire relational movement are criticized as ignoring psychic conflict and the unconscious. The French remain as ever critical of the object-relations school, especially of Fairbairn and his affirmation that drives are not pleasure-seeking but object-seeking, and they tend to lump together the object-relations school with Ego psychology. This critical stance hails back to Lacan's condemnation of Ego psychologists, which, as we know, was partly due to his unresolved conflict with Loewenstein, his former analyst. Even though the French are aware that the relational movement and the Self psychology movement were developed in reaction to Ego psychology, Lacan's anathema continues to weigh down on their knowledge of contemporary developments in American psychoanalysis.

Thus, Mitchell's important contributions are virtually unknown in France, and none of his books have been translated into French. The review *Psychoanalytic Dialogues* is never mentioned in bibliographies. The French have no idea of the relational concepts developed by Mitchell, and even if they did they would view them as one more development of American antimetapsychology. Indeed, a classical French analyst cannot read such statements as "Some of [Freud's] ideas are anachronistic and need to be discarded" or "the dimension of Freud that seems important to me to reject is his drive theory" without being shocked (Mitchell, 2000, p. 266). And no classical French analyst would agree to his revision of Freudian determinism, his assertion that the patient can exercise his or her will and be free of repetitions and unconscious forces thanks to elucidation and knowledge. For the French, anything referring to cognitive processes, to notions of will and change, belongs to motivational theories and is incompatible with the very idea of the unconscious.

This movement of rejection began with the concept of the self and its gradual replacement of the Freudian ego. The French consider that in terms of metapsychology, the "self" is an overextended and ill-defined notion emphasizing experience and neglecting the unconscious. In particular, the notion of psychic conflict becomes secondary and nearly fades away. The idea of an a-conflictual zone of the ego that can be extended through treatment is viewed as typically American, stemming from an ideology of adaptation and motivation that gives precedence to external reality and actual relationships. The self, for the French, is an exaggerated simplification of the structural model; the emphasis on the "here and now" of the session tends to establish a confusion between the unconscious and the preconscious, or even subjectivity (Tessier, 2005) Expressions such as "self-awareness" or "nonawareness" are considered clearly borrowed from cognitive psychology. If the term "unconscious" no longer refers to the sexual unconscious but only to what is not perceived or felt by the subject, then the entire topographical model becomes obsolete along with the entire foundation of Freudian theory. When the subject becomes "aware," he or she is in fact aware, or conscious, of what he is feeling: this quest for meaning remains purely descriptive and ignores the process of discovery of the unconscious based on the drives. The idea of a subject with a unified sense of self gained through understanding and experience is completely at odds with the French conception of a subject divided by the very nature of what constitutes the psyche, that is, infantile sexuality, fantasy, and repression.

Relational psychoanalysis thus finds itself accused of reducing the dimension of otherness; indeed, otherness, both in relation to the Other and to oneself, is central to the French conception of the desiring subject. For the followers of Lacan, the "Real" is precisely what is unknowable in the Other, that which cannot be understood. French psychoanalysts are hostile to the notions of negotiation or even symmetry developed by the intersubjectivists; they believe that accepting them would blur the difference between metapsychology and ordinary psychology, even if it is phenomenological. Indeed, if, according to this conception, intrapsychic conflict is more important than intersubjective issues, then the importance of present relationships in resolving the patient's conflicts and patient-analyst conflicts cannot possibly be acknowledged. The idea of a primarily intersubjective and interactive psychic life is objectionable to the advocates of a theory based on desire and its counterpart, conflict: the relationship with the Other is no more than a means of expression of this conflict, which is the foundation base of the psyche. Thus, from the French perspective, the intersubjective movement distorts all the key Freudian notions, beginning with the notion of representation, renamed "idea"—a mistranslation of the Freudian concept of "Vorstellung" in that it ignores its hallucinatory aspects and approximates it with perception.

Or yet again the word *repression*, which underscores only the defensive aspects of the concept of *Verdrängung* (as opposed to the French *refoulement*). Similarly, the extensive use of the notion of splitting to explain all unconscious movements seems quite insufficient to French theoreticians. And last but not least, the near disappearance of the notion of *Nachträglichkeit*, in French "*après-coup*," poorly translated into English by "deferred action" or afterwardsness" and reduced to an aspect of trauma. If everything can be resolved through sharing and recognition, there can be no unresolved remains, the "fueros" Freud mentions in Letter 52 to Fliess (Freud, 1919).

Another criticism touches upon the central role given by the intersubjectivists to affect, thereby diminishing the role of verbal associations during the session and consequently the function of interpretation. If the analyst's interpretations are by essence just as subjective as the patient's own experience and both are considered equivalent, then the only thing that matters is shared meaning and knowledge. Thus, according to many French analysts, the relational and intersubjective schools are tantamount to theories of communication. Bernard Brusset, for example, believes that such concepts turn psychoanalysis into an "exploration of conscious thought and conscience through cognitive elaboration . . . avoiding anything that might give rise to manifestations of the unconscious, proper" (Brusset, 2000, p. 109). He disagrees with the importance given to relations as experienced in reality because this position encourages the avoidance of the question of fantasy, of the uncontrollable force of transference, and the patient's inevitable resistance. In his view, the "realistic" goal orients the treatment toward secondary processes and the reality principle, leaving little space for desire in the form of hallucinatory wish fulfillment.

But for the French, the most critical issue is the nonrecognition of the death drive by Anglo-Saxon psychoanalysis: Fairbairn, Winnicott, and Kohut's assertion that the death drive is an unnecessary postulate indicates a refusal to consider destructiveness as a core aspect of the psyche. Whereas the Anglo-Saxons understand the death drive as the result of a failure of the environment, and consequently a pathology of the self, the French see it as the cornerstone of human conflict, as such necessarily intrapsychic. The idea of a strong or coherent self is over-reminiscent of the Ego psychology that they so dislike. Destructiveness and hatred cannot be erased simply through recognition and empathy: according to Jean Laplanche's theorization, the compulsion to repeat cannot be separated from what he terms "extended sexuality" and internal drive impulses (Laplanche, 2007).

Anglo-Saxon optimism concerning the resolution of destructiveness appears as one more expression of the American credo in the vein of Obama's "yes we can." It could be that French pessimism is tied to the experience of two world wars on their soil. Even Winnicott, despite his popularity in France, is criticized for his irenic approach, his belief that a good enough environment and creativity can overcome destructiveness. His skill at avoiding difficulties while constantly questioning the drive theory and the death drive enabled him to escape most of the criticism leveled at his object-relations colleagues. Another possible reason could be that what he had to offer was so much needed by psychoanalysts that he was "forgiven" his unorthodox assertions. However, French interest in Winnicott did not lead to new openings: on the contrary, the fear that any slight shift in paradigm might destroy the entire Freudian edifice, and particularly the drive theory, has led to a reinforcement of orthodox positions.

THE LIQUIDATION OF THE DRIVES AND THE END OF FREUDIAN SEXUALITY

In a short article entitled *"Contre-courant,"* Jean Laplanche, who died in June 2012, insists that metapsychology must not be discarded like an old shoe (Laplanche, 2001) Transcending the debate between advocates of psychoanalysis versus advocates of psychotherapy, Laplanche defends a view of psychoanalysis based on the reference to what he calls "the sexual," that is, sexuality in the wider sense of the term, to be distinguished from sexuality in the strict sense. "The sexual" is for Laplanche what comes from the subject's and the Other's infantile sexuality. This is what governs the unconscious, repression and fantasy. Laplanche avoids Freud's biological impasse and suggests that the enigma represented by the Other entails psychic consequences that cannot be resolved through elucidation and understanding. What he calls the "fundamental anthropological situation" is marked by a radical dissymmetry necessary to the child's survival: the child is dependent on the adult and as such subject to "generalized seduction" (p. 302). This situation leads to an infinite number of nonverbal modes of communication. The child faces the constant difficulty, or even impossibility, of deciphering the enigmatic messages received from those who take care of him or her—messages carrying their own unconscious load. Laplanche sees the work of analysis as a form of hermeneutics in the sense that it always is an attempt to translate the analysand's productions as coming from his and the Other's sexual unconscious. Thus, Laplanche cannot accept the loss of the sexual and of the drives, which for him are the very foundation of psychic life and not the result of environmental failure. For the same reason, the analyst-patient relationship cannot be seen as equal and merely contractual because the analyst's and the patient's unconscious contain unknowable traces of their own parents' unconscious. According to Laplanche, the idea of resolving conflict, and resulting anxiety, through shared understanding and elucidation can only be a defensive stance vis-à-vis the drive impulses and their strange and inexplicable nature: the dissymmetry of the analytic relationship is analogous to the primary dissymmetry, also named primary seduction. Any attempt to disregard this dissymmetry and the resulting hermeneutic movement triggered by this situation is the result, in his words, of "vulgar" pragmatism (p. 306). We can see how clearly his thought contradicts the tenets of the intersubjective movement.

JESSICA BENJAMIN: A NEW WAY OF THINKING

In this context, the decision of Payot, the famous publisher of Freud, to follow my recommendation and publish Jessica Benjamin's book *Like Subjects, Love Objects* represented a genuine challenge (Benjamin, 1995). However, I believe that unprejudiced analysts curious of the recent developments in American psychoanalysis should take great interest in her work. Thanks to her refusal to choose between the drive theory and the relational theory, to her deep knowledge of Hegel, Lacan, and in general of French psychoanalytic theory and her sophistication, her work may help to transform misunderstanding into genuine dialogue. Benjamin adheres to the critical social theory of the Frankfurt school; she became interested in psychoanalysis while "reading Freud and Marcuse with the hope of finding in psychoanalysis the answer to the great social questions of the 1960s" (Benjamin, 2000). Her work should appeal to French thinkers inspired by Michel Foucault, Gilles Deleuze, and Jacques Derrida, all of whom have reflected on the relationship between mental illness, power, and domination. Her reference to dialectics and philosophy would certainly interest French contemporary psychoanalysts; however, they would probably disagree with her claim to resolve the conflict of mutual recognition, considered by classical psychoanalysis a core human conflict, bound to remain unresolved. Today, Benjamin's ideas concerning the binary logic of domination between the sexes, the mother-child dyad and its impact on love relationships, are gradually finding an echo in French psychoanalysis. Her criticism of traditional feminist positions, which she considers overessentialist—especially concerning the discourse on "nature" and gender polarity—should necessarily be of interest to those concerned with "gender studies." However, we must remember that in France, readership in this field is still limited, and that psychoanalytic thinking remains reluctant to open up to these new currents for the reasons mentioned earlier.

Nonetheless, many here would agree with her on the role of parents: her criticism of the repudiation of mothers, considered the main obstacle to individuation, is powerful and has important clinical consequences. Jessica Benjamin denounces the "chauvinism of repudiation" and challenges classical psychoanalysis, which has remained fixated on the depreciation of the maternal/feminine and idealization of the paternal/masculine. She debunks the "counter-myth of a harmonious maternal ideal," which refuses to recognize the fundamental otherness of the preoedipal mother in order to better denigrate her. Benjamin shows how the idealization of the first mother-child dyad is a product of a rigid oedipal discourse, creating frozen categories such as "mother for attachment" and "father for separation." The father's preoedipal role is denied, and as a result, child and mother are also denied a part of the emotional basis that founds future relations. Her proposal to reinclude the father in the preoedipal period corresponds to what is currently observed with the phenomenon of "new fathers": modern fathers are creating new models of fatherhood and no longer have to choose between a "mothering father" model and a patriarchal ideal devoid of caring and tenderness; a genuine "primary paternal preoccupation" is emerging (Korff-Sausse, 2009). In the same vein, she revisits the concept of thirdness. Benjamin, well versed in Lacanian theory, contradicts Lacan's understanding of the concept whereby the third is essentially oedipal, language-borne, paternal, and representing prohibition. Benjamin is closer to Daniel Stern, for whom thirdness exceeds language and begins earlier with nonverbal communication and emotional tuning. She develops a new conception of thirdness that rehabilitates the dyad, too often considered the source of psychosis. Her critique of attachment theories, particularly those of Margaret Mahler, opens interesting avenues for understanding how a relation is built, with a reflection on the necessary tension between recognition of the Other and self-affirmation. By suggesting that one should analyze the psychic processes that sustain dissociation and support domination, without designating them as good or bad or linking them to masculine or feminine qualities, Benjamin offers novel ideas on human relations that take into account social change without reducing psychoanalysis to a psychosociology dominated by ideology.

CONCLUSION

For many French analysts, psychoanalysis as it is practiced in the United States is at best a psychotherapy, necessarily of lesser value because, as Freud wrote, psychotherapy "alloys the pure gold of psychoanalysis with the copper of suggestion"(Freud, 1919). Today, many analysts have reinterpreted this formulation, in particular child analysts or those working with nonneurotic patients, giving rise to new developments in the definition of the analytic process; nonetheless, the debate between "pure psychoanalysis" and "psychotherapy" still holds strong, especially concerning issues of frame and setting. Psychoanalysts are still afraid of losing their "purity," and this fear triggers a great deal of resistance toward novelty. Mitchell's (1988) audacity in replacing the drive theory with the relational theory is perceived as a danger, a Trojan horse that could destroy psychoanalysis from within; therefore all such attempts must be fought. Of course, America's extreme eclecticism has given rise to rather esoteric movements that are psychoanalytical only in name. The fact that these trends have gone along with the gradual desertion of psychoanalysis throughout the world does provide a case for Freudian orthodoxy, whose best advocates are some great French psychoanalysts. However, maintaining a "fortress" attitude could sign a death warrant for psychoanalysis. The spirit of Masada lives on, and refusing to open up to the world in the name of purity is not only dangerous but also suicidal. Let us hope that Jessica Benjamin and others will enable psychoanalysts to "steer a course between the Scylla of rigid orthodoxy and the Charybdis of opportunistic heterodoxy," to quote Merton Gill (1954), who nearly sixty years ago had already expressed concern that psychoanalysis might become fossilized or even extinct.

REFERENCES

Anzieu-Premmereur, C. (2000). Que sont devenues les pulsions? Histoire des débats Américains autour de la métapsychologie [What has become of the drives? An overview of American debates on metapsychology]. In: *Sur les controverses Américaines dans la psychanalyse [American Controversies in Psychoanalysis]*. Monographies de Psychanalyse. Paris, France: PUF, pp. 23–37.

Benjamin, J. (1988). *The Bonds of Love: Psychoanalysis, Feminism and the Problem of Domination*. New York, NY: Pantheon.

———. (1995). *Like Subjects, Love Objects: Essays on Recognition and Sexual Difference*. New Haven, CT, and London, UK: Yale University Press.

———. (2000). Response to commentaries by Mitchell and Butler. *Studies in Gender and Sexuality*, 1, 291–308.

Brusset, B. (2000). Au cœur des divergences: La scientificité, la relation d'objet et l'intersubjectivité [At the center of the disputes: Scientificity, object-relations and intersubjectivity]. In: *Sur les controverses Américaines dans la psychanalyse [American Controversies in Psychoanalysis]*. Monographies de Psychanalyse. Paris, France: PUF, pp. 85–119.

Butler, J. & David-Ménard, M., eds. (2009). *Sexualités, genres et mélancolie: S'entretenir avec Judith Butler [Sexuality, Gender and Melancholia: Conversations With Judith Butler]*. Paris, France: ed. Campagne Première.

Durieux, M.-C. & Fine, A. (2000). *Sur les controverses Américaines dans la psychanalyse [American Controversies in Psychoanalysis]*. Monographies de Psychanalyse. Paris, France: PUF.

Freud, S. (1919). Lines of advance in psycho-analytic therapy. *Standard Edition*, 17. London, UK: Hogarth Press, 1961, pp. 157–168.

Gill, M. M. (1954). Psychoanalysis and exploratory psychotherapy. *Journal of the American Psychoanalytic Association*, 2, 771–797.

Korff-Sausse, S. (2009). *Eloge des pères [In Praise of Fathers]*. Paris, France: Hachette Littératures.

Laplanche, J. (2001). Contre-courant [Against the current]. *Revue Française de Psychanalyse*. Paris, France: PUF, pp. 299–311.

———. (2007). *Freud and the Sexual, 2000–2006*. International Psychoanalytic Books, 2012.

Mitchell, S. A. (2000). Juggling paradoxes: Commentary on the work of Jessica Benjamin. *Studies in Gender and Sexuality*, 1, 251–269.

Renik, O. (1995). The ideal of anonymous analyst and the problem of self-disclosure. *Psychoanalytic Quarterly*, 64, 466–495.

———. (1996). The perils of neutrality. *Psychoanalytic Quarterly*, 65, 495–517.

Tessier, H. (2005). *La psychanalyse Américaine [American Psychoanalysis]*. Paris, France: PUF.

Beyond Intersubjectivity: Science, the Real World, and the Third in Psychoanalysis

Martin Altmeyer, Psy.D.
Bund Deutscher Psychologinnen und Psychologen

Jessica Benjamin's seminal contribution to the intersubjective turn of contemporary psychoanalysis raises some general issues that are discussed. Is the relational turn owned by psychoanalysis? No, we should recognize important relational findings of other human sciences. Does relational psychoanalysis rely too much on beliefs and confessions? Unfortunately yes, but as a human science it should instead be based on interdisciplinary knowledge. Is psychotherapy only an encounter of patient and therapist? No, besides subjectivity and intersubjectivity there is the objective reality as the "missing" third. Can we get rid of the psychoanalytic attachment to the past? No, there is no patient without his or her biography. Do we have to reconsider our epistemology of radical constructivism? Yes, we should stick to the "weak" constructivism of Winnicott claiming that reality has to be found and invented at the same time. Finally, some remarks on the current crisis of psychoanalysis: the issue is modernization versus fundamentalism.

The earth continued to revolve since the first appearance of *The Bonds of Love: Psychoanalysis, Feminism and the Problem of Domination* (Benjamin, 1988). Outer reality changed rapidly, and inner reality often could not keep pace with it. The unstoppable process of globalization brought different cultures, religions, and secular beliefs closer to each other, with new conflicts of nearness emerging, together with dangerous dynamics that we still fail to understand. The worldwide expansion of market-oriented capitalism has led to the economic rise of once underdeveloped countries (like India or China) but has simultaneously challenged their traditional cultural systems in ways that created social and mental problems unknown thus far. The digital revolution penetrated the everyday life of people whose intersubjective relations are increasingly mediated by the intensive use of the Internet, electronic mail, multifunctional smartphones, and social media. The expansion of such forms of media in global society opened universal spaces of mirroring and echoing formerly reserved for the beauties, the important, and the rich, spaces that can now be utilized by everyone to present himself or herself or his or her work with the hope of finding an interested public. All these changes pose an enormous challenge for contemporary psychoanalysis that—as a modern discipline and, according to Freud, as "science of the unconscious" (Leuzinger-Bohleber, 2010)—had to change and still continues to change in order to contribute to the never ending process of enlightenment and human self-enlightenment.

When Jessica Benjamin's mesmerizing book, focusing on human relations, especially gender relations, appeared in the late 1980s, she challenged not only fashionable poststructural theorizing—with Lacan, Foucault, Derrida, and Kristeva as the intellectual heroes of those days—but also the monadic limitations of the one-person psychology that epistemologically dominated psychoanalysis then. The German translation (published in 1990) had carefully turned *The Bonds of Love* into *Die Fesseln der Liebe*, which literally means *chains* or even *handcuffs* but figuratively also the *charming* or *attractiveness* of love. So the ambivalent semantics of *bonds* was maintained if not increased. In Frankfurt, where Jessica had spent some time studying critical theory—namely, Horkheimer, Adorno, and Habermas—we were all excited about her book, a book written in our familiar tradition of theory building, bringing together philosophy, social studies, and psychoanalysis while adding two new ingredients: on the one hand modern feminism and on the other a post-Freudian notion of intersubjectivity and recognition based on Winnicott and infant research.

Jessica Benjamin's special contribution to feminist theory is extraordinarily strong and needs no further acclamation: in fact she was one of the pioneers, a front woman of the liberation movement, and her book was read and celebrated by women and men all over the world. The great contribution of feminism to the cultural progress of mankind needs no further mention, or rather, there are others who are more qualified to do so than myself. I therefore concentrate on Jessica's contribution to change in psychoanalysis. Her book contributed to a paradigmatic shift we nowadays call the relational or intersubjective turn. This process of "modernizing psychoanalysis," as Helmut Thomae and I (Altmeyer and Thomae, 2006a, p. 5f) propose to call it, is still ongoing and needs further discussion. So I try to honor Jessica Benjamin's seminal work by pointing to her particular approach to intersubjectivity and discussing some problems that arise in this context. In some parts of this text I refer to an International Association for Relational Psychoanalysis and Psychotherapy (IARPP) online debate on the present and the past in relational psychoanalysis, which took place in 2009; in what follows, I use the arguments made jointly by Martin Dornes and myself because we contributed to this debate as one discussant.

My considerations begin with a proposal: to look at the intersubjective turn in psychoanalysis, a turn that came rather late comparatively, as part of a relational turn in the human sciences in general. I then raise the question of our professional identity: Is psychoanalysis, especially relational psychoanalysis, based on empirical and interdisciplinary validated knowledge or on a set of confessions based on good beliefs and noble values; and because psychotherapy is not a science but an intersubjective piece of art, what is the connection between our basic theory on the human mind and the psychotherapeutic encounter? Discussing Jessica Benjamin's core conception of intersubjectivity as the third between two subjectivities—what two people share—brings up the question of objectivity: Isn't there an objective reality out there we all have to recognize as our common third despite the fact that we might look at it differently? I then look at the relevance of reality in our clinical field, where it sometimes arises as a matter of the true past of the patient or what really happened to him or her versus a subjective narrative or a more meaningful coconstruction in the course of the psychoanalytic process. The question of a specific epistemology in contemporary psychoanalysis and Jessica's (and others') relational approach to this question is raised. I close my contribution with some general remarks on the modernization of psychoanalysis at the edge of its decline.

THE RELATIONAL TURN IS AN OVERARCHING MOVEMENT IN HUMAN SCIENCES BASED ON BETTER KNOWLEDGE, NOT ON BELIEF

Jessica Benjamin became influential in many fields especially by contributing to the relational turn in psychoanalysis, which came late compared with other human sciences like philosophical anthropology (from Buber to Gadamer), linguistic philosophy (from Wittgenstein to Davidson), symbolic interactionism (G. H. Mead), attachment theory (Bowlby), infant research (from Trevarthen to Stern and Dornes) or social sciences (Habermas, Honneth). This delayed turn moved a discipline fragmented into multiple schools—proponents of classical instinct theory; ego and self psychology or object-relation theories of all kinds; contemporary Freudians; contemporary Kleinians; neo- and post-Kleinians; Bionians; late disciples of C. G. Jung, Alfred Adler, and other dissidents in the history of the psychoanalytic movement—toward intersubjectivity as its new "common ground" (Wallerstein, 1990).

Through this process of renewing, even "revolving"—as Stephen Mitchell (2000) preferred to say in *Relationality: From Attachment to Intersubjectivity*—contemporary psychoanalysis in relational terms has gained speed, depth, and momentum since 1988. Far from being only another metapsychological approach or a new school of psychoanalysis, its intersubjective turn reflects the modernization of the psyche itself. As if moving outward, the human mind shows overtly its formerly hidden psychic connections with others, corresponding to the growing interconnectedness of global life in the 21st century. The legend of the isolated self—primordially narcissistic and becoming social only through the need to be satisfied or the constraints of society (cf. Altmeyer, 2000)—has been dismissed and replaced by the growing knowledge that human beings are related to each other. This new understanding of the social character of human "nature" is generally spreading from scientific communities to the intellectual world: the individual is a "social animal" as *The New York Times* columnist David Brooks (2011) recently put it in his same-titled book (subtitle: "The Hidden Sources of Love, Character, and Achievement"), collecting and presenting a whole body of relational knowledge in the human sciences including psychoanalysis and its conception of the unconscious. From birth on there is a "virtual other" (Bråten, 1992; Dornes, 2000) within our self.

Thus the relational turn of the human sciences including psychoanalysis is based on better knowledge instead of other beliefs. The psychoanalytic version of the "amoeba-saga" lost ground only when infant research and attachment theory empirically demonstrated the intersubjective nature of psychic functioning (Trevarthen 1979; Stern 1985; Dornes 2000, 2006, 2012). Further support for a theory of primary intersubjectivity came from other human sciences like evolutionary anthropology; social philosophy; and last but not least and with an enormous impact, by the advanced and highly sophisticated domain of brain research and its revolutionary discovery of a system of "mirror-neurons," which might prove to be the neurobiological equivalent of mental relatedness. Considering that neurobiology and psychoanalysis used to fight each other like warring clans over decades in the 20th century, the current convergence of both disciplines seems like an irony in the history of human sciences.[1] Like scientific twins

---

[1] Freud himself was ambivalent toward empirical research. Sometimes he counted on neurobiology and its findings to eventually validate the speculative assumptions of his metapsychology or reject them and deliver better foundations. Sometimes he rejected empirical data—"it can do no harm" to the psychoanalytic method (Freud, 1934, in a letter to Saul Rosenzweig quoted by Gay, 1988, p. 523; cf. Grunbaum, 1984, p. 1)—when it was brought to him; he said the data from the psychoanalytic process was all he needed (I owe this reference to Joseph Schachter, personal communication, August 2012).

they share their object while competing in perspectives (brain vs. mind) and should try to integrate their insights.

In fact it is not only the discovery of an intersubjective "mirror-system" bringing modern neuroscience and modern psychoanalysis together but also other relational findings and assumptions of brain researchers. For example, they nowadays agree with our general assumption that early interactions are internalized during the development of the psyche, building mental structures on the different levels of memory including the implicit (unconscious) one. Whether you call those structures "representations of interactions generalized" (Stern's RIG), internalized object-relations, interactive patterns, metarepresentations, or "scenes" depends on the school you belong to: this seems to me a relational approach to the dynamic unconscious. For example, the American neuroscientist Antonio Damasio (2004) suggests that even the unconscious background of our emotions is filled with visual interactive scenes going back to personal experiences made by the emerging self with others in the past, interactions that transform—in a process of "docking"—inborn affects into human emotions: this would indicate the relational character of our feelings. The hypothesis of a decentered "neuronal self" is a third example for the relational turn in advanced neurosciences. Because a central unit of regulation or a hierarchical sort of control is missing in our brain and cerebral processing is instead wired by decentralized connections, the well-known German neuroscientist Wolf Singer came to assume that the self is potentially a "cultural construct" stored as a metarepresentation in the implicit memory; our subjective perception of a coherent self might thus emerge—by overtaking the perspective of the other mediated and "broken" by all kinds of subjective, intersubjective, and objective contingencies of life—from social interactions, originating in an intimate early relation that transforms the "You" of the mother (or other care persons) into the "Me" respectively the "I" of the child (Singer, 2002, p. 73ff.).

WE SHOULD NOT GRACE OUR BELIEFS BY CALLING THEM THEORIES: ON RELATIONAL KNOWLEDGE AND THE THERAPEUTIC PROCESS IN PSYCHOANALYSIS

The relational turn in psychoanalysis is due in no small part to good-enough research requiring a new paradigm as well as good-enough "research [that] followed the development of the relational paradigm" (Joseph Schachter, personal communication, August 2012). At the end relational thinking should be more a matter of empirical findings and theoretical conclusions instead of group confessions or personal values as some leading relationalists might think. Lew Aron (1996), for example, explained the divergence of psychoanalytic schools by divergent "personal and professional value-systems" (p. 7) liable for the deep disagreement in metapsychology and clinical approach and strongly promoted relational values. So it did not come as a surprise that there has been a growing tendency to establish relational psychoanalysis as a new school of confession organized in own institutions with the IARPP as its umbrella organization founded in 2001.

In order to illustrate how I experience the almost religious character of this tendency I cite from my closing comment at the end of a 2-week online discussion on the significance of the past for relational psychoanalysis, which took place in December 2009 (IARPP, 2009). I might unjustly generalize my personal experience, but this is what I wrote:

> The second week gradually shifted to an ideological reassurement of relational psychoanalysis: how much we appreciate one another, how sensitive we are towards the needs of our patients, how deeply

we recognize the perspective of the other (as if other psychoanalytic schools, humanistic psychologies and even the bunch of esoteric therapeutic approaches would not claim the same sensibility). An atmosphere of worshipping was gradually generated with "relation" as the new "god." The inner dynamics of this relational "service" became very suggestive, encouraging to join the swelling stream of enthusiasm and self-appreciation. The sublime rise of an emotional climate of collective narcissism could be observed: "Look how great we are!" More emotion and affective closeness was asked in the community instead of a rational discourse. There was no distance anymore. Differences disappeared or were ignored.

Referring to this climate of worshipping and group narcissism I draw a line to the history of splitting in psychoanalysis because our discussion on the attachment of psychoanalysis to the past seemed to reflect and in a certain sense repeat the drama of psychoanalysis in the course of the 20th century, namely, shifting from a human science to a confession. At the end of the 19th century psychoanalysis had been born as a child of the enlightenment, emerging as a new scientific approach that generated knowledge—instead of and against religious belief systems of all kinds—of the *conditio humana*. As Freud frankly conceded there were some speculations but he was steadily trying to replace speculative knowledge by empirical data and valid assumptions. Yet under the persisting pressure of a hostile social and academic environment he tried on the other side to hold the young psychoanalytic movement together by demanding its members to subscribe to certain theoretical positions. Those demands shaped what Freud called the psychoanalytic "Schibboleth": the recognition of infantile sexuality and the validity of drive theory, later adding the existence of transference and resistance in the psychoanalytic process. Freud's politics of "Schibboleth" inaugurated a fatal process shifting psychoanalysis slowly from knowledge to a belief system of its own kind. Convictions and confessions were asked, not an attitude where doubts should pave the road to psychoanalytic truth. This was one of the main the reasons psychoanalysis after the death of its founding father finally fragmented into different schools fighting each other on the basis of a "narcissism of minor differences" (Freud, 1930, p. 114). The long list of dissidents, as we all know, contains the names of John Bowlby, Harry Stack Sullivan, Erich Fromm, and Karen Horney, among others.

Ironically the track of intersubjectivity and relationality—by the way more than half a century ago sharply attacked for its "revisionism" of Freud's revolutionary drive theory by the rather orthodox Adorno (1952)—once excluded by mainstream psychoanalysis sticking to *drive* as its "truth" back then has become the leading track in contemporary psychoanalysis. But it seems to me another irony that relational or intersubjective psychoanalysis is in danger of derailing and getting stuck in its own "Schibboleth" with *intersubjective relation* as the new "truth" you have to pray to. However, we do not need to confess, we do not need a strong belief system. We can afford to abdicate any ideology because we have better things on our side: there is the factual reality of social life; there is the inherent intersubjectivity of the self, of human emotions, language, communication, and acting; and there are the convergent findings of modern human sciences that mental life is basically relational. That should be enough—a sufficiently strong fundament for relational psychoanalysis.

But what about therapy? Psychotherapy is not a science, isn't! There is of course a fundamental difference between a scientific attitude toward basic theory (or metapsychology, which Freud used to ground in the scientific knowledge of his times) and clinical sensibilities in the psychoanalytic process. Psychotherapy is a human encounter of a very special sort, with a very special end, in a very special process: the therapeutic encounter is an intersubjective piece of art. Basic theory is about the developing, structuring, and operating of the psyche in general: it is based on contemporary knowledge gathered by human sciences. Building and incorporating theories is different from treating patients; psychotherapy is not applied science. But what then is the connection between the two, between our basic theory on the human mind we once called metapsychology and the human encounter we call psychoanalysis?

Our theories influence the way we think about what is going on between us and our patients, our conscious and unconscious; our implicit or explicit theories modify our attitude, perspective, and behavior as therapists—they are all experienced by our patients. This may be the reason that case studies of the Kleinians quite obviously differ from those of self psychologists or relationalists or classical Freudians—because they are theory biased. This is why we have to consider and reconsider those theories in order to discover our blind-spots preventing us from really seeing the patient and how he is relating to us just as we are to him. The practice of this permanent reconsideration is not limited to the critical self-reflection of our countertransference or to supervision; it goes far beyond: psychoanalysts have to be aware and to receive what is going on in neighboring sciences dealing with the human mind.

What does the view across the borders of our discipline reveal? In short: that modern human sciences interdisciplinarily converge in that the human mind is a dynamic relational network objectively based on material processes in the brain and subjectively constructed by the successive internalization of interactions that are stored on different memory levels. This is the summed-up contribution of contemporary infant research, nonreductionist neurobiology, and developmental psychology to the discovery of the human mind. And we should be highly sensitive to this contribution because it may change our own psychoanalytic theory; it may show that some of our suggestions about the psychic condition are just wrong and untenable. It may even support some of our convictions. We should use "good" empirical findings and "well-justified" theories, which means valid conceptions in the field of human sciences to validate our own convictions. So it is good news for the relational approach in psychoanalysis that according to the findings of other human sciences, the mental world seems to be constructed like an inner relational world. But this convergence is no coincidence. The rise of the relational idea—the intersubjective turn in psychoanalysis—began in sync with the interactive turn in infant research.

In the history of psychoanalysis infant research had been disrespectfully called "only observational" and "nonpsychoanalytic": Melanie Klein versus John Bowlby; the early Heinz Kohut versus the "baby-watchers"; André Green versus Daniel Stern; Hanna Segal versus the whole Mischpoke of Balint, Kohut, Winnicott, and the British Middle group, which she blamed for missing the psychoanalytic "truth" and for thinking and acting in an "unpsychoanalytical" way by recognizing the personal influence of the analyst on the therapeutic process (Segal, 2006).[2] The developmental theory of relational psychoanalysis is dominantly based on attachment theory and infant-parent research (see Beebe and Lachmann, 2003). And it is not by

---

[2]"In further developments, the Middle Group... established a new model of the mind, deriving from Ferenczi and developed by Balint, Winnicott, and, later in the United States, by Kohut.... A new concern emerged... that did not rest on attaining truth and that considered the personal influences of the analyst—e.g., his support, advice, and comfort—to be integral to the analytic process. Here the changes in technique were of a kind that made them essentially nonanalytic. They went against the psychoanalytic effort to bring about change through the search for truth" (Segal, 2006, see pp. 288ff.).

contingency that Stephen Mitchell passionately honored the work of Bowlby in his illuminating book *Relationality: From Attachment to Intersubjectivity* (2000)[3] and that Jessica Benjamin in *The Bonds of Love* (1988) relied on the peculiar paradoxes of Winnicott, whose developmental theory she continues to adopt until last.

On the other hand, contemporary psychoanalysts, including relationalists, are at least skeptical toward empirical research on psychoanalytic process and outcome. Irwin Hoffman earned standing ovations for his antiscientific talk "Doublethinking Our Way to 'Scientific' Legitimacy: The Desiccation of Human Experience" at the 2007 winter meeting of the American Psychoanalytic Association (Hoffman, 2009). What attitudes and values of analysts may have been reflected in their spontaneous applause? Arnold Cooper suggested "that the audience was reassured in their ignorance" (Cooper, 2008, p. 5). Denigrating evidence-based systematic research as a submission to political pressure Hoffman implicitly even recalled George Orwell's (1949) objection to totalitarian thought control in *1984*—"doublethink" is an Orwellian term—in order to place psychoanalysis off limits for scientific study in the name of human dignity. In his talk on the perils of systematic empirical research "potentially damaging both to the development of our understanding of the analytic process itself and to the quality of our clinical work" (Hoffman, 2009, p. 1044) and allegedly dehumanizing patients by using classifications of mental disorders Hoffman emphasizes the "uniqueness of each patient" (p. 1059) and "the 'consequential uniqueness' of each interaction" (p. 1043) arguing that "systematic empirical studies simply do not control for the consequential uniqueness of the analyst, of the patient, of their relationship, and of the moment" (p. 1050).

Rejecting the "authoritarian objectivism" of empirical studies and advocating single case studies instead he ignores the serious and well-known problems of case studies, especially the fact that they usually tell not the history of an interaction between analysand and analyst (cf. Kaechele, Schachter, and Thomae, 2009, 2012). Those studies are inevitably filled with the reporting analysts' uncontrolled subjectivism: implicit or explicit theories, blind spots, lapses of memory, sometimes self-righteousness. As we all know this subjectivism often generates those familiar and usually fruitless debates at case presentations Hoffman seems to appreciate by arguing that the ambiguity and openness of the "data" from single case studies would not "prevent people from mounting critiques of the work, from suggesting alternative formulations of what went on in the process, and from offering suggestions as to better ways the analyst might have intervened and participated" (Hoffman, 2009, p. 1052). David Wolitzky (2010) is right in his "Critique on Hoffman's Paper" that "claims of therapeutic effectiveness based only on clinical case reports can readily be dismissed as analysts' self-congratulatory testimonials" (p. 12).

Irwin Hoffman—he once shared Merton Gill's empirical approach to psychotherapy before turning to his own hermeneutic epistemology of "dialectical constructivism"—triggered a lot of critical reactions among psychodynamic researchers. They ask for more science, not less. So do I: the undecidable controversy between competing schools on psychoanalytic convictions and values should be transformed into an accountable discourse about scientifically validating our specific theories of the human mind and the efficiency of psychoanalytic treatment—instead of validating both by our own case material. We know and we should be aware that this material does not exclusively belong to the patient; it is profoundly "contaminated"—not only through

---

[3]Mitchell's *Relationality* (2000) is a highly "ecumenical" book, which I had the pleasure to translate into German.

our conceptions and personal attitudes, which are consciously as well as unconsciously experienced by the patient, but also by the relationship itself: by the interaction between patient and therapist, which can be carefully observed and examined.

THERE IS MORE THAN TWO PEOPLE RELATING TO EACH OTHER: REALITY AS THE MISSING THIRD IN RELATIONAL PSYCHOANALYSIS

As I mentioned previously, the relational approach is in good concordance with contemporary human sciences. Our social constructivism is not and has to be reflected upon. This epistemology has once been useful to deconstruct the classical idea of an objective therapist observing the inner world of his or her patient. Psychoanalysis is a common enterprise of two people. Nowadays we know that what happens in the psychoanalytical situation is coconstructed. However, we overdrew our radical constructivist view, which is still prevalent in relational psychoanalysis and urgently needs to be reconsidered. We went too far in epistemologically dismissing reality itself. The fuzzy debate on the third in psychoanalysis, which emerged in the 1990s, is an enduring consequence of this dismissal. In this section I make a plea for reality as the third beyond subjectivity and intersubjectivity (cf. Cavell, 2006b).

Recognizing the relational findings of infant research and the insights in the inherent intersubjectivity of psychic functions and structures we had to learn that inner reality is not self-contained—as the Kleinians still keep on claiming (cf. Cavell, 2006a, p. 1)—but deeply connected with external reality, connected in fact to the deepest levels of the unconscious self. This is why we claim that the psyche itself is functioning as a "social network" (Altmeyer, 2011) and have chosen the metaphor of the "interconnected soul" (*Die vernetzte Seele*) as the title of our anthology on the intersubjective turn of psychoanalysis (Altmeyer and Thomae, 2006a). This volume includes Jessica Benjamin's brilliant essay "Beyond Doer and Done to: An Intersubjective View of Thirdness" (Benjamin, 2004), which we now take a closer look at.

In her essay Jessica Benjamin (2004) depicts mental thirdness as intersubjective and cocreated on a range from the affective attunement between mother and child (its earliest formation) to highly elaborated forms of a symbolic or even moral third (including differentiation). And this specific kind of a third is also represented within the therapeutic situation where it shows up as the mutual recognition between therapist and patient evidenced by their common surrender to the analytic process: "In the space of thirdness, we are not holding onto a third; we are . . . sur-surrendering to it" (p. 8). In her effort "not to reify the third, but to consider it as a principle, function, or relationship, rather than as a 'thing' in the way that theory or rules of technique are things" (p. 7), Jessica designs a third that enables "the felt experience of the other as a separate yet connected being with whom we are acting reciprocally" (p. 6), a shared third that "mediates 'I and Thou'" (p. 8). Thus the intersubjective third arranges for two people to be and to stay together and plays a crucible part in the well-functioning of human relationships, serving as a strong remedy against the disintegration and disruption of interpersonal relations, against the breakdown of mutual recognition she already described in *The Bonds of Love* (1988; cf. Honneth, 1992). Without this connecting force of the shared third, interpersonal relations would fall to pieces, the therapeutic process would end in misunderstandings, impasses or deadlocks, each party blaming the other for the failure.

Considering the third as an observing function of the neutral analyst (classical model) or as a way the analyst relates internally to psychoanalytic theory (Kleinian model) may lead to a situation where the patient feels "excluded, and therefore attacks" this kind of a third (Benjamin, 2004, p. 20)—as Jessica Benjamin rightly detected in a case study reported by Feldman (1993)—and the therapist gets involved in malignant enactments while desperately trying to maintain his hierarchic role as the one who knows better. If the patient cannot participate in the dialogue between analyst and theory he may become the child who is excluded from the relation between father and mother, unable to see or to hear what they secretly are doing together. Stephen A. Mitchell (1997) cited the same case study of Feldman before generalizing his suspicion "that a certain portion of the destructive envy that is so prominent a feature in Kleinian case descriptions is an iatrogenic consequence of a rigid hierarchy in the definition of analytic roles" (p. 141).

The contemporary Kleinians of British provenience tend to model the clinical triangulation as a triple relation of a specific kind. At first the relation between patient and therapist is conceptualized along the line of early childhood, precisely as the relation between infant and primary object, that is, the breast of the mother. Thus the analytic dyad becomes the "nursing-couple" (Joseph, 1989, 256 ff.) with the "alimentary milk" of the "good breast" delivered by the analyst via true interpretation or threatened by the "poisoned milk" of the "bad breast" unconsciously experienced as such and refused by the patient. Because milk/interpretation comes from a higher source, namely, the Kleinian or Bionian theory, a third party is involved that completes the triad taking the form of patient/infant—analyst/mother—analyst/mother in sync with psychoanalytical theory/father. No wonder that the excluded patient feels infantilized by the oedipal couple with the options of either subjugating or attacking if not leaving the field.

Missing the intersubjective third within the psychoanalytic process—this is what Benjamin (2004) essentially is pointing out in her article—leaves only the choice between to do or to be done to: becoming either the perpetrator or the victim. Thus she adds intersubjectivity as a shared third, shared by the two subjectivities involved so that her formula for triangulation appears to read: subjective self—subjective other—intersubjectivity. However, we are always doing or being done to in rather specific surroundings and under rather specific circumstances. Perpetrating or being victimized does rarely happen without a relation to a certain real environment. Subjectivity and intersubjectivity are not enough: we act and interact not in an empty space but in a material and social reality—a factual reality we sometimes are not fully aware of.

It is certainly true that our views of reality may differ and that meanings have to be negotiated between the partners of the psychoanalytical process. But we do not get rid of reality itself when we acknowledge our different views of reality and concede negotiable meanings. Phil Ringstrom is right when he suggests that each of us at best can only have "our perspective on reality" and that there is subjective meaning in each of our different "versions of reality" (personal communication from December 2009 in the context of the aforementioned IARPP online colloquium of 2009 I take a closer look at in the next section), but this does not dismiss reality in its own right. We should not conflate objective reality with our different constructions and coconstructions of reality: constructed is only the meaning, the perspective, not reality itself.

So what about the objective world outside the mutual relationship of two people or in and between groups? When people interact, when they talk with each other or work together, when they argue and exchange ideas, feelings, and opinions, they usually refer to the real world that they have in common. And even if they might look at it differently they hopefully come to know that they share the same world they live in together. It seems to me that Jessica Benjamin lacks a concept of reality in her relational approach to the psychoanalytic third, that she is missing a concept of objectivity in addition to subjectivity and intersubjectivity. This is not only an epistemological question of purely academic meaning and possibly oversophisticated. Beyond the sensibilities of our psychoanalytic epistemology it is a question of enabling psychoanalysis to return to a scientific discourse we left long time ago, a question of replacing our discipline within an interdisciplinary community, a question of regaining reputation in a modern society of knowledge.

In order to illustrate what I mean by the real world, by the field of objectivity beyond the fields of subjectivity and intersubjectivity, let us take a short look on the enduring conflict in the Middle East, where Jessica Benjamin is deeply engaged. She does (and in fact must) have a view on the real situation in the "Holy Land," on the long history of the conflict, and on a possibly better future. When she is passionately advocating a new era of peace and reconciliation, when she personally is intervening as a moderator between Palestinians and Israelis in order to bring the fighting parties together, to understand and respect each other, she in fact must (and certainly does) have such a view on a multifaceted reality there: the continuing occupation on the West Bank, the Jewish settlements in occupied areas, the treatment of the Palestinians and the Arab population in Israel on the one side; the persisting attacks against Israel from Gaza, the anti-Semitic charta of Hamas and its financial and ideological support by Iran, the Islamization of the Palestinian movement, the corruption of the Fatah administration on the other side. There are many more facts you have to deal with in such a conflict as the situation in Jerusalem, the question of water from the Jordan River, the growing religious induction of the conflict, the obscure interests of all the allies engaged, and—last but not least—a substantial amount of irrationality on both sides. It is necessary but not sufficient that the parties respect and recognize each other. They have as well to accept facts and mutually recognize realities. Thus intersubjectivity is not enough to solve the conflict between Israel and the Palestinian people in the Middle East. It needs a concept of reality shared by both sides in order to come to a peaceful arrangement.

Far from criticizing Jessica Benjamin's engagement—which on the contrary I am strongly in favor of and engaged myself by occasionally commenting on the conflict in German newspapers[4]—I use this disastrous conflict between the two warring groups to make a plea for the recognition of reality as the missing third beyond subjectivity and intersubjectivity. Jessica has her intellectual roots in the Frankfurt school of critical theory, which used to analyze social as well as mental structures in the materialistic terms of the early Marx enlarged by a freudomarxistic version of sociology and a social philosophy of its own. *The Bonds of Love* (Benjamin, 1988) is reality soaked in a way that we learn a lot about the history, the sociodynamics, and the power play of gender relations while rereading her book. Thus she might consider enriching her formula of triangulation *subjective self—subjective other—intersubjectivity* with reality as the third, which would then read *subjectivity—intersubjectivity—objectivity*.

We can shed more light on those epistemological distinctions with regard to modern infant research. How do infants come to learn that there is an objective outside world? The surprising answer to this difficult question is given by the British psychoanalyst and developmental theorist

---

[4]Cf. *Kultur der Niederlage* [Culture of Defeat] (Altmeyer, 2006) and *Antisemitismus von links* [Anti-Semitism from the Left] (Altmeyer, 2009); both articles appeared in the Berlin *tageszeitung* (taz).

Peter Hobson in his book *The Cradle of Thought: Exploring the Origins of Thinking* (2002): not in a sheer maturation process but within a triangular relationship. In the first months of life the baby is restricted to dyadic relationships; he or she communicates *either* with mother (or father or any other person he relates to emotionally) *or* with an object of his interest. Only later the infant starts communicating *with his mother about an object* they both look at, a third in their common field of vision and interest. Let's say the third is a baby bottle. The infant may register that the mother has an approving attitude toward that bottle, which is different from his own rejecting attitude. Thus the baby learns that there are two attitudes toward the same object. In fact he learns that his seemingly natural attitude is only a perspective. He learns more generally that there are perspectives in the case of the bottle: two different subjective perspectives—the negative one of his own and the positive one of his mother—but only one real object. He learns at the end that meaning is not in the object, not part of the object, but attributed by himself or his mother. The world has meaning not only for me but also for others, and the different meaning of an object for the other may change its meaning for me.

This is the birth of symbolic thinking: allowing the child to separate meaning from things and subject from object and negotiating meaning and perspectives with the mother. According to Hobson (2002) and challenging traditional theory the child is not adopting the different perspective of the mother and abandoning his own. He or she does not capitulate. Far from overtaking the perspective of the other, the child begins to think. However, this early process of experiencing an independent reality is based on a good-enough relationship between mother and child; otherwise an endless "arguing" will begin, usually ending with the baby desperately being forced to drink by an equally desperate mother.

Isn't this what relational psychoanalysis is all about: two people in a good-enough relationship bringing their subjective perspectives into communication—in the unique psychoanalytic setting with complementary but asymmetric roles. Both are negotiating meaning by intersubjectively referring to an external reality. And this is what the legendary Sufi master from Mali Tierno Bokar meant by saying, "There are three truths: my truth, your truth, and the truth" (Hampaté Bâ, 1957). He was adding the truth of objective reality to our unquestionable certainties in order to avoid our getting lost in mere subjectivity and intersubjectivity. Thus reality may actually be "the fact of life," the missing triangulating third in psychoanalysis that we all need to recognize.

THERE IS NO PERSON WITHOUT A HISTORY OF LIFE: THE ATTACHMENT OF RELATIONAL PSYCHOANALYSIS TO THE PAST

To look at the question of reality more precisely and in our familiar context let us go back to the clinical field where in the course of its intersubjective turn contemporary psychoanalysis has been focusing on what really happens between analyst and analysand. This therapeutic relationship—mutual but asymmetrical by its very nature, modulated by specific rules and roles—has no end in itself. It may be considered a conversational medium, a kind of "broken" mirror in which the history of the patient's relational life can be reexamined and reflected upon by both partners in a particular exchange. And in his or her relation to the therapist the patient hopefully develops new mental representations that will allow different ways of relating to other people. Psychoanalysis is neither about endlessly "just analyzing" nor about the pure pleasure of being together and relating to each other: work has to be done. The end of the analytic process is to enable the patient to "reappropriate" those relational experiences that have been repressed, denied, projected, or otherwise excluded from the self in the past: to bring into communication and consciousness what has been mentally excommunicated, to reintegrate what has been disintegrated during earlier life and therefore keeps on unconsciously affecting the actual life. Thus a relational perspective in psychoanalysis will never get rid of the real past in favor of the present or the future—neither in terms of its clinical theory nor in terms of its metapsychology: "Every reification means falling into oblivion" as Theodor W. Adorno and Max Horkheimer (1947, p. 263) once asserted in "Dialektik der Aufklaerung": "Alle Verdinglichung ist ein Vergessen."

Contrary to classical psychoanalytic theory and in accordance with the findings of modern human sciences such as infant research and neurobiology, we suppose that the dynamic unconscious does not consist of drives and their destinies but of relational experiences including both—the self and the other—in interaction. This is why relational psychoanalysis needs a developmental theory based on empirical research of interactions between the child, his or her caretakers, and the environment. We need to abandon untenable metapsychological suppositions: the inner world of the infant is interpersonal, not monadic; subjectivity is emerging from intersubjective contexts; psychic development means processing interactions and transforming them into mental structures.

That is, by the way, what Freud said in *The Ego and the Id* (1923): the ego is the sediment of former object-choices, containing the history of our object-relations. In modern terms we suggest that it is the history of mentally "dispossessed" interactions that is probably sedimented in implicit memory where it may determine unconsciously the patient's present life. It is the history of a somehow derailed track of interactions, mentally excluded, locked in the darkness of the unconscious, which is hopefully enlightened, reconsidered, and freed during the analytic process. The end of this process is marked by the analysand's mental "repossession" of his interaction-history—in the helpful presence of an analyst whom he is emotionally relating to and who is emotionally relating to him. The theoretical shift of psychoanalysis, our relational turn, is from drive to relation, not from past to present.

The initial statement opening the 2009 IARPP online colloquium on the past I mentioned earlier declared that "achieving knowledge of how one's past affects the present" was one thing, "establishing awareness of the transformative potential of human relationships" the other (IARPP, 2009). This seems to be a false opposition, which needs to be integrated. Because we know how crucial good-enough relationships are for the development of the individual self and how badly the failures and disruptions of childhood relations affect the growing self, we need to be highly aware of the patient's relational past. Because this past affects his or her present also in the transference of the analytic situation, we can experience such relational past via empathy, countertransference reactions or enactments of all kinds. The curative value of psychoanalysis is in the transformation of the "old" (neurotic, psychotic or otherwise disturbed) relational world of the patient including his or her disturbed self-relation into a "new" (healthier, more adequate, less disturbed) world of relations.

In the course of this debate Doris Silverman worried about developmental theory neglecting the unique individuality of human beings: "If you believe in the exquisite uniqueness of each individual," she stated, "the idea of a coherent developmental theory obscures the matchlessness of the individual. I argue, instead, that a position that considers empirical data should not maintain a linear perspective or a credo of one line of development for all. Change and transformation is critical in understanding development'' (personal communication, December 2009). It was the same argument against developmental theory that has been used by Hoffman (2009) against systematic research: the uniqueness of the individual. Those worries reveal an obvious misunderstanding of human science, as if an empirically based developmental theory would be leveling the differences between human beings because it makes general statements. A general statement of modern infant research, for example, is this: There is primary intersubjectivity, not primary narcissism (cf. Trevarthen, 1979; Altmeyer, 2000; Dornes, 2000). Another one: Psychic growth is mediated by human relations and interactions that are internalized and represented as relational knowledge in the memory systems (cf. Stern, 1985). The difference between individuals, Doris Silverman is insisting on, lies in the peculiar kind of such earlier processes of internalization we clinically try to discover with our patients in order to invent new ones.

The analytic process should allow for new experiences in the present and future by revoking irrational constraints and suspending the determining power of the past. The working-through of his or her past permits the patient to overcome what he might experience as a "causality of nature" and to transform it to a "causality of destiny" like Juergen Habermas (2005) once put it referring to Kant and Hegel. After the analytic process the individual should be able to tell the story of his or her real life as truthfully as possible, fairly corresponding to his personal history from the past up to the present. It is a story of his life reconsidered, reconstructed as well as constructed in a "Winnicottian" sense.

This kind of reconsideration makes the psychoanalytic process not just another encounter where two people talk with each other intensively. In their dyadic effort there is always a third both analyst and analysand jointly refer to, namely, the outer reality that can take shape in many forms: the past of the patient, his or her actual social reality, the objective world both partners share with each other—up to the objective limitations of the analytic setting. This is why Helmut Thomae (1999) once called the analytic dyad a "triad minus one": the "one" stands for the missing yet present reality in the psychoanalytic dyad. Focusing only on the "here and now" of the analytic encounter runs the risk of forgetting why analyst and analysand come and work together. Overstressing the relationship runs the risk for the dyadic encounter to become symbiotic or even incestuous.

RECONSIDERING THE EPISTEMOLOGY OF CONTEMPORARY PSYCHOANALYSIS

Psychoanalytic pluralism has grown over the last 30 years. Influential schools of contemporary psychoanalysis that put the analytic encounter itself in the center of considerations tend at the same time to dismiss objective reality from theory and clinic substituting it by all kinds of "third." The whole discussion on the "third in psychoanalysis" may be considered a symptom of this dismissal, the sprawling debate as a side effect of a delayed effort to keep up with a fashionable postmodernism in social sciences and cultural studies that was already in decline. Radical constructivism, its leading epistemology, had declared terms like reality, truth, or past are illusions: it's all constructed. When past, truth, or reality do not exist, no wonder that the psychoanalytical goal to truthfully reconstruct a personal life story becomes a myth (cf. Bohleber, 2007).

However, there are differences between schools. Constructing instead of reconstructing, neglecting the real world and concentrating on the analytic situation itself—this shift had different outcomes, according to the theory applied. In the narrative tradition an analyst is satisfied when he or she together with his patient can coconstruct a coherent story without necessarily referring to an objective reality and irrespective of how the life story of this patient might really have been. Thus the biographical narrative may contain a subjective coherence and may be intersubjectively authorized by the analytical couple but it may at the same time fail the biographical truth. Such narratives can be deeply tempted by social tendencies toward self design and identity construction. Psychoanalysis in cooperation or collusion with these tendencies of the "Zeitgeist" loses its claim of being a science of enlightenment; instead of strengthening the self it might contribute to that defensive façade-like construction Winnicott (1960) once called the "false self."

The contemporary Kleinians (Schafer, 1997) on the other hand—some of them inspired by Bion's mystic philosophy of "no memory, no desire" (Bion, 1967), even suggesting that "history is rumor" (Grotstein, 2007)—conceptualize the analytic situation as an enduring early infancy: the patient is the infant; the analyst is the mother, delivering good (or bad) milk through interpretation. But what about the missing third, keeping the analytical relation in a certain distance? The third is the Kleinian analyst's own theory: he or she is in constant dialogue with what might upset the patient. Consequently we learn in clinical vignettes of the Kleinian School much more about the analytic microcosm of transference and countertransference than about the biography of the patient. Significant and revealing that transference phenomena, which once were understood as resistance against unbearable memories, are now under suspicion for being in the service of resistance against the transference-relation (an elaborated critique in Bohleber, 2010).

Self psychology, which has developed an intersubjective systems theory, also tends to fade out the objectivity of outer reality, including the objective reality of the patient's past. Driven by the hermeneutic phenomenology of Hans-Georg Gadamer (1975), it represents an overempathetic conception of intersubjectivity by destroying "myths" like the isolated self or the neutral, indifferent analyst but also "the myth of objectivity" and replacing those myths by deep intersubjective experience. According to Orange, Stolorow, and Atwood (2006) only the intimate folding and interweaving of both the analyst's and the analysand's personal world of experiences make the analytic process work. In a personal case study Donna Orange reports of a severely traumatized patient who needed a therapist talking about his own traumata in order to come in emotional touch with another. As if this kind of self-disclosure by the therapist—which seems to us far across the borderline—only would open an access to the inner world of the patient.

Relational psychoanalysis, although competing with an intersubjectively evolving self psychology on the ownership of intersubjectivism (see Benjamin, 2004, p. 6), tends to share with its competitor the shading of an objective reality, which is obscured by its constructivist epistemology. The other—the object in classical terms—is a subject in his or her own right. Because every human being has his own subjective perspective on reality, in psychotherapy, the patient as well as the therapist, the analytical process aims at the intersubjective widening of this restricted perspective, restricted on both sides. Thus, because "outer" reality does not matter and subjective "inner" reality is not enough, intersubjectivity is considered the third so that the relational mental triangle is formed by the patient (one subject), the therapist (second subject) and their mutual exchange in the process creating their relationship (intersubjectivity) leaving hardly space for objectivity.

In accordance with neighboring human sciences we propose the slightly different relational triangulation of *subjectivity—intersubjectivity—objectivity*. Epistemologically we favor a "weak constructivism" following the paradoxes of Winnicott, which might offer a common ground with Jessica Benjamin: There is a real world outside but it has to be invented. There is a significant past that can be reconstructed but must be constructed at the same time. There is a biographical truth that can be found but has also to be created within the therapeutic process. The biographical structure of our individuality is contained in all realms of memory, explicit and implicit, declarative and procedural, episodic and semantic. That said, relational psychoanalysis should claim that our discipline as a clinical enterprise keeps closely attached to the present and past reality of the patient and as a contemporary human science keeps in dialogue and cooperates with other human sciences so that we can elaborate and validate our metapsychology, development theory, and clinical conceptions.

CURB YOUR ENTHUSIASM: SOME REMARKS ON THE MODERNIZATION OF PSYCHOANALYSIS

Modernizing psychoanalysis (cf. Altmeyer, 2004) is manifold, inevitable in order to survive, and in fact proceeding. There seem to me three interwoven lines of modernization:

- *Common ground:* On the first line our disintegrated discipline is reintegrating under the overarching paradigm of intersubjectivity and—hopefully—will reintegrate institutionally as well. We are reapproaching our "common ground."
- *Human science:* On the second line there are strong efforts to regain its scientific status both as a proven treatment of mental disorders controlled by research of clinical process and outcome and as a basic science of mental functioning, which is not self-contained but deeply related to the outside world.
- *Interdisciplinarity:* On the third line psychoanalysis is reestablishing the interdisciplinary discourse with the academic community abandoning the self-referential track of collecting idiosyncratic knowledge outside the framework of universities and other research institutions.

However, there is also strong resistance against modernizing psychoanalysis because this ongoing progress is touching and unsettling the well-cultivated identity of many psychoanalysts (cf. Bohleber, 2010). At least three different kinds of such countercurrents—interwoven as well—can be outlined: a fundamentalist one against the "contamination" of psychoanalytical truth, an epistemological one against "scientism," and an identity-based one against the loss of a privileged access to the psyche:

- *Psychoanalytic fundamentalism:* The most powerful resistance against the modernization of psychoanalysis comes from the Neo-Kleinian School (Betty Joseph, Elizabeth Bott-Spillius, Michael Feldman, John Steiner, Ronald Britton, to name only a few whose works are too numerous to list them all) adhering to their special ontology of a self-contained innerworld founded on speculations of a dominating death drive and its derivatives in the emerging psyche and insisting on the existence of a paranoid-schizoid and a depressive position while denouncing discordant findings of infant or brain research as irrelevant to psychoanalysis being a discipline of its own right. Because the contemporary Kleinianism likes to speak in the name of "true analysis" or "psychoanalytic truth" (Segal, 2006), which have to be defended against all contamination, especially against interactional flattening, and because the Kleinians—under the influence of the late Bion (1992)—tend to mystify psychoanalytic insights as an exclusive knowledge of revelation, Helmut Thomae and I (2006a, p. III; new foreword 2010) called this current a countermodern "psychoanalytic version of fundamentalism."

- *Preoccupation toward science:* A second countercurrent against the modernization of psychoanalysis is founded on an antiscientific resentment, an affective resistance against evidence-based research allegedly dictated only by the "Zeitgeist." This tendency resides not only in the erratic French psychoanalysis, from Lacan up to Laplanche, Chasseguet-Smirgel, or André Green (cf. Altmeyer and Thomae, 2006b) but seems endemic also to American intersubjectivism (to aggregate relational psychoanalysis, intersubjective systems theory, Interpersonalists, and the Postkleinian approach) where it is philosophically armed with hermeneutics, phenomenology, or social constructivism in order to reject the alleged empirism, positivism, or essentialism of the scientific approach.
- *Fear of identity-dissolution:* The third resistance originates in our professional identity possibly being threatened by a modernized psychoanalysis. One is worried that the intrapsychic core of psychoanalysis might get lost, our peculiar concept of the unconscious damaged, when we address ourselves to the "superficial" phenomena of interaction and communication. One is worried that embracing methods of observation might devaluate empathy and introspection as our legitimate sources of knowledge. And one is especially worried that the process of modernization would endanger the whole profession at the end: psychoanalysts should better defend their privileged access to psychic truth instead of sharing and diluting our wisdom with other human sciences.

In a certain sense those worries appear historically comprehensible. They indicate a latent fear of losses: the loss of interpretational sovereignty, the loss of personal and professional identity, but also loss of social power and cultural dominance. Because psychoanalysis has already lost much of its former influence by not keeping up with the changes in modern societies of knowledge, we risk losing even more by anxiously defending what we are and what we have instead of renewing and developing our discipline in an interdisciplinary sense and on an empirical basis.

Contemporary psychoanalysis is still suffering from its own "overspecification" and "overcomplexity," as Peter Fonagy (2010, p. 2) recently brought it to the point, an "oversupply" of theoretical and clinical concepts generated by the plurality of divergent schools. On the other side there is an obvious lack of core theory, which could be expanded over generations—as is the case in other sciences—by the convincing logics of good-enough research. Thus we have to reduce our overweight body of knowledge in order to come to the core of psychoanalysis. Without such a core theory we remain in a situation of incessantly reinventing the wheel once more. Relationality belongs certainly to psychoanalytic core theory. But mental relatedness reaches much beyond the relation of the self to the other (i.e., intersubjectivity); it includes consciously and unconsciously the psychic relation of individuals and groups to the real world, which should be part of our core theory too. This is why the complex relations between subjectivity, intersubjectivity, and objectivity need further examination in a relational psychoanalysis, modernized. Let us go, Jessica.

REFERENCES

Adorno, T. W. (1952). Die revidierte Psychoanalyse. In: *Theodor W. Adorno: Gesammelte Schriften, Vol. 8*, ed. R. Tiedemann, Frankfurt/Main, Germany: Suhrkamp, 1997, pp. 20–41.

——— & Horkheimer, M. (1947). Dialektik der Aufklaerung: Philosophische Fragmente. In: *Theodor W. Adorno: Gesammelte Schriften, Vol. 3*, ed. R. Tiedemann, Frankfurt/Main, Germany: Suhrkamp, 1997, pp. 7–295.

Altmeyer, M. (2000). Narzissmus und Objekt: Ein intersubjektives Verstaendnis der Selbstbezogenheit. Göttingen, Germany: Vandenhoeck u. Ruprecht.

———. (2004). Inklusion, Wissenschaftsorientierung, Intersubjektivitaet: Modernisierungstendenzen im psychoanalytischen Gegenwartsdiskurs. *Psyche–Z Psychoanal*, 58, 1111–1125.

———. (2006). Kultur der Niederlage. In: tageszeitung (taz) Berlin 07.08.2006.

———. (2009). Antisemitismus von links. In: Tageszeitung (taz) Berlin 23.01.2009.

———. (2011). Soziales Netzwerk Psyche: Versuch einer Standortbestimmung der modernen Psychoanalyse. *Forum der Psychoanalyse*, 27, 107–127.

——— & Thomae, H., eds. (2006a). *Die vernetzte Seele: Die intersubjektive Wende in der Psychoanalyse*, 2nd ed. with a new foreword. Stuttgart, Germany: Klett-Cotta.

——— & Thomae, H. (2006b). Einführung: Psychoanalyse und Intersubjektivitaet. In: *Die vernetzte Seele: Die intersubjektive Wende in der Psychoanalyse*, 2nd ed. with a new foreword, eds. M. Altmeyer & H. Thomae, Stuttgart, Germany: Klett-Cotta, pp. 7–31.

Aron, L. (1996). *A Meeting of Minds: Mutuality in Psychoanalysis*. Hillsdale, NJ: Analytic Press.

Beebe, B. & Lachmann, F. (2003). Die relationale Wende in der Psychoanalyse. Ein dyadischer Systemansatz aus Sicht der Säuglingsforschung [The relational turn in psychoanalysis: A dyadic systems view from infant research]. In: *Die vernetzte Seele: Die intersubjektive Wende in der Psychoanalyse*, eds. M. Altmeyer & H. Thomae. Stuttgart, Germany: Klett-Cotta, 2006, pp. 122–159.

Benjamin, J. (1988). *The Bonds of Love: Psychoanalysis, Feminism, and the Problem of Domination*. New York, NY: Pantheon. German: *Die Fesseln der Liebe: Psychoanalyse, Feminismus und das Problem der Macht*. Frankfurt/Main, Germany: Stroemfeld/Roter Stern, 1990.

———. (2004). Tue ich oder wird mir angetan? Ein intersubjektives Triangulierungskonzept [Beyond doer and done to: An intersubjective view of thirdness]. In: *Die vernetzte Seele: Die intersubjektive Wende in der Psychoanalyse*, eds. M. Altmeyer & H. Thomae, Stuttgart, Germany: Klett-Cotta, 2006, pp. 65–107.

Bion, W. R. (1967). Notes on memory and desire. *Psychoanalytic Forum*, 2, 279–281.

———. (1992). *Cogitations*. London, UK: Karnac Books.

Bohleber, W. (2007). Erinnerung, Trauma und kollektives Gedaechtnis: Der Kampf um die Erinnerung in der Psychoanalyse. *Psyche–Z Psychoanal*, 61, 293–321.

———. (2010). *Destructiveness, Intersubjectivity and Trauma: The Identity Crisis of Modern Psychoanalysis*. London, UK: Karnac Books.

Bråten, S. (1992). The virtual other in infants' minds and social feelings. In: *The Dialogical Alternative: Towards a Theory of Language and Mind*, ed. A. Wold, Oslo, Norway: Scandinavian University Press, pp. 77–97.

Brooks, D. (2011). *The Social Animal: The Hidden Sources of Love, Character, and Achievement*. New York, NY: Random House.

Buber, M. (1923). Ich und Du. In: *Das Dialogische Prinzip*, Vol. 4. Heidelberg, Germany: Lambert Schneider, 1979, pp. 7–121.

Cavell, M. (2006a). *Becoming a Subject: Reflections in Philosophy and Psychoanalysis*. New York, NY: Oxford University Press.

———. (2006b). Subjektivitaet, Intersubjektivitaet und die Frage der Realitaet in der Psychoanalyse. In: *Die vernetzte Seele: Die intersubjektive Wende in der Psychoanalyse*, eds. M. Altmeyer, & H. Thomae, Stuttgart, Germany: Klett-Cotta, pp. 178–200.

Cooper, A. M. (2008). American psychoanalysis today: A plurality of orthodoxies. *J. Am. Acad Psychoanal Dyn Psychiatry*, 36(2), 235–253.

Damasio, A. (2004). The neurobiology of emotions. International Psychoanalytic Association (IPA), Plenary Address 43th Congress, March, New Orleans, LA.

Dornes, M. (2000). Die emotionale Welt des Kindes. Frankfurt/Main, Germany: Fischer.

―――. (2002). Der virtuelle Andere: Aspekte vorsprachlicher Intersubjektivitaet. *Forum der Psychoanalyse*, 18, 303–331.
―――. (2006). *Die Seele des Kindes*. Frankfurt/Main, Germany: Fischer.
―――. (2012). *Die Modernisierung der Seele*. Frankfurt/Main, Germany: Fischer.
Feldman, M. (1993). The dynamics of reassurance. In: *The Contemporary Kleinians of London*, ed. R. Schafer, Madison, CT: International Universities Press, pp. 321–344.
Fonagy, P. (2010). Unconscious theories of psychoanalysts expressed as metaphors. Unpublished manuscript.
Freud, S. (1923). The ego and the id. *Standard Edition*, 19. London, UK: Hogarth Press, 1961, pp. 1–66.
―――. (1930). Civilization and its discontents. *Standard Edition*, 21. London, UK: Hogarth Press, 1961, pp. 64–145.
―――. (1934). Letter to Saul Rosenzweig, February 28, 1934. Quoted by Peter Gay in *Freud: A Life for Our Time*. New York, NY: Norton, 1988, p. 523.
Gadamer, H. G. (1975). *Truth and Method*, 2nd rev. ed. New York, NY: Crossroad.
Grotstein, J. S. (2007). *A Beam of Intense Darkness: Wilfred Bion's Legacy to Psychoanalysis*. London, UK: Karnac Books.
Grunbaum, A. (1984). *The Foundations of Psychoanalysis*. Berkeley: University of California Press.
Habermas, J. (2005). *Zwischen Naturalismus und Religion: Philosophische Aufsaetze*. Frankfurt/Main, Germany: Suhrkamp.
Hampaté Bâ, A. (1957). *Vie et Enseignement de Tierno Bokar, le Sage de Bandiagara*. Paris, France: Editions du Seuil, 1980.
Hobson, P. (2002). *The Cradle of Thought: Exploring the Origins of Thinking*. London, UK: Macmillan.
Hoffman, I. Z. (2009). Doublethinking our way to "scientific" legitimacy: The dessication of human experience. *Journal of the American Psychoanalytic Association*, 57, 1043–1068.
Honneth, A. (1992). *Kampf um Anerkennung: Zur moralischen Grammatik sozialer Konflikte*. Frankfurt, Germany: Suhrkamp, 2003.
International Association for Relational Psychoanalysis & Psychotherapy (IARPP). (2009, December). Online colloquium: On the attachment of psychoanalysis to the past.
Joseph, B. (1989). *Psychic Equilibrium and Psychic Change: New Library of Psychoanalysis*, Vol. 9. London, UK, and New York, NY: Tavistock/Routledge.
Kaechele, H., Schachter, J., & Thomae, H. (2009). *From Psychoanalytic Narrative to Empirical Single Case Research: Implications for Psychoanalytic Practice*. New York, NY: Routledge.
―――. (2012). Single case research. In: *Psychodynamic Psychotherapy Research*, eds. R. Levy, S. Ablon, & H. Kaechele, New York, NY: Humana, pp. 495–510.
Leuzinger-Bohleber, M. (2010). Psychoanalysis as a "science of the unconscious." IPA Anniversary Celebration— Contemporary Perspectives on Psychoanalysis. Unpublished manuscript.
Mitchell, S. A. (1997). *Influence and Autonomy in Psychoanalysis*. Hillsdale, NJ: The Analytic Press.
―――. (2000). *Relationality: From Attachment to Intersubjectivity*. Hillsdale, NJ: Analytic Press. German: *Bindung und Beziehung: Auf dem Weg zu einer relationalen Psychoanalyse*. Gießen, Germany: Psychosozial-Verlag, 2003.
Orange, D., Stolorow, R. D., & Atwood, G. E. (2006). Zugehörigkeit, Verbundenheit, Betroffenheit: Ein intersubjektiver Zugang zur traumatischen Erfahrung. In: *Die vernetzte Seele: Die intersubjektive Wende in der Psychoanalyse*, eds. M. Altmeyer, & H. Thomae, Stuttgart, Germany: Klett-Cotta, pp. 160–177.
Orwell, G. (1949). *Nineteen Eighty-Four*. New York, NY: Harcourt, Brace & Co.
Schafer, R., ed. (1997). *The Contemporary Kleinians of London*. Madison, CT: International Universities Press.
Segal, H. (2006). Reflections on truth, tradition, and the psychoanalytic tradition of truth. *American Imago*, 63, 383–292.
Singer, W. (2002). *Der Beobachter im Gehirn*. Frankfurt/Main, Germany: Suhrkamp.
Stern, D. N. (1985). *The Interpersonal World of the Infant: A View from Psychoanalysis and Developmental Psychology*. New York, NY: Basic Books.
Thomae, H. (1999). Zur Theorie und Praxis von Übertragung und Gegenübertragung im psychoanalytischen Pluralismus. *Psyche–Z Psychoanal*, 53, 820–872.
Trevarthen, C. (1979). Communication and cooperation in early infancy: A description of primary intersubjectivity. In: *Before Speech: The Beginning of Interpersonal Communication*, ed. M. Bullowa, New York, NY: Cambridge University Press, pp. 321–347.
Wallerstein, R. S. (1990). Psychoanalysis: The common ground. *International Journal of Psycho-Analysis*, 71, 3–20.

Winnicott, D. W. (1960). Ego distortion in terms of true and false self. In: *The Maturational Process and the Facilitating Environment: Studies in the Theory of Emotional Development*, ed. D. W. Winnicott, New York, NY: International UP Inc., pp. 140–152.

Wolitzky, D. (2010). Critique on Hoffman's paper. *IARPP eNews*, 9(2).

"Here I Am!"—Irreducible Invocation of the Other

Noreen O'Connor, Ph.D.
International Association of Relational Psychoanalysis and Psychotherapy

The Bonds of Love (Benjamin, 1988) continues to inaugurate new horizons for critical reflection on the psychoanalytic theorizing of human relationships in terms of unconscious-conscious dynamics with its inevitable insertion in different sociocultural constructions of power practices. I follow Benjamin philosophically through post-Hegelian critical social/political theorists, particularly Habermas, and psychoanalytically through her respect for Winnicott's analyses of early developmental struggles for individuality in the face of fear of loss and destructiveness. Philosophical/Psychoanalytic inspiration carries her quest. This article excavates questions weaving throughout the book: Is an ideal of recognizing ourselves and others as "free" individual subjects possible? Could a psychoanalytical dialectics help us to live more responsibly with each other's differences not withstanding ineradicable past trauma? Is there possibility of life together, even in our gender differences, beyond the dialectical spell of erotic domination/submission?

INTRODUCTION

In this article I highlight Jessica Benjamin's originality in critically reconfiguring the parameters of psychoanalytical theorizing of human relationships. Her questioning and theorizing of unthematized yet operative assumptions of the sociocultural constructions of power in gender relationships opens new horizons for psychoanalysts. This is a challenge to develop our psychoanalytic practices, to respect the individuality of own critical thinking rather than sinking into authoritative compliance with constructions that are not alive to the nuanced day-to-day, listening/speaking relationships with our patients. I think that a decisive move in such theorizing requires a critique of foundational dualisms in psychoanalytic metapsychology such as, for example, mind/body, thinking/language. Uncritical acceptance of such dualistic speaking/thinking risks repeating and reinforcing the frightened bewilderment of patients struggling with trust in their own embodied speaking/responding to others.

A person seeking analysis can often experience a struggle between a courageous resolve to seek help from someone with the expertise, the knowledge, that will enable them to shift from the pain of their emotional impasse, of wanting the analyst to know and at the same time not to know *who* one is. Is everything I say about myself interpreted by the analyst in a language I don't know? Where does this leave my speaking? Do I become alienated from possibilities of relating to others resulting from an incongruence between the analyst's theories and his or her listening/responding? Does not the heart of analytic practice lie in the irreducible dynamic creativity of the speaking relationship between patient and analyst where there is not a split, a dualism, between mind/body, thinking/speaking, where language is not construed as a nominalism, a representation that names things such as, for example, objects of thought that exist in a private mind?

Benjamin's (1988) critiques of the relationships of power and knowledge open possibilities for exploring the relevance to psychoanalytic practices of contemporary philosophical critiques of language and thinking, language and subjectivity. To this end I include a brief account of the baby's language learning, that is, of his or her becoming a body-subject, elaborated by the French psychologist/philosopher Maurice Merleau-Ponty: I refer to the psychoanalyst John Foehl's phenomenological account of distance in "difficult to reach patients." In line with Benjamin's power/knowledge critique of gender I draw on the contemporary philosopher Tina Chanter's work on the marginalization of slavery in her work on *Antigone*. I show the relevance of Emmanuel Levinas's challenging critiques of the hegemony of Greek ontology to questions of recognition and intersubjectivity. Levinas highlights ways in which such ontological "knowledge" of the other is privileged over responsive relationship. This is not a utopian claim to transcend the hard painful work of understanding and attempting to resolve conflicts but a call to remember that the living time, speaking, of another is different, cannot be rationally appropriated by me. The other not only relates to me from a cultural context but also carries meaning in his or her evocative originality.

The wealth of psychoanalytic theories/praxes that have developed over the past century gives us ever renewed resources for our understanding of our subjectivity/intersubjectivity. This wealth is not superseded by philosophy but enhanced by its critical ethos of written or oral questioning across thousands of years and all cultures.

The Bonds of Love (Benjamin, 1988) initiated an original interpellation to psychoanalysis: How can we speak about and respond to the uniqueness of individual subjectivity? How can we hear the speaking of the present, specific rhythmic poiesis of daily struggles and triumphs, of dreams of love and loss, of persecutory terrors, of the impossibility of finding words for the long slow suffering, of the awful shame of embodiment, of the driven desires, if we do not question a vital feature of sociocultural gender construction, namely, the domination-subjection power-speech of masculinity-femininity? This psychosocial questioning is relevant to every one of us, lesbian, gay, bisexual, transgendered (LBGT), heterosexual, queer, celibate. Jessica Benjamin has courageously faced the challenge in her analytical critique marking the intercuts of post-Hegelian philosophical debates on the "nature" and function of human interactions with reflective experiential narratives of the practice, praxis, of psychoanalysis. Benjamin's focus on the relationship between the particular and the universal, the individual and culture/society, emerges from her working engagements with the dynamic interweaving of horizons of critical theorists and of relational psychoanalysts.

COMPLEXITY AND AMBIGUITY: SOCIAL PSYCHES

On the one hand Benjamin accuses Freud of blocking conceptual explorations of the inevitably constitutional character of relationships within society. From this perspective Freud's notion of social relationship is that of a rational authority repressing unbridled instinctual nature for our own good. On the other hand Benjamin positively acknowledges his contention that an individual's obedience to laws of civilization are motivated not by fear but rather love for those with the power to give and withhold, figures who command obedience from our earliest infancy. Both

Hegel, with his conceptualization of dialectical dynamism, and Freud, with his conceptualization of a dynamic unconscious, shift the conceptual ground question of individuality and authority from that of a monadically rational human nature interpreting its "reality" to one that allows for analyses of human relationships in terms of changing dynamisms of psychic/social life. Benjamin wonders about the two-way participant process of love and domination. Her aim is "to understand how domination is anchored in the hearts of the dominated" (Benjamin, 1988, p. 5). She draws on Hegel's discussion of the genesis of conflict between self and other. He claims that the social construction of subjectivity generates matrices of competitiveness between the self's need for absolute independence and its need of recognition by the other. Thus the self's conscious struggle to be free of the need of others is compromised not just by the other existing as a separate center of consciousness but also by the realization that the absoluteness of my world, my self-consciousness, depends on the recognition by the other's self-consciousness. But is our goal of being certain about our experience of ourselves, in control, paradoxically rendered impossible because it can only be achieved through recognition by the other, who, although posited as a sovereign free subject, also needs my recognition?

WHO ACHIEVES FREEDOM OF TRUE SUBJECTIVITY?

Many sociopolitical ideals, of whatever de facto authority-citizens organization, dictatorship, monarchy, autocracy, fascisms, communisms, variations of democracies, function powerfully with rhetorics of goodness and truth. "*Truths*" derived from perceptions of units of society such as the family, tribe, religious or ethnic group, are based on the notion that truthful perception is known, and to be known, at least in principle, by the powerfully rightful or insightful leaders. Their claim to authority is based on claims to know what is best for the survival and promotion of what is designated as their population. Significantly such *knowledge rendered rhetorically* commands allegiance to the speakers' actions, laws. Warring factions inevitably justify their killings in rhetorical terms whether of nationalistic land ownership or ethnic or religious righteousness. Authoritative leaders employ persuasive strategies that extoll the interconnection between their knowledge of the good and their power of achieving and implementing it. Such leaders argue that there is symmetry between the *truth and the goodness* of what they know to be best for a group/individual. Political strategists emphasize their claims to rationality in judgments of truth and concomitantly of goodness in legislating personally/politically for human relationships. Reflection on politics does matter as we practice analysis, enjoy and struggle with life and love in our daily lives because political systems affect how we interpret ourselves and others. Groups and individuals who rule on the basis on power/knowledge affect how we relate with one another: "Levinas argues that the power of 'mind' has become so dominant that Western philosophy has become identified with the substitution of ideas for persons, the theme for the interlocutor, and interiority of logical relations for the exteriority of interpellation" (O'Connor, 1982, p. 186). Although relational psychoanalysts assume such critical conceptualization, it continues to be the case that some institutes and organizations who pride themselves on the 'scientific' rigor of their psychoanalytic practices dismiss cultural political, especially sexually political, critiques of their epistemological, ontological, and ethical claims as irrelevant to and incompatible with their metapsychologies and practices. "I am attempting to explore not just the institution or the content of psychotherapy but rather the complex matrices that unravel *how* it is practised" (O'Connor, 2010, p. 45).

MIND/BODY DUALISMS IN ACTION

Benjamin highlights the extraordinarily confining focus of theorizing, including Freud's, on masculinity in the delineation of the parameters of debates and knowledge claims for authority. She cites the ubiquitous reliance of father-son metaphors in explanatory theories of power struggles that figure dominantly in attempts to explain the emergence of fascist movements. In line with the Western philosophical tradition (until the 20th century) Freud shares the assumption of women's subordination to men. Psychoanalysis in its conscious and unconscious unquestioning assumption of women's subordination to men has functioned to occlude issues of authority and gender relations in its narrative construction. Its analytic discourses of psychosexual relationships fail to include questioning of its own premises and assumptions. Thus traditional psychoanalytical oedipal explanations of socialization in their explorations of human development in terms of normality and its deviations have precluded possibilities of identifying and questioning enactments of the power dynamics in gender differences. Benjamin acknowledges her indebtedness to de Beauvoir's original characterization of relationships between men and women as dualistic in the sense that the "natural" woman submits as object to the superior "rationality" of the man who is the dominant subject. Gender domination, dependency and autonomy "thus establish the coordinates for the position of master and slave" (Benjamin, 1988, p. 7). In his analysis of imperialism and colonization Edward Said points out that, with the notable exception of feminists, cultural critiques of power/authority emanating from 20th-century French theorists, including psychoanalytic, remain silent on the interpellation of imperialistic struggles of mastery/slavery in "Third World" countries (Said, 1994, p. 336).

Benjamin resists rushing to a logical solution to oppositional gender identifications. She develops a relational psychoanalytical critique of gender binarism through her reading of critical theory, particularly from Habermas's interpretation of the concept of "I" in Hegel's *Philosophy of Mind* (Habermas, 1974, pp. 144–145). Subjectivity of the "I," rather than being a self-consciousness knowing itself, is a matter of achievement of self-experience through learning to see oneself through the eyes of others. Through the *dialectical* struggle for recognition each "I" becomes a subject though the formative processes of communicative action in a group, for example, the family. Through this developmental active participation in the third, group, society, the "I" becomes an identity of the universal in the singular (Habermas, 1974, p. 156). Here "the intersubjectivity in which the 'I' can identify with another 'I' without relinquishing the nonidentity between itself and the Other..." can be achieved (Habermas, 1974, p. 163).

Rather than reproduce any essentialist feminist reversal of binary dualism Benjamin holds that theorizing/practicing adequate politics of psychosocial relationships requires an examination of lived contradictory irrationalities in the dialectical gender conflict to win recognition. We remain in varying kinds of dependency on others throughout our lives. An infant's struggle for separation-individuation requires acknowledgment of the child's need of recognition of his or her independence by those on whom the child is most dependent. For Benjamin, refusal to trust that existence for oneself implies existing with/for another and results in a kind of psychic deterministic dialectic of domination/subordination. Alienated denial of the vulnerability of our individual inevitable mortality results in the fantasy of oneself as freed from need and desire, identification of oneself as master or slave. This is a de facto abdication of the vulnerability of responding to the unpossessable differences of the other in favor of a fantasy of free choice on the part of each dominant-submissive participant. For Hegel, in order to find the meaning of my individual free existence I require the other's existential recognition: the dialectical struggle of subordination submission is infinitely played out.

INDIVIDUATION BY/OF THE PHALLUS?

The complexity and ambiguity of Benjamin's analysis of domination and submission is exemplified by her critical reading of Bataille's claim that erotic violation is the only way of negotiating the inevitability of our lived isolation, "connected yet separated by a sea of death" (Benjamin, 1988, p. 63). Analysis of the asymmetrical dynamics of erotic submission and domination constitutive of the master/slave relationship reveals that desire for the infliction of and submission to pain is the crossing of the "sea" boundaries of our embodied lived discontinuities. Benjamin maintains that in this violation of the body, which is characteristic of "sadomasochistic fantasies and relationships we can discern the 'pure culture' of domination—a dynamic which organises both domination and submission" (Benjamin, 1988, pp. 51–52). The fantasy of voluntary erotic domination embodies the paradox of achieving freedom through slavery. Benjamin focuses on Pauline Reage's *Story of O* as a powerful depiction of conflicting desires for autonomy and recognition whose only resolution is confined to self-renunciation. Benjamin values Reage's courageous exploration of ways in which submission can derive not from women's fear of another but as complicit with their deepest desires.

The woman in the story masochistically seeks satisfaction from the powerful other who, she fantasizes, paradoxically can through his indifference to her desire bestow the craved-for recognition. She loses any agency, subjectivity, and becomes merely an object body open to violation. Transgression of her boundaries is achieved through such abdication of her "self"; she must always be "available and open" (Benjamin, 1988, p. 57). The woman's masters are not identified with the living contingency of "selves" either; rather their desires are in a sense formalized, represented by the penis. It is this indirect representation that asserts their sovereignty: "Their acts are carefully controlled: each act has a goal that expresses their rational intentions" (Benjamin, 1988, p. 57). The master's sadistic pleasure is achieved not by enjoyment of her pain but through the visible exhibition of power over her. Benjamin concludes that the penis in its symbolism of male mastery signifies a radical asymmetry that precludes the woman's knowledge or agency yet whose object status is required by the penis master.

The snare of this scenario of lived subjectivity is its depiction of the ideal of "freedom" achieved by reason. Indigent, needy, and insecure mortality is paradoxically transcended through attachment to the cutting deliberations and deliverances from death by the powerful indifference of the Master. Benjamin sees Bataille's depiction of erotic violation, the sadomasochistic fantasy of the master/slave relationship, in terms of its literary enactment of the Hegelian dialectic. In her critical analyses of Sophocles' *Antigone*, Chanter (2011) argues that Hegel's rejection of the feminine results from his distrust of feelings that, because of their random contingency, cannot become elevated to the purity of the spirit, that is, masculinity. This is why, for example, he confines Antigone to the ethical realm of the familial, the private, in subservience to the state: "Antigone is made to stand for the state of nature that both precedes and threatens to disrupt the contractual obligations with which Hegel associates his masculinist account of the social contract..." (Chanter, 2011, p. 52). It is evident that such positioning of women produces that which Benjamin highlights as "the more common form of masochism: adult ideal love" (Benjamin,

1988, p. 116). Possibilities for women' own agency and desire are dissolved in their identification with the powerful other who embodies these. Benjamin quotes de Beauvoir's interpretation of this "dream of annihilation," namely, that it expresses "an avid will to exist." In giving herself completely to the one she idealizes "she hopes that he will give her at once possession of herself and of the universe he represents" (Benjamin, 1988, p. 116).

Benjamin's reading of Freud through Hegel generates a crucial discussion of the relation between domination and omnipotence. She explores Freud's notion of erotic domination as manifesting a fusion of eros and the death instinct. From a Hegelian point of view, "the self refuses the claim of the outside world (the other) to limit its absoluteness. He asserts omnipotence" (Benjamin, 1988, p. 67). According to Freud, domination simultaneously involves an absence of tension and a creation of tension in order to dissolve appropriation by and of the other. She refers to Laplanche's psychoanalytic distinction between eros, which dynamically seeks synthesis of lived existence and psychic life, and sexuality, which drives the repetition compulsion yet works as the antithesis of the erotic drive: "Laplanche argues, rightly I think, that sexuality can be alloyed either with Eros or with death and destruction, but the great discovery of psychoanalysis was this latter, negative form of sexuality, which opens up to us the peculiar attraction of death and destruction" (Benjamin, 1988, p. 263). Benjamin phenomenologically describes the circularity of numbness and exhaustion in domination and, in so doing, identifies the breakdown of recognition between self and other. Departing from both Hegel and Freud, she argues for an intersubjective interpretation: the omnipotence of the dominating subject has its source in an earlier breakdown in the recognition of self and other. This is "destined to repeat the original breakdown unless and until the other makes a difference" (Benjamin, 1988, p. 68).

ALONE IN THE PRESENCE OF THE OTHER

Benjamin identifies the toddler's struggle with the realization that the exercise of her own freedom is dependent on the other as decisive in relational development. She holds that this is a dialectically paradoxical moment of realization that recognition of *myself* depends on the other's recognition of me, which in turn requires my recognition of the other. Benjamin characterizes this moment as necessarily contradictory. The achievement of differentiation cannot be specified by a linear logic of noncontradiction but rather through the dynamic tensions "from subject to subject, from self to other and back" (Benjamin, 1988, p. 36)

Benjamin contrasts the notion of destruction as domination, creating differentiation through objectification, with Winnicott's theory of destruction derived from his experience of the developmental relationship between the infant's aggression and the mother's survival. In his intersubjective theory such destructiveness can produce recognition of the other. He describes disengagement and engagement between self and other, which allows the safety of having and being in one's own space: "Prior to self-consciousness, this experience will appear to the child as that of the self alone; but later it will be understood as a particular way of being with the other" (Benjamin, 1988, p. 42). Mutual recognition cannot be achieved by either aggression or repression but through child and parents growing to tolerate the child's aggression, and their own, without retaliation. Rather than being perceived as a brake on narcissistic aggression, otherness can be felt as a shared enhancement of reality, the world.

EXPRESSIVE ENGAGEMENT WITH THE OTHER

Benjamin questions how the prevalent psychoanalytic tendency to explain "mature" development in terms of universal essentialisms can allow for reciprocity between individuals. In our book *Wild Desires and Mistaken Identities* Ryan and I emphasize that "the gendered split between desire and identification which typifies the classical Oedipus complex appears to us to rest on a prior assumption that the complementary necessity for each other as male and female constitutes the source of 'real' desire" (O'Connor and Ryan, 1993, p. 269). John Foehl (2011) points to psychoanalytic presuppositions of the separation of subjects, of mind and body, language and thought, in theories that are developed in order to bridge those presupposed gaps or splits. He wonders "how might things look if we begin with an assumption of our fundamental interconnectedness?" (p. 609). This not an argument for a reinvented notion of rational understanding that guarantees some innate mutual recognition of complementary re-presentations of reality, of each other. Neither is it a denial of thinking in favor of random solipsisms. Rather it is to shift perspective on the problem of self and other toward an intersubjectivity that is theorized in terms of embodied meaning, perception.

At birth the baby is "thrown into language" of family, culture. Don Ihde, the phenomenologist, argues that in the living body "the concrete experience of speech and language is always... one of embodied meaning" (Ihde, 1998, p. 68). Ihde's conceptualization is central to Merleau-Ponty's theorizing of intersubjectivity. Merleau-Ponty praises Freud's construction of the notion of libido as an intersection of sexuality and existence, thereby marking the individual's history. However, he is critical of the naturalistic assumptions guiding Freud's a-linguistic, a-cultural theories of child development. Merleau-Ponty's account of embodiment in terms of intentional subjectivity "challenges dualistic distinctions between 'internal' and 'external' worlds and situates the subject within a world of language, gestural and spoken, allowing for the embodiment of different cultural meanings" (Ellis, 2010, p. 79).

BIRTH: BEING THROWN INTO LANGUAGE

For Merleau-Ponty, the baby's original feeling its way in its new environment occurs through its babbling with its melody, intonation, and musicality. This nonverbal affective communication is necessary for the formation of words. Babbling is polymorphic language in which the baby responds to its environment through imitation, which "concerns the melody of the sentence just as much as the words, because the child tries, as it were, to speak in general" (Merleau-Ponty, 1973, p. 11). The baby imitates the acts of others. This ability presupposes that the child directly responds to the bodies of others as carriers of structured behavior while simultaneously experiencing its own body as capable of realizing gestures as meaningful. There is simultaneous apprehension of others' behavior and a sense of the baby's own self as "noncontemplative" but motor subject, an "I can" (Merleau-Ponty, 1973, p. 36). The baby is already itself in relation to others. Language as the indissoluble extension of all physical activity and dynamically renewed in that activity. Thinking is not "internal" and "does not exist independently of the world and of words... we can silently recall to ourselves... through which we acquire the illusion of an inner life..." (Merleau-Ponty, 1962, p. 183). Speech emerges from gestures, mimicries, yet it is transformational. The relation of the word-sound to its meaning cannot be conventional; it is intersubjectively situational. Merleau-Ponty criticizes classical psychology for claims that thought precedes expression but he does maintain that there is a significant gap in the child's language development, namely, the discontinuity of the central instant when the child's grasp of individual elements moves to grasp the significance of the whole. Judith Butler's analysis of psychic inceptions crucially illustrates the relationship between "the one who speaks... and the necessary conditions of such speech. ... Interpellation works by failing, that is, it institutes its subject as an agent precisely to the extent that it fails to determine such a subject exhaustively in time. ... The inaugurative scene of interpellation is one in which a... failure to be constituted becomes the condition of the possibility of constituting oneself" (Butler, 1997, p. 197).

The immediacy of psychotherapeutic speaking/listening culturally mediated testifies to the vital place of theorizing language in its different inceptions, not only within the relational specificity of patient-analyst but also in the recurrent irruptions of the language/s that carry our intersubjective lives. This sense of growing up with collective life and identity is movingly evident to me in Eyal Rozmarin's account of his work, "Dori" (2011), and Benjamin's equally personally moving response to him: "Rozmarin's patient confronts him head-on with the narratives of exile and redemption..." (Benjamin, 2011, p. 58). She points to the longing for the utopian community, home, the seductive fantasy of redemption that fails us. Is this because such transcendental longing leaves us lost in the precariousness of our mortal identity? Instead of identifying the self in terms of reflective self-possession Benjamin follows Keats's poetic path of negative capability in its tolerance of, and openness to, uncertainty.

EXILE AND SELF-IDENTITY

The relationship between exile and uncertainty is recurrently present in Levinas's work. In speaking of self-identity in the relationship of self and other Levinas describes the noncoincidence of self/rationality as the notion of exile: "Uniqueness, identity of uniqueness, precisely *me* or *I* that is not just a metaphor for the identical, but its original meaning in the saying... of of the I it expresses" (Levinas, 1993, pp. 155–156). This is a postulation of the notion of "self" as not having an identifiable essence that can be possessed by gathering the moments of our lives into a synthetic history or known truth. Chronological time presents the other as an image that distances him or her from me. For Levinas, the relationship of self and other is expressed as being in two times, that is, a diachronic relationship that is outside of recuperable, linear, time. The notion of exile, of vulnerability, expresses the "identity" of the self as rupture of an essentialist definition. Rather, identity of self is in the proximity of responding to the other in the diachronic difference. Here we are, each of us, where in relating to each other in our face-to-face speaking we are moved to listen to an unencompassable otherness.

CRITICAL COURAGE

Benjamin has courageously grasped the nettle of reconfiguring psychoanalysis *in relation* to critical theory. Against the establishment of utopian psychoanalytic claims for gender identifications and desire, she interweaves nuances of psychoanalytical conceptualizations of development with a post-Hegelian dialectical critique in order to trace new perspectives for the development of psychoanalysis in relational terms. In her rigorous questioning and exegesis she avoids "adding on" philosophical arguments to established psychoanalytic intrapsychic explanations in terms of conscious/unconscious dynamics. Instead, through her attention to operative philosophical presuppositions of psychoanalysis, such as claims about knowledge, reality, ethics, politics, she enhances our understanding of developmental dynamics. Benjamin avoids rejecting philosophical argument despite some philosophical critiques of psychoanalysis that characterise it as, for example, folk psychology or imaginative free associations claimed to be objective knowledge. Her account of psychoanalysis as relational theory/practice is a refusal to split philosophical reflection on subjective-intersubjective human living from daily analytic practice.

Benjamin's openness to listening and responding to voices of differences starkly contrasts with the developmental history of the psychoanalytic movement with its faction fighting and exclusion of those who think/practice differently from interpretations derived from their own transferentially received truths of "the" unconscious.

REFERENCES

Benjamin, J. (1988). *The Bonds of Love*. New York, NY, and Toronto, Ontario, Canada: Random House.
———. (2011). Facing reality together. In: *With Culture in Mind: Psychoanalytic Stories*, ed. M. Dimen. New York, NY, and Hove, East Sussex, UK: Routledge, pp. 49–63.
Butler, J. (1997). *The Psychic Life of Power*. Stanford, CA: Stanford University Press.
Chanter, T. (2011). *Whose Antigone?* New York: State University of New York.
Ellis, M. L. (2010). Shifting the ego towards a body subject. In: *Questioning Identities: Philosophy in Psychoanalytic Practice*, M. L. Ellis & N. O'Connor. London, UK: Karnac, pp. 59–84.
Foehl, J. (2011). A phenomenology of distance: On being hard to reach. *Psychoanalytic Dialogues*, 21, 607–618.
Habermas, J. (1974). *Theory and Practice*. Boston, MA: Beacon Press.
Ihde, D. H. (1998). *Expanding Hermeneutics: Visualism in Science*. Evanston, IL: Northwestern University Press.
Levinas, E. (1993). *Outside the Subject*, trans. ed. M. B. Smith. Stanford, CA: Stanford University Press.
Merleau-Ponty, M. (1962). *Phenomenology of Perception*, trans. C. Smith. London, UK, and Henley, UK: Routledge and Kegan Paul.
——— (1973). *Consciousness and the Acquisition of Language*, trans. ed. H. J. Silverman. Evanston, IL: Northwestern University Press.
O'Connor, N. (1982). Intentionality analysis and the problem of self and other. *The Journal of the British Society of Phenomenology*, 13, 186–192.
———. (2010). Is Melanie Klein the one who knows who you really are? In: *Questioning Identities: Philosophy in Psychoanalytic Practice*, M. L. Ellis & N. O'Connor. London, UK: Karnac, pp. 35–45.
——— & Ryan, J. (1993). *Wild Desires and Mistaken Identities: Lesbianism and Psychoanalysis*. London, UK: Virago, 1993. London, UK: Karnac, 2003. New York, NY, and Chichester, West Sussex, UK: Columbia University Press, 1993.
Rozmarin, E. (2011). Dori. In: *With Culture in Mind: Psychoanalytic Stories*, ed. M. Dimen. New York, NY, and Hove, East Sussex, UK: Routledge, pp. 35–40.
Said, E. (1994). *Culture and Imperialism*. London, UK: Vintage, Random House.

Reading Jessica

Andrea Celenza, Ph.D.

Harvard Medical School, Boston Psychoanalytic Society and Institute, and Massachusetts Institute for Psychoanalysis

The Bonds of Love, by Jessica Benjamin (1988), is a book written with both the structure and spirit of contemporary psychoanalysis. Any analyst interested in the analytic process as an evolving discipline will have read it, been impacted by it, and been transformed, even in ways unconscious. This article follows my personal and professional evolution as I trace a trajectory through retrospective, current and prospective lenses. I have selected some favorite excerpts from *The Bonds of Love* and describe my own transformation in response to each. The article reveals a continuous dialogue with Jessica as I discuss how my past and present have been impacted by this elegant book.

This is a story of a productive use of envy. It ends with gratitude and follows a circuitous but transformative route. The story itself starts well before my reading *The Bonds of Love* (1988), against a backdrop of my own college days. I had unwittingly enrolled in a university that will remain nameless (Cornell) wherein the psychology program was staunchly behavioral. Because I had made a commitment to myself since age 8 that I would major in psychology, I forged ahead nevertheless. I minored in philosophy, having always been inexplicably drawn to existential phenomenology. It perpetually bewildered me that my philosophy classes touched my inner being whereas my psychology classes did not. This dilemma (you could say opposition) in my experience between psychology and philosophy generated enormous conflict in me as I refused to give up one for the other.

Rats not being my favorite animal, I became increasingly disenchanted with psychology. I had almost abandoned my lifelong project of becoming a clinical psychologist when I finally read Guntrip, Fairbairn, and Shapiro. Years later, I came across *The Bonds of Love* and witnessed Benjamin weaving her tapestry of Hegel and Freud. The feeling was that distinct mix of excitement and dread upon encountering a like mind: on the one hand, a relieving confirmation that one is not alone, a feeling of communion and understanding that steadies the shaking limbs; on the other, that preposterous conceit that someone else had already written what I might have if only it had occurred to me! (If only I had the expansive intelligence, the sharpness of wit and the courage... big caveats, I realize.)

Rather than get caught up in this self-critical reactivity, I have selected some favorite excerpts from *The Bonds of Love* and describe my own transformation through a more constructive (yet no less true) prism. Refracted through a retrospective lens, I aim to shine a light on moments of synchrony, many beyond my self-awareness at the time. These moments, I now see, have been hugely generative as my long-standing admiration of Jessica's boldness has facilitated my own ability to harness inner forces. Perhaps this is a felicitous reconstruction that braids a friendship as the third strand. So be it.

Wholeness can only exist by maintaining contradiction [Benjamin 1988, p. 63].

The Bonds of Love is a major opus and for many of us has become the foundational organizer of an abundance of knowledge from diverse areas of scholarship. Surely, philosophy and psychoanalysis find an integration here but also developmental psychology, attachment research, sociology, literary criticism, and feminism. Jessica's scholarship and experience is no less vast than her ability to synthesize findings from each, no doubt reflecting a striving for wholeness within her own mind.

In this elegant book, Jessica takes on a series of dualisms underlying Western thought and demonstrates the ways in which we are drawn to discriminate, divide, polarize, and finally choose among our various potentials. Now, I am not one to choose unless I can check the last box "All of the Above" and after reading Chapter 2, I distinctly remember uttering (I think even aloud), "I don't have to choose!" I felt freed to integrate Merleau-Ponty, Marcel, and Sartre with my psychoanalytic formulations, the humanist and the universal along with the individualistic and the particular.

Another way the problem came to me is that I could identify with being *both* the master *and* the slave; more generally, there were ways in which I felt both the patriarch and the feminist. Jessica opens the way by focusing on the structure behind a set of dualisms without yielding to the temptation of a simple reversal. The book is an application of astute dialectical reasoning, especially in its relevance to gender relations. Among the pertinent binaries, Jessica discusses recognition/destruction, autonomy/dependency, reason/nature, subject/object, and male/female, thus examining the various "gender polarit[ies] ... that establish the coordinates for the positions of master and slave" (p. 7).

Jessica incisively observes (and I'm paraphrasing here) that Western society, despite its formal commitment to equality, has failed to dislodge these dualisms from gender-power hierarchies. She employs psychoanalytic processes to unearth the psychogenesis of the psychic structures that serve to maintain them.

Well, psychoanalysis, for me, has always been about unearthing deep structure but not always about bringing together; indeed it more often seems to pull apart. For me, this kind of thinking represents a shift from ego psychology's press toward compromise formation wherein the resolution of an either/or forced choice resides in a muted (and rather unexciting) trophy of ambivalence. Jessica moves us toward sustaining a tension between the heights and depths of human passion.

The wish to restore early omnipotence, or to realize the fantasy of control, never ceases to motivate the individual. In Hegel's terms, "Self-consciousness wants to be absolute. It wants to be recognized by the other in order to place itself in the world and to make itself the whole world [Benjamin 1988, p. 54].

I tend to see my life as a series of awakenings, and indeed, some have been rude. There are no straight lines, nothing is pure, experience is rife with contradiction. Some of these contradictions even fail to oppose each other (reason and passion, for example). *The Bonds of Love* has been integral to this journey, revealing the binary as a false dichotomy; as a forced choice set up as either/or because of an unconscious drive toward privilege—the temptation toward hierarchy. But I had the persistent problem that no matter which side I found myself on, I felt nagged.

Reading Jessica, I felt freed from the renunciatory model of development. Having been liberated from the pressure to "give up" one desire or another, I could now admit that I had persistently failed at this task anyway. I found myself writing about universal fantasies of love, the seductiveness of unconditional acceptance and commitment, fueled and intensified by (a) the desire for *unity,* to be loved totally and without separateness; (b) the desire for *purity,* to be loved unreservedly without hate; (c) the desire for *reciprocity,* to love and be loved in return; and finally, (d) the desire for *omnipotence,* to be so powerful that one is loved by everyone everywhere at all times (Celenza, 2006a, 2007).

To write in passionate extremes is to edge closer to raw experience, the ways in which our desires reside unmetabolized and uncivilized in our unconscious, perhaps as a melody only angels would hear (Benjamin, 1994). I discuss how all of these universals figure prominently in fantasies of romantic perfection and are stimulated in the treatment setting because the treatment contract partly instantiates their gratification (Celenza, 2006a, 2007).

> The discussion of erotic domination has shown how the breakdown of the tension between assertion and recognition becomes associated with the polarization of gender identity [Benjamin 1988, p. 85].

In "Woman's Desire" (Chapter 3), Jessica presages herself by examining the way in which gender identity is recruited to situate and entrench power inequities. This is a foreshadowing of her exquisite tracking of the cultural repudiation of femininity in her third book, *The Shadow of the Other* (Benjamin, 1998).

No piece of writing has planted seeds in my mind evolving into a current preoccupation than has Jessica's discussion of women's sexual subjectivity (or lack thereof). She writes of the "doer/done to" in gender complementarity, that is, "man expresses desire and woman is the object of it" (Benjamin, 1988, p. 86). This will (or should) grab most women and did so for me because, for one, during my training it was illegitimate to use the term *subject* at all. We had *object* in reference to libido, representations, or other persons (as in love object); however, it was prohibited to use the term *subject* (and, by extension, *subjectivity*) not because of the repudiation of feminine subjectivity so much but simply because the term did not exist within the psychoanalytic lexicon. And not for want of need but because Freud and his direct successors had not used it, wedded as they were to Enlightenment-era fantasies of objectivity.

Jessica makes woman her subject. She takes on many contested themes that are especially relevant for female subjectivity, including nominal gender, the active-passive binary, the repudiation of femininity, and the centrality of the Oedipus complex (Benjamin, 1998). Intertwined within all of these is woman's struggle to maintain attunement with her desires in an active, agentic manner despite the ways in which Western culture embeds power relations in gender constructs, defining and thereby influencing the individual's psychological and subjectively experienced construction of a gendered self (Goldner, 2002; Dimen, 2003; Harris, 2005). Here too, the question of nature versus nurture is resolved. Jessica writes of the internalization of culture as embedded in self-other relational patternings and how these become the structures of subjectivity in concordance with culturally sanctioned power hierarchies.

> The mentality of opposition...pits freedom against nurturance: either we differentiate or remain dependent; either we stand alone or are weak; either we relinquish autonomy or renounce the need for love [Benjamin 1988, p. 172].

Binaries serve power grids that are embedded in language, a major conveyance of culture. Naming itself reflects membership in a group that denotes *this* (some particular way of being) and not *that* (usually its polar opposite). Hence a binary surfaces along with a relentless or seemingly inevitable tendency to privilege one pole over the other, thus refracting through and instantiating within a hierarchical relation. These power hierarchies are reflected, accepted, and embedded in discourse, cultural practices, and rituals that are so commonplace as to disappear from view. In these ways, many types of subjugation are nonreflectively perpetuated through the social and cultural order.

Jessica's experience with infant development takes us back to the rudimentary self when linguistic capacities are beginning to develop. Gender is one of many difference markers (Goldner, 2002) that pose a binary facilitating the organization of an early self as the preoedipal child awakens to gender differences. We name "me" and "not me" by creating a gendered split that forms the basis of various segregated or dissociated aspects of the self (gendered or otherwise). These will later press to be recuperated and reconnected as in the postoedipal recuperation of earlier bisexual self-other identifications (Bassin, 1996; Benjamin, 1998; Elise, 2002).

The bigendered aspects of the self and its complimentary disclaiming, the feminine/masculine binary and the passive/active binary, as Jessica has so thoroughly investigated (Benjamin, 1998), have prompted me to develop ways in which analysts may clinically facilitate reintegrations of disclaimed aspects of bigendered selves. Especially for those patients who struggle with sexual aspects of their erotic lives, I find it helpful to engage a related polarity (receptivity and potency) that has stereotypically defined femininity and masculinity, the poles of which are not actually opposite (thereby are not mutually exclusive)—in effect, *a binary that is not one*.

Various self-states can be described in terms of the extent to which phenomenal experience within these states is *receptive* (feelingful) and *potent* (agentic). As fundamentally embodied subjects, embodiment is sensate *receptivity* to feeling and affective aliveness. The capacity to harness one's *potency* (power or authority) is what is meant by being a subject, the experience of articulated selfhood. It's easy to see how these poles can be gendered and I propose that a healthy state of mind is maximally both. Who could choose? (Yet we do.)

> People do not want freedom and truth which only cause deprivation and suffering; they want miracle, mystery, and authority. The pain that accompanies compliance is preferable to the pain that attends freedom [Benjamin 1988, p. 5].

Jessica's paraphrase of Dostoyevsky (1880) seeks to reveal the elusive part of the psyche that is drawn to domination, that willingly submits. I have always been drawn to complexity and have my own journey as a reluctant feminist, struggling with so-called victimology as an oversimplification, as in you-monster, me-angel polarizations. Jessica, too, writes of her objection to a certain strand of feminist thinking that allies with the patriarchal creation of "a victimized woman, too weak or brainwashed or hopeless to resist her degradation" (p. 55). Culture imposes only where there is a ready receptacle and psychoanalysis promises to examine these receptor sites, the whys and ways we participate in our own subjugation.

I always want psychological truth to be complicated, ironic, and paradoxical—otherwise it would neither hold my interest nor ring true. Studying race relations in college, I was interested in the psychology of the racist and the ways in which racist beliefs enslave the master, indeed, the ways in which the master *needs* the slave. In graduate school, it was the psychology of the abuser that captured my attention; in practice, the psychology of the sexual boundary transgressor (Celenza, 2007). (I've imagined another coinciding between me and Jessica in her journey with the Frankfurt School and the examination of Nazi sympathizers.)

I am interested in victims of exploitation; certainly, sympathy for those who are hurt by power hierarchies is easy to evoke. Too often, however, this sympathy becomes trapped in the same binary we aim to deconstruct. Jessica elaborates formulations on both sides. Developing a different framework that allows for resolution, she cites Foucault (1980): "If [power] never did anything but to say no, do you really think one would be brought to obey it?" (Benjamin 1988, p. 4). In this way, she grapples with the victim's willingness to submit to power, converting the underlying epistemological structure from either/or to both/and, "conceiv[ing of] domination as a two-way process, a system involving the participation of those who submit to power as well as those who exercise it" (p. 5). No one is off the hook.

At the same time, Jessica's insightfulness renders each participant's engagement humanly meaningful. She reveals the way in which "inflicting pain is the master's way of maintaining his separate identity" (p. 62). This proved enormously helpful to me as I attempted to unravel my engagement in a sadomasochistic enactment that involved a murder fantasy (my patient, Michael, wanting to murder me) and my ability to realize his unconscious project: *I murder therefore I am* (Celenza, 2006b).

> The equation of masculinity with desire, femininity with object of desire does reflect the existing situation; it is not simply a biased view. ... But this situation is not inevitable. ... The psychological integration of biological reality is largely the work of culture—of social arrangements that we *can* change or direct [Benjamin 1988, p. 90].

Jessica is not anything if she is not a social activist. We know ourselves through seeing our force, flexing our muscles, and seeing its effects (our potency). Her action has prompted action on my part. As mentioned, I am now working on the elaboration of a dialectic: receptivity and potency. Translated into the language of sexuality, we might say holding and penetration; in the language of the body, openness and backbone; or, in traditional stereotypic language, the feminine and masculine.

One aim of clinical practice is to liberate our patients from constraint and degradation in the construction of self-referents, of which gender is often a foundational organizer. My stance is to engage and elaborate the meaning of this binary, receptivity and potency, as it is instantiated and lived out in my patients. It is a binary that has stereotypically defined femininity and masculinity yet the poles are not actually opposite and thereby are not mutually exclusive. *Most important, I view these poles as liberated from any hierarchic power relation in that neither pole is privileged,* though in any particular individual one may be.

As treatment progresses, it becomes possible to transcend cultural stereotypes (of gender, race, ethnicity, age, etc.) and expand self-experience and gender repertoire (Elise, 1998) or one's gender portrait (Balsam, 2001). (I suspect Jessica would disagree with the use of a binary in order to transcend binaries, but I know she would appreciate the paradox.) This expansion involves the acceptance and inclusion of binarial, oppositional categories in a both/and multiplicity, in effect to achieve a *unique gender blend.*

My thinking has evolved from there. And so now I find myself writing, "The binary is not dead; it is not even binary."

***

I hope I have shown the ways in which Jessica's work has actively prompted and reworked my own. I suppose this has been a personal love letter that charts the course of a relationship Jessica did not know she had. It is not for me to chart a different course, such as the place of *The Bonds of Love* in feminist discourse or its impact on relational psychoanalysis. But I know well the effects the book has had on me, a woman with a dearth of female mentors searching for a psychoanalysis that would speak to me. I have found my place, both as mentee and author, and I have Jessica to thank for the influence and generativity of her work on my own. Is it not the highest compliment, indeed a sign of love, to trace the outlines of the shadow of the other imprinted on one's soul?

REFERENCES

Balsam, R. (2001). Integrating male and female elements in a woman's gender identity. *Journal of the American Psychoanalytic Association*, 49, 1335–1360.

Bassin, D. (1996). Beyond the he and the she: Toward the reconciliation of masculinity and femininity in the postoedipal female mind. *Journal of the American Psychoanalytic Association*, 44S, 157–190.

Benjamin, J. (1988). *The Bonds of Love*. New York, NY: Pantheon.

———. (1994). What angel would hear me? The erotics of transference. *Psychoanalytic Inquiry*, 14, 535–557.

———. (1998). *Shadow of the Other: Intersubjectivity and Gender in Psychoanalysis*. New York, NY: Routledge.

Celenza, A. (2006a). Hyperconfidentiality and the illusion of the dyad. Paper presented at the Philadelphia Psychoanalytic Society and Institute, January, Philadelphia, PA.

———. (2006b). The threat of male-female erotic transference. *Journal of the American Psychoanalytic Association*, 54, 1207–1232.

———. (2007). *Sexual Boundary Violations: Therapeutic, Supervisory and Academic Contexts*. New York, NY: Aronson.

Dimen, M. (2003). *Sexuality, Intimacy, Power*. Hillsdale, NJ: Analytic Press.

Dostoyevsky, F. (1880). *The Brothers Karamazov*, trans. C. Garnett (rev. by R. E. Matlaw). New York, NY: Norton Critical Edition, 1976.

Elise, D. (1998). Gender repertoire: Body, mind and bisexuality. *Psychoanalytic Dialogues*, 8, 353–372.

———. (2002). The primary maternal oedipal situation and female homoerotic desire. *Psychoanalytic Inquiry*, 22, 209–228.

Foucault, M. (1980). Truth and power. In: *Power/Knowledge: Selected Interviews & Other Writings*, ed. C. Gordon, New York, NY: Pantheon, p. 119.

Goldner, V. (2002). Toward a critical relational theory of gender. In: *Gender in Psychoanalytic Space*, eds. M. Dimen, & V. Goldner, New York, NY: Other Press, pp. 63–90.

Harris, A. (2005). *Gender as Soft Assembly*. Hillsdale, NJ: Analytic Press.

A Day at the Zoo Through the Lens of Jessica Benjamin's *Bonds of Love*

Donna Bassin, Ph.D.
Pratt Institute

In this photo-based essay I bring Jessica Benjamin's project of transforming relationships of domination to a day at the zoo. The interrogation of the human/animal dualism illuminates relational moments of mutuality across species. Managing the tension between sameness and difference without collapse into hierarchical configuration, the human-animal connection may take its place in the project of transforming relationships of domination and extending the circle of ethical care.

It is well known that the impact (or imprint) of Jessica Benjamin's work is widespread and visible not only in psychoanalysis or gender studies but also across many disciplines. In my photo-based essay I bring Jessica along as a companion, to think with, as I attempt to understand the nature of our relationship(s) to animals—specifically the creation of psychic structures, which support the destructive cycles of subject-object domination and foreclose new relational moments across species. Work within the field of animal studies has suggested that the interrogation of the human/animal dualism is a necessary condition for all ethical questions.

THE BONDS OF LOVE, REVISITED

For much of my life I have related to animals as objects—objects of entertainment, education, food, and clothing—even pets I cared for were essentially objects of my own subjectivity. And as for many of us living in the Western civilized world, other than occasional sightings of rogue animals trespassing human space, or visits to the zoo, animals were a very small part of my social world.

As a mental health consultant to first responders at Ground Zero following 9/11, I had the opportunity to observe encounters between those working in the pits and the therapy dogs we brought to mitigate stress and trauma. Recently, a number of my patients have gotten companion dogs and regularly bring these dogs to their therapy sessions. Thoughts of bringing a therapy dog to my office brought me back to Freud's chow chow, Yofi, who participated in his analytic hours, identifying and comforting anxious patients as well as signaling the end of the hour. Increasing curiosity about the impact of our relationships with animals (or lack thereof) and pressed to connect with animals since the loss of a beloved pet, I have begun to photograph life at the zoo.

THE BONDS OF LOVE, REVISITED

Life in progressive zoos for apes and certain monkeys has changed. No longer displayed in cement cages with painted faux replicas of their native habitat and visitors, animals at the Bronx Wildlife Conservation Park are increasingly housed in some recreation of their natural habitat. Gorillas live and freely roam in a 6.5-acre natural lowland rain forest. Built inside and snaking within the gorilla habitat is the human habitat—a mostly glass tunnel-shaped and climate-controlled enclosure, complete with toilets, benches, and educational material.

It is along this meandering glass edge, where animal and human habitats intersect, that Jessica Benjamin's theoretical commitments to the deconstruction of the unethical master-slave dichotomy may be usefully employed and her radical vision of transformed relationships, even across species, might be briefly enjoyed.

THE BONDS OF LOVE, REVISITED

THE BONDS OF LOVE, REVISITED

THE BONDS OF LOVE, REVISITED

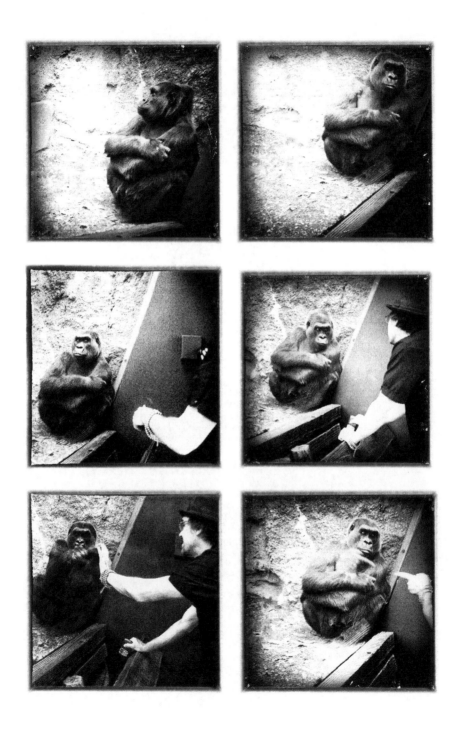

THE BONDS OF LOVE, REVISITED

Despite the language barriers between the human visitors and the gorillas, instances of call-and-response through gesture and gaze define cross-species encounters. Gorillas, no longer mere passive captives, become active subjects initiating and responding to attempts of attunement and assertion. These borderlands of relational activity, according to Jessica Benjamin, are opportunities where identity and subjectivity may be negotiated.

Cautionary stories regarding our relationship to apes reflect and fortify the master-slave relationship. Menacing King Kong must be captured, constrained, and killed for transgressive behavior, acting as a subject in love. Or in an instructive flip, apes once slave to humans transform into hyperintelligent master of humans in *Planet of the Apes.*

Animal rights activists, in the service of increased ethical responsibility toward animals, have generally sought to dissolve the boundary between animals and humans, making animals more like humans and thus deserving human treatment. However, and inadvertently in doing so, some animal rights activists might be charged with anthropomorphism, a different form of domination. That is, in their attempt to relate to animals humanely, they call for a destruction of their difference from us. In contrast, Jessica Benjamin's project of recognition, I suggest, may be a useful addition to the efforts of animal studies scholars, who, in resisting the anthropomorphic perspective, seek to open up new spaces of relationships across species. Recognition here, as I understand and extend Jessica's work, requires that we resist the destruction of the unique differences of the other as subject. That is, we must recognize the animal's animality and struggle to manage the oscillating tension between these dichotomies—animality and humanity—in the service of transforming relationships of domination.

THE BONDS OF LOVE, REVISITED

Surely, as Jessica Benjamin has argued, transcending tragic repetitions of master-slave enactments in the service of true ethical relationships requires that we manage the tension, without collapse into hierarchical configuration, between sameness and difference, and therefore the human-animal connection must take its place, alongside male-female, subject-object, us-them, as another set of opposites in tension for the project of transforming relationships of domination and extending the circle of ethical care.

Index

abuse 52–4
accommodation: mutual 64–6
acknowledgement 54, 88; mutual 74, 90–1, 99
activism 75, 161
activity 53, 70, 83
Adler, A. 121
Adorno, T. 19, 22, 120, 123; and Horkheimer, M. 130
African National Congress (ANC) 9
afterwardsness (*Nachträglichkeit*) 20, 114
agency 20, 50, 57, 80, 142
aggression 6, 12–13, 48–9, 52–4, 77; narcissistic 143
AIDS (acquired immunodeficiency syndrome) 37–8, 42
alienation 87
Ally, S. 13
Althusser, L. 34, 37–9
Altmeyer, M. 3, 119–37; and Thomae, H. 120
American psychoanalysis 111–15
American Psychoanalytic Association (APsaA) 125
Amichai, Y. 54
anger 15, 53
animal rights 161
animals 154, 157; social 121
anthropology 115; evolutionary 121; philosophical 121
anthropomorphism 161
Antigone (Sophocles) 139, 142
antipornography movement 62
anxiety 52, 115
Anzieu-Premmereur, C. 112
apartheid 4, 9–15
Apartheid Archive Project 13–15
Aron, L. 49, 66–7, 122
arousal: sexual 50–1
assertion 93–4, 161; self- 68, 94
Association of Black Women Historians (ABWH) 15

asymmetry 66, 76–81, 86–7, 142
Atlas, G. 48–55
attachment 19–22, 54, 65, 112, 116, 121, 124, 148
attunement 65–6, 161
Atwood, G.: Orange, D. and Stolorow, R. 132
Aury, D. (Pauline Reage) 61, 142
authority 60, 112, 141
autocracy 140
automatism: repetition 77
autonomy 29, 42, 49, 68, 81, 141–2, 148
awareness: self- 113

babies 62–5
Baleful Head, The (Burne-Jones) 56
Barnes & Noble 32–3, 38
Barthes, R. 81
Bartkowski, F. 2, 56–8
Bassin, D. 3, 153–63
Bataille, G. 61, 142
Beauvoir, S. de 59–60, 71, 141–3
Beebe, B.: and Stern, D. 63
behavior 105, 144
Benjamin, W. 62
Bernfeld, S. 63
Beyond Doer and Done to: An Intersubjective View of Thirdness (Benjamin) 102–3, 126
binarism 149–51; gender 49–50, 60, 141
Bion, W.R. 35, 88, 121, 127, 132–4
Bloch, E. 62
body 27, 51–2, 57
Bollas, C. 65
bondage 102; erotic 37; psychic 22
bondless love 32–47
bonds 32–3, 36–7, 50–2; dissociated 37–8; emotional 22; loosening 17–31; risky 33–5; timeless 38–41
Bourdieu, P. 34
Bowlby, J. 123–5
Brooks, D. 121

165

INDEX

Brusset, B. 114
Burne-Jones, E. 56
Bush, G. 32, 37–8
Butler, J. 18, 23, 49, 69, 79–80, 112, 145

caretakers 4–14, 51
Celenza, A. 2, 147–52
certainty: sense- (*sinnlicheGewißheit*) 99–101
Chanter, T. 139, 142
Chasseguet-Smirgel, J. 134
child development 18, 144, 150
childcare 11–13
childhood 4, 7–15, 27, 33–7, 82; early 127; education 63
Chodorow, N. 2, 17, 50, 60
chreode 74–92
civil rights 15
Civitarese, G. 35
class 27–8, 37, 42
Cock, J. 9
cognition 77, 111–13
colonial oppression 85
communication 63, 77, 80, 123, 129; nonverbal 115–16, 144
Communism 62, 140
complementarity 98; gender 149; split 83–6, 89
complexity 62, 139–40
compulsion: repetition 77, 91
comradeship 88
conflict 57, 89, 114–15, 140; ethnic 75, 81, 84; intrapsychic 114; Israeli-Palestinian 75, 84–90, 128; psychic 113
conformity 29, 62
consciousness 97–102, 124, 138, 145; self- (*Selbstbewußtsein*) 99, 140
constraints 48, 77
constructivism 119; dialectical 125; radical 119, 126, 131; social 112, 126, 134; weak 119, 133
contemporary psychoanalysis 1–3, 120–2, 131–4, 147
Contre-courant (Laplanche) 115
control 22, 52–3, 57
Cooper, A. 125
Corbett, K. 2, 40–1, 68
Corrigan, E.: and Gordon, P. 51
countertransference 51, 124, 130–2
Cradle of Thought: Exploring the Origins of Thinking, The (Hobson) 129
creativity 115, 138–9
critical theory 19, 62, 120, 128, 138, 141, 145
critical thinking 138
cultural domination 134
cultural studies 57–8, 131

culture 17, 29, 42, 56
Culture of Narcissism (Lasch) 10, 34
cyberspace 41–2

Damasio, A. 122
Davidson, D. 95
death drives 115
deconstruction 21
Deleuze, G. 116
democracy 33–5, 140
dependency 20, 32, 36, 48–9, 53, 65, 148; gender 141; masculine 51
Derrida, J. 49, 112, 116, 120
Descartes, R. 80, 94
desire 20, 50–2, 57, 68, 71, 144–5, 149; homoerotic 32–3, 41–2; mutual 44; online 43; power of 62; subjective 29
destruction 32–3, 41, 49, 64–5, 148
destructiveness 114–15, 138
deus ex machina 28
development 38, 125, 130–3, 141, 146, 149; child 18, 144, 150; gender 36; psyche 113, 122, 154; relational 143; sexual 49
Dewey, J. 32–4
dialectics 99, 116, 138, 145, 151; master-slave 61, 75–80, 141–2, 157, 161–3
Dialektik der Aufklaerung (Adorno and Horkheimer) 130
difference 22–3, 143, 153, 163; crisis of 6; problem of 65; social 63
Dimen, M. 2, 33
Dinnerstein, D. 17, 60
disclosure: self- 112, 132
discourse 24, 37, 42
domination 48–50, 70, 74–5, 79–80, 93–110, 116, 140–3; cultural 134; destruction of 143; erotic 138, 142; gender 141; ideological 41; interpersonal 79; masculine 18; problem 97; sexual 60; social 60, 79
Dornes, M. 120
Dostoyevsky, F. 93, 150
doublethinking 125
Doublethinking Our Way to 'Scientific' Legitimacy: The Desiccation of Human Experience (Hoffman) 125
drive theory 115–17, 123
dualism 60, 138–42, 149–54
Dworkin, A. 18
dyadic relationships 74, 79–85, 89, 129

education: childhood 63; lacking 10; vouchers 34–5
ego 21–5, 41–3, 51, 60, 63, 121, 130

INDEX

Ego and the Id, The (Freud) 130
ego psychology 111–14, 148
Eigen, M. 109
Ellis, M.L. 144
emotional bonds 22
emotions 8, 22, 51, 66, 71, 108, 122–3
empathy 11, 14, 38, 65, 130
empiricism 111–12
employment 9–10, 13
engagement 63; mutual 90
enlightenment 123, 149; self- 120
enslavement 22
entwinement 103–4
envy 147; penis 18, 67
epistemology 90, 94–9, 102, 126–8, 140; constructivist 132; hermeneutic 125
eros 32–3, 41–2, 143; homo- 23, 26
erotic bondage 37
erotic domination 138, 142
eroticism 23, 40–5, 142–3; collective 32; liminal 37
essentialism 134, 144
ethics 15, 79, 90–1, 140, 146, 153–4, 161–3
Ethics of Psychoanalysis, The (Lacan) 79
ethnic conflict 75, 81, 84
ethnicity 28, 80
excitement: sexual 50–3
exhibitionism 42
existence 95, 99, 109, 144
experience 51, 95, 108; intrapsychic 39; self- 151; social 34; subjective 93
exploitation 52–3, 65; female 15

Faculty of Israeli and Palestinian Peace (FFIPP) 84
Fanon, F. 80
fantasy 12, 40–1, 113; active 45; intrapsychic 39; sadomasochistic 142; universal 149
fascism 140–1
Fast, I. 21–3, 69
fatherhood 8, 20, 50, 68, 116, 141; identificatory 25; primal 25
Feldman, M. 127
female exploitation 15
female oppression 59–60
femininity 20, 26, 49, 60–2, 69–70, 116, 139, 142, 148–51
feminism 17–31, 48–50, 56–9, 62–4, 70–1, 141, 148–52; collective 60; heterosexual 70; intersubjective 111; lesbian 57; modern 120; traditional 116
Ferenczi, S. 54, 67
Fifty Shades of Grey (James) 57, 70
Foehl, J. 139, 144

Fonagy, P. 134
Foucault, M. 37, 70, 80, 112, 116, 120, 151
Foulkes, S.H. 85
Frankfurt school 19, 116, 128
freedom 20, 79, 93–4, 102, 140–3
French psychoanalysis 111–18, 134, 141
Freud, S. 17–26, 66–9, 76–8, 113–15, 119–24, 130, 139–44, 147–9
friendship 56
Fromm, E. 19, 123
fundamentalism 119, 133

Gadamer, H-G. 132
Gaza Community Mental Health Program (GCMHP) 84
Gaza Strip (Palestine) 84, 87–8
gender 21–9, 36–7, 57, 70, 139–41, 145, 149–51; binarism 49–50, 60, 141; relations 4–8, 12, 79–80, 120, 138, 148; studies 111–12, 116, 154
Gender Trouble (Butler) 18
gene pool 74–5
gestures 144; identificatory 43
Ghent, E. 61–2, 102–3
Gill, M. 117, 125
Gilligan, G. 17
Ginsberg, R. 13
Glasnost 36
Goffman, E. 7
Goldner, V. 2
Gonzalez, F.J. 2, 17–31
Gordan, P.: and Corrigan, P. 51
Grand Inquisitor, The (Dostoyevsky) 93
Green, A. 124, 134
Green, C. 40
Grindr 32–3, 43–5
Group Psychology and the Analysis of the Ego (Freud) 17, 20–3, 29
groups: problem of 17–31
Guntrip, H. 147

Habermas, J. 19, 63, 120, 131, 141
habitus 37, 41
Hadar, U. 3, 74–92
Harris, A. 2, 21, 27
Hartman, S. 3, 32–47
Hegel, G.W.F. 60–1, 64–5, 75–7, 93–104, 116, 131, 138–47
helplessness 52, 93
hermeneutics 115, 134
heterosexual feminism 70
heterosexuality 6, 20–1, 25–9, 49, 58, 68–70, 139
hierarchy 148–51
history 25, 59–62, 91; interaction 125, 130

INDEX

Hobson, P. 129
Hoffman, I. 125, 131
homo-eros 23, 26
homoerotic desire 32–3, 41–2
homoerotic identity 23
homoeroticism 23, 26, 43–4, 67–8
homosexuality 18, 23, 26, 45, 68
Horkheimer, M. 19, 120; and Adorno, T. 130
Horney, K. 49–50, 67, 123
hostility 53; interethnic 79; mutual 85; persistent 84
Huffington Post 42
human relations 1, 4, 120, 126, 131, 140
human sciences 121–6, 130–4

idealization 68, 116
identificatory gestures 43
identificatory love 21–6, 37–8, 67–71
identity 23, 132–4, 144, 150; homoerotic 23; paternal 20; self- 145
ideology 24, 37
Ihde, D. 144
imperialism 141
impression: sense- 99–100
In a Different Voice (Gilligan) 17
Independence and Dependence of Self-Consciousness, The (Hegel) 98
infancy 5–6, 27, 63–5, 139, 150
infant research 19, 71, 121, 124, 130
infantile sexuality 111–15, 123
inhibition: sexual 44
injury 74–5, 90; narcissistic 32–3
intelligibility 28, 70
intentionality 79–84, 90
interaction 66, 122, 125–6, 130–1, 139; internalization of 124; social 122; symbolic 121
interconnected soul (*Die vernetzte Seele*) 126
interdisciplinarity 128, 133
International Association for Relational Psychoanalysis and Psychotherapy (IARPP) 120–2, 130
Internet 32–3, 37, 119
interpellation 39, 71, 88–9, 139
intersubjectivism 132–4
intersubjectivity 35–9, 51–4, 74–82, 93–8, 101–4, 108–22, 144–6; beyond 119–37; primary 63; self 123
intimacy 4–16, 49, 53, 56–8
intrapsychic spaces 25, 32, 38–40, 97
Islamization 128
Israel: Israeli-Palestinian conflict 75, 84–90, 128, *see also* Palestine

Jameson, F. 79–80
Jung, C.G. 37, 121
justice 8, 61

Kaës, R. 25–6, 29
Kant, I. 90, 131
Keats, J. 145
Klein, M. 18, 36, 39, 63, 121, 124–7, 132–4
knowledge 1–3, 34–5, 121–2, 139, 146; empirical 120; idiosyncratic 133; interdisciplinary 119–20; modes 99–101; objective 146; objects of 58; ontological 139; relational 122–3, 131; speculative 123; validated 120
Kohut, H. 65, 114, 124
Kojève, A. 61, 98
Kristeva, J. 120

Lacan, J. 25, 74–84, 90, 111–13, 116, 120, 134
language 25, 78–81, 84, 123, 138–9, 144–5; barriers 161
Laplanche, J. 51, 114–15, 134, 143
Layton, L. 39, 49
Lazarre, J. 64
lesbian feminism 57
lesbian, gay, bisexual, transgender (LGBT) 57–8, 139
Lesbians are not women (Wittig) 2
Levinas, E. 139, 145
liberation 29, 45, 59, 120
libidinization 36, 41
libido 39, 44, 144, 149
Like Subjects, Love Objects (Benjamin) 96, 115
Loewald, H. 95
Lukacs, G. 19
Lyotard, J-F. 112

MacKinnon, C. 18
Mahler, M. 116
Maids and Madams (Cock) 9
Mandela, N. 9
Marcel, G. 148
Marcuse, H. 19
Marx, K. 19, 60, 63, 71, 80, 128
masculine dependency 51
masculine domination 18
masculinity 19–20, 25–9, 48–52, 70, 116, 139–41, 148–51
masochism 57
master-slave dialectic 61, 75–80, 141–2, 157, 161–3
mastery 36, 49–50, 60, 142, 148
maternal subjectivity 60, 63, 66
Meade, G.H. 63
media 70, 119

INDEX

melancholy 23, 26, 42, 69
memory 122, 130–3
mental disorders 116, 119, 125, 133
mental health 85
Merleau-Ponty, M. 139, 144–5, 148
Mermaid and the Minotaur, The (Dinnerstein) 17
metapsychology 36, 111–15, 122–4, 130, 133, 138–40
Miller, E.: and Rice, K. 88
mind 28–9, 51–2, 57, 79, 124; racialization 4–16
mirroring 28, 65, 68, 121–2
misattunement 65
misogyny 40
misunderstanding 111–18
Mitchell, J. 8, 17, 25, 56
Mitchell, S. 19, 36, 66, 113, 117, 125–7
modern feminism 120
modernization psyche 121
Moments 98–103
morality 42, 77–9, 90–1
Mother Knot, The (Lazarre) 64
mother-child relations 5, 48–51, 116, 129
motherhood 8–14, 20, 56, 59, 62, 67, 82
Mourning and Melancholia (Freud) 23
multiplicity 71, 100–1
Mutual Acknowledgement Project 74–5, 84–90
mutual recognition 26–8, 42–4, 52–4, 63–6, 83–5, 97–104, 107–11
mutuality 6–8, 57–8, 63–7, 93–4; relational 153

Nachträglichkeit (afterwardness) 20, 114
Nanny 4–16
narcissism 10–12, 19, 32–3, 36, 42, 121–3, 131
narcissistic aggression 143
narcissistic injury 32–3
narratives: personal 56–8
Nation at Risk, A (Gardner) 34
needs 51, 64, 93
negotiation 6, 111
neoconservatism 35, 38
networks: social 126
neurobiology 124, 130
neuroscience 111, 122
New York Times, The 121
New York University (NYU) 59–60, 64–5
1984 (Orwell) 125
Nixon, R. 38
nonrecognition 38, 60, 114
normativity 40–2, 61–2, 71
nurturance 20, 62, 66

Obama, B. 114
Obamacare 38

objectification 10–13, 143
objectivity 93–7, 101–2, 109, 120–2, 126–8, 132–4; fantasy of 149; rationalist 19; subjective 106
objects 43, 52, 66, 80, 83, 96, 148–9; collective 37, 44
O'Connor, N. 3, 138–46; and Ryan, J. 144
Oedipus 17–22, 27–9, 42–3, 49–50, 69–70, 116, 127
Oedipus complex 67–8, 88, 144, 149
Ogden, T.H. 104
omnipotence 6, 12, 52–3, 61, 143, 149
ontology 41, 93, 97–102, 133, 139–40
oppression 4, 8–9, 15–16, 90; colonial 85; extreme 5, 9, 15; female 59–60; social 62
Orange, D.: Stolorow, R. and Atwood, G. 132
Orwell, G. 125
Otherness 41–2, 58–60, 80–4, 90, 96–8, 102–3, 112–16; dimension 113; engagement with 144; invocation 138–46; presence 143; recognizing 60; subjective 128; tyranny 78; use 48–55; virtual 121
overinclusiveness 21–3, 67, 71

Palestine: Gaza Strip 84, 87–8; West Bank 75, 86–8, 128
parenthood 19, 67, 124
Paris Psychoanalytical Society (SPP) 112
passivity 53, 69–70, 83
paternal identity 20
patient uniqueness 125
patients 132
patriarchy 18, 54, 57, 69, 148
Peirce, C. 81–2
penis envy 18, 67
perception (*Wahrnehmung*) 99–102, 144
Person, E.S. 43
phallus 67, 142–3
phantasy 6, 12–14, 39–40
phenomenology 132–4, 139, 143, 147
Phenomenology of Mind, The (Hegel) 97–9
Phenomenology of Spirit, The (Hegel) 60
philosophy 81, 93–5, 99, 116, 120, 139–41, 148; continental 74; linguistic 121; political 112; social 121, 128
Philosophy of Mind (Hegel) 141
pleasure 79, 96, 113, 142
plurality 99–103
Poe, E.A. 77, 82
polarity: gender 50, 116
political correctness 62
politics 18, 29, 32–3, 56, 138, 146
Popper, K. 81

INDEX

postmodernism 19, 112, 131
postoedipal complex 69–70
potency 150–1
power 20, 78–81, 84, 116, 141; of desire 62; gendered 18; hierarchy 148–51; relations 14–15, 57–8, 139, 151; social loss of 134; state 34
powerlessness 10, 13
practical reason 90
preoedipal complex 49–50, 68–9, 95, 116
primal horde 21, 24
Pro-Life 35
promiscuity 43
psyche 41, 77, 114, 124, 133, 150, 154; development 113, 122, 154; modernization 121; quasi-autonomous 39; social 139–40
psychic bondage 22
psychoanalysis 17–33, 48–50, 56–64, 69–71, 94–7, 141–3, 146–8; American 111–15; biological 75; clinical 59; contemporary 1–3, 120–2, 131–4, 147; development 84; epistemology 131–3; French 111–18, 134, 141; intersubjective 76, 123; mainstream 123; postcolonial 80; pure 117; relational 19, 23, 35–8, 41, 64, 113, 119–20, 123–34, 139–40, 152; therapeutic 74, 122–3
Psychoanalysis and Feminism (Mitchell) 17, 56
Psychoanalytic Dialogues 113
psychoanalytic thirdness 119–37
psychology 2, 79, 111–12; classical 144–5; cognitive 113; developmental 124, 148; ego 111–14, 148; folk 146; group 23–4; individual 24; one-person 19, 37, 120; self- 65, 68, 113, 121, 124, 132; sexual 49
psychotherapy 66, 115–20, 123–5, 132, 145
Purloined Letter, The (Poe) 77, 82

queer theory 21, 69–70
queerness 2, 28, 71, 139

Rabinbach, A. 62
race 4–5, 12, 12–13, 28, 37
racialization: mind 4–16
racism 4–5, 10–12, 15
Rand, A. 37
rationality 18–20, 60, 145
Reagan, R. 17, 37–8
Reage, P. (Dominique Aury) 61, 142
real world 119–37
reality 114, 126–9, 144–6; inner 119, 132; material 127; objective 127, 132; outer 119, 132; social 127
Realpolitik 36
reason 148; practical 90
receptivity 150–1

reciprocity 8, 54, 67, 144, 149
recognition 40–4, 49–51, 58–60, 63–8, 74–7, 93–6, 139–42; adverse 38; alienation of 61–2; collective 43; emotional 71; erotic 42; failure 4–16; gender 26; group 28; involuntary 102; meaning 61; mutual 26–8, 42–4, 52–4, 63–6, 83–5, 97–104, 107–11; paradox 96–8; problem 58; rhythmic 36; self 36, 143; subject 61; two-way 83; unconscious 41; voluntary 102
Recognition and Destruction: An Outline of Intersubjectivity (Benjamin) 96–8
reconciliation 89–90
reflection: philosophical 146; political 140; self- 124
regulation 70–1; mutual 64, 67, 76–7; self- 50–1
Reis, B. 103
relatedness 96, 121, 134
Relational Concepts in Psychoanalysis (Mitchell) 19
relational psychoanalysis 19, 23, 35–8, 41, 64, 113, 119–20, 123–34, 139–40, 152
relationality 40, 59, 71, 116–17, 121–4, 128, 161
Relationality: From Attachment to Intersubjectivity (Bowlby) 125
relations 4–5, 12–13, 27, 52; adult 10; cross-ethnic 88; developmental 143; dyadic 74, 79–85, 89, 129; gender 4–8, 12, 79–80, 120, 138, 148; human 1, 4, 120, 126, 131, 140; interethnic 75, 79; interpersonal 6, 12, 49; mother-child 5, 48–51, 116, 129; mutual 5; object- 67, 81, 94–6, 111–15, 121–2, 130, 154; patient-analyst 114, 139; power 14–15, 57–8, 139, 151; psychosexual 141; subject- 37, 78, 81, 94–6, 154
relationships: dyadic 74, 79–85, 89, 129
Renik, O. 112
repression 113–14, 143
Reproduction of Mothering, The (Chodorow) 17
reproductive rights 35
resistance 13, 123
respect: mutual 49, 107–8
responsibility 5, 8–9, 15–16, 54, 90, 161
Revue Française de Psychanalyse 112
Rice, K.: and Miller, E. 88
rights 87; animal 161; civil 15; reproductive 35
Ringstrom, P. 127
risk 33–9
Roiphe, K. 70
romance 43–5
Rorty, R. 95
Rozmarin, E. 1–4, 22–4, 33, 145
Ryan, J.: and O'Connor, N. 144
Ryan, P. 37, 43

sadism 12–13, 142
sadomasochism 70–1, 142, 151

INDEX

sadomasochistic fantasy 142
Said, E. 141
sameness 22–3, 26, 37, 103, 153, 163
sanity 20, 109
al-Sarraj, E. 84–5
Sartre, J-P. 60, 80, 148
satisfaction: sexual 24–6
Schmidt, V. 63
sciences 119–37; human 121–6, 130–4; social 121, 131
scientism 133
Searles, H. 103
Second Sex: Thirty Years Later, The (NYU, 1979) 60–2
Second Sex, The (de Beauvoir) 59
seduction: generalized 115
Segal, H. 124
self 42, 122, 145; false 132; neuronal 122; social 42; subjective 127–8
self-assertion 68, 94
self-awareness 113
self-consciousness (*Selbstbewußtsein*) 99, 140
self-enlightenment 120
self-identity 145
self-psychology 65, 68, 113, 121, 124, 132
self-reflection 124
self-regulation 50–1
Sennett, R. 60
sense-certainty (*sinnliche Gewißheit*) 99–101
sense-impression 99–100
sensibility: relational 66
sensuality 54
separation 20–1, 67, 116, 141
sex 12, 36, 53–4, 62
sexual development 49
sexual domination 60
sexuality 12, 22–6, 28–9, 40–2, 48–58, 144; extended 114; infantile 111–15, 123; intersubjective 51
Shadow of the Other, The (Benjamin) 9, 149
Shaffer, T. 12–14
Shalgi, B. 2, 93–110
shame 48–55, 70–1, 85
She Came to Stay (de Beauvoir) 60
Sherbon, C. 44
Shibboleth 17, 123
Silverman, D. 130–1
Simmel, G. 49
Simons, M. 60
Singer, W. 122
slave-master dialectic 61, 75–80, 141–2, 157, 161–3
slavery 11, 36, 49, 60, 95, 98, 139, 142, 148
social difference 63

social domination 60, 79
social interaction 122
social networks 126
social oppression 62
social psyche 139–40
social sciences 121, 131
social theory 138; critical 60, 63, 71, 116
socialization 63, 141
sociology 94, 112, 128, 148
solipsism 97, 144
Sophocles 142
soul: interconnected (*Die vernetzte Seele*) 126
sovereignty 134, 140–2
spaces: intrapsychic 25, 32, 38–40, 97
speech 77, 80, 139, 145
split complementarity 83–6, 89
splitting 19, 28, 89, 114, 123
Stein, R. 40, 53, 69
Stern, D. 60, 63–5, 116, 124; and Beebe, B. 63
Stoller, R.J. 50, 53, 112
Stolorow, R.: Atwood, G. and Orange, D. 132
Story of O (Reage) 19, 57, 61, 70–1, 142
Straight Mind, The (Wittig) 2
Straker, G. 2–16
Studies in Gender and Sexuality 2–4, 33, 71
subject formation 32–3, 140
subject positioning 82–3
subjectification 38–40
subjectivity 15–20, 35–45, 64–6, 75–84, 88–97, 125–30, 133–4; collective 25; constitution of 24; feminine 94, 149; group 28; homosexual 28; individual 20, 29; intentional 144; liminal 36; lived 142; masculine 94; maternal 60, 63, 66; objective 94–6; recognition 26, 61; sexual 149; social 28, 140; subjective 94; true 140
subjects 15–16, 76–80, 83, 90, 148–9
subjugation 20, 150
submission 5–8, 11–13, 48, 61, 94, 98, 141–2; erotic 138, 142; feminine 50
Suchet, M. 4, 14
suckling 51–2
Sullivan, H.S. 123
superego 21–2
surrender 61, 83, 93–110
survival 41, 65, 143
symbolic interaction 121
symbolic order 8, 25, 83–4
symbolism 142
symmetry 66, 71, 76, 81

technocracy 35
therapy 75, 80, 106, 109–11, 124–6, 129, 132–3

INDEX

thinking 80, 115–16, 129, 138–9; critical 138
thirdness 36, 74–5, 81–90, 103, 116; co-created 104; intersubjective 127; mental 126; missing 126–9; psychoanalytic 119–37; rhythmic 66; shared 104
Thomae, H. 131, 134; and Altmeyer, M. 120
traditional feminism 116
transference 51, 68–9, 78, 91, 112–13, 123, 132; erotic 52, 68
trauma 53, 88, 155; group 85–6, 89
Trevarthen, C. 63
triangulation 127–8, 133
Tronick, E. 64
truth 108, 124, 133–4, 140
Truth and Reconciliation Commission (TRC) 9
tyranny: maternal 20

Ullman, C. 91
unconsciousness 26, 56, 119–20, 124, 138, 145; sexual 113–15; social 112
understanding (*Verstand*) 99
unemployment 10
unity 99–103, 149
Universal (*Das Allgemeine*) 99–100
Use of an Object (Winnicott) 61

validation 96, 100
Verdrängung 114
victimhood 62
victimology 150
violence 86–8; personal 18; racial 12
Vorstellung 114
voyeurism 42
vulnerability 53–4

Waddington, C.H. 74
Waintrater, R. 2, 111–18
Weber, M. 19, 60
weltanschauung 94
West Bank (Palestine) 75, 86–8, 128
Wild Desires and Mistaken Identities (O'Connor and Ryan) 144
Winnicott, D.W. 60–3, 96–7, 103–4, 114–15, 119–20, 124–5, 131–3
Wittig, M. 2
Wolitzky, D. 125
Woman's Desire (Benjamin) 68, 149

Zeitgeist 94, 132–4
zoos 153–63